EXPORTING 'MADE-IN-AMERICA' DEMOCRACY

The National Endowment for Democracy & U. S. Foreign Policy

Colin S. Cavell

University Press of America,® Inc.
Lanham · New York · Oxford

**Copyright © 2002 by
University Press of America,® Inc.**
4720 Boston Way
Lanham, Maryland 20706
UPA Acquisitions Department (301) 459-3366

PO Box 317
Oxford
OX2 9RU, UK

ISBN 0-7618-2440-5 (paperback : alk. ppr.)

Dedication

This book is dedicated to a transformed world where democracy is not accompanied by hunger, starvation, torture, genocide, lies, and war.

Contents

List of Tables

Preface

The promise of democracy, as an Enlightenment ideal, has been to specifically transcend the dichotomy of ruler and ruled by establishing self-rule of the people themselves as the normative basis of governance in the modern world. Reproduction of societies and the socioeconomic form this takes along with associated ideological constructs which legitimize such formations, however, have produced various understandings of just exactly what is meant by democracy as well pitting one conception against another. The Cold War between the U.S. and the Soviet Union (1945-1991) brought the question of democracy to the forefront of modern political debate, and the subsequent collapse of the Soviet model on December 25, 1991 has motivated the U.S. to place its own capitalist democracy forward as a model to be exported abroad through agencies like the National Endowment for Democracy and emulated thoughout the world. The present study examines this democracy-promotion project of the U.S. through the NED, exploring the various contradictory tensions which this form of democracy produces in the context of an increasingly capitalist globalization of the world that has accelerated in the post-Cold War period and into the 21st century.

Acknowledgements

For the aid, friendship, care, memories, companionship, example, laughs, solidarity, opposition, criticism, support, and love, I wish to acknowledge my associates, acquaintances, comrades, friends, and family—all of whom contributed in some way to this dissertation and now book. I give you all my thanks. Especial thanks are given to Joe R. Hicks of the University of Massachusetts Office of Information Technologies for computer assistance and to my book compositor Cynthia Antoinette Therrien.

Introduction

The recent conjuncture of a form of democracy with the practice of hegemony in United States foreign policy is the focus of the present study.[1] Specifically, the practice of democracy as a form of governance previously restricted to internal state politics—that is, a pattern of political behavior either enforced by law and/or norms within state boundaries—has become the major ideological means by which the United States seeks to transform its internal political philosophy into an instrument for hegemony in international politics in the, presumably, anarchical post-Cold War world. And, more importantly, what makes this conjuncture worthy of a closer analysis, as opposed to previous chauvinistic aspirations along these lines, is precisely the relatively broad success (cf. Sklar and Berlet, 1991-92, p. 12) which the United States has obtained in this regard while avoiding the necessity of direct and continuous United States military involvement.[2]

The success of democratic transitions in Latin America during the 1980s, away from the dominance of bureaucratic-authoritarian regimes, is evidence of this success (O'Donnell, et al., 1986; Wiarda, 1990). Also, the capitulation of former communist regimes in eastern Europe and the Soviet Union as the decade of the 1990s began was showcased as the highlight of this new U.S. foreign policy which seeks to promote democracy (or, more precisely, democratic capitalism) abroad (cf. NED Strategy Document, 1992, p. 1). Currently, the transformation of authoritarian regimes to liberal forms of democracy has also altered the political landscape of many countries in Africa. Worldwide, according to Freedom House (which is officially a nongovernmental agency but often works to support U.S. foreign policies), 65 countries and 50 related territories were rated as politically "Free" at the end of 1990, four more than in 1989, with only 33% of the world's 5.323 billion people (1990 estimate), or 50 nations and 9 territories, classified in the "Not Free" category (McColm, 1991, p. 36).[3] By the beginning of 1998, of an estimated world population of 5.771 billion people in 191 sovereign states and 59 related territories, 22% or 81 countries and 44 related territories were rated as "Free" while 39% or 53 countries and 11 related territories were deemed to be "Not Free" (Karatnycky, 1998, p. 4).[4] And as the new century begins, Freedom House's survey classifies 85 of the world's 192 countries or 44.27% as Free, another 60 countries or 31.25% as Partly Free, while only 47 countries or 24.45% of all states fall under the Not Free category. Overall, the survey concludes that at the beginning of the year 2000, "38.9 percent of the world's population lives in Free societies, 25.58 percent lives in Partly Free states, and 35.51 percent lives in Not Free countries" (Karatnycky, 2000).

It would be an exaggeration to link all of these transitions to U.S. actions alone or even to claim U.S. involvement as the proximate cause leading to a democratic transition in each particular case. Still, because this distinct type of democracy, which is being heralded by Freedom House and other U.S. allied organizations, differs substantially from what are known as "peoples' democracies" in communist or former socialist bloc countries, and which, in fact, is closely modeled upon the U.S. model of democracy depicted below in Chapter 4, it is one of the underlying assumptions of this study that regimes which meet U.S. "democratic" criteria are, in large measure, recipients of prior and/or current U.S. interventionist action and aid to promote its brand of democracy abroad.[5] U.S. efforts in this regard thus can be said to constitute a persistent interventionist and external variable in either effecting these transitions or at least in influencing the form they take. Furthermore, to the degree the U.S. does claim credit for these transitions (cf. NED SD, 1992, p. 1; Bush, 1992, p. A16; NED Annual Report 1999, 2000, p. 4, Albright, May 16, 2000), it is important to analyze this claim in order to examine the specific impact on the construction of U.S. policy. Moreover, utilization of passive, non-military instruments to foster compliance with U.S. policies amongst foreign populations recognizes that the reconstruction of U.S. hegemony in the post-Cold War world and the reestablishment of American supremacy (either in the Western bloc itself or in the world generally) requires more than domination "through the application of force in the world economy," a point made by Augelli and Murphy (1988, p. 198). As such, one of the questions examined herein is to what degree the U.S. export of democracy abroad constitutes the ethical aspect of American hegemony, given the present conjunction of U.S. economic and military dominance. As well, the practice of democracy promotion raises questions as to whether this is a wholly new practice undertaken by the U.S., what type of democracy is being advocated and/or exported, and for whose benefit?

The nature of these democratic transformations and specifically the U.S. role in effecting them requires an examination of the now institutionalized overt role which is being played by the National Endowment for Democracy (NED), the agency first officially proposed by President Reagan in a June 8, 1982 speech to the British Parliament.[6] In order to counter Soviet totalitarianism, he said it was necessary to

> foster the infrastructure of democracy—the system of a free press, unions, political parties, universities—which allows a people to choose their own way, to develop their own culture, to reconcile their own differences through peaceful means (Reagan, 1982, p. 549).

Enacted into law by Congress in November 1983, the NED is, curiously, a privately incorporated organization which, nonetheless, happens to be funded by the U.S. government and subject to the oversight and review procedures of Congress. It has been suggested that this contradictory basis of the NED structure is a way to get government funding on the one hand, while its private status "enables it to deflect criticism from the U.S. government when its policies and programs go awry or prove embarrassing" (Wiarda, 1990a, p. 150). But while the supposedly private status of the NED may keep its activities out of the purview of the American public, its status in the eyes of other governments and dissident organizations is not so ambiguous and, in fact, subjects the agency to their immediate suspicion and hesitation, especially when it claims to be promoting democracy (cf. Weaver and Barnes, 1991, pp. 138-40; Grey, May 21, 1998; Parenti, 1995, p. 53; Blum, 2000, p. 183).

Because the focus of this dissertation rests primarily on the National Endowment for Democracy (NED), which is only one instrument amongst many which the U.S. utilizes to effect its policies abroad, a more accurate assessment of the overall impact of U.S. foreign policy on democratic transitions abroad would require analyses not only of these other agencies, programs, and practices but as well detailed comparisons of their impact in the c ountries w here su ch democratic g overnmental f orces emerge. Consequently, whatever conclusions herein reached can only be said to be tentative, partial, limited, and derived from an examination of only one instrument of U.S. foreign policy, viz. the NED. As Cohen notes, the NED's budget is but "0.2 percent of America's $16 billion foreign operations budget and just 0.01 percent of its $300 billion defense budget" (2000, p. 848). Indeed, he points out, even if the NED's average annual budget of around $32 million were "increased tenfold, to $320 million, this would amount to less than 2 percent of the more than $16 billion in the U.S. budget for foreign operations and State Department appropriations, and 0.1 percent of the $300 billion defense budget" (Cohen,

2000, p. 852). Admittedly, this is an acknowledgement of the limitations of this dissertation's c onclusions, and the reader is thus provided with a caveat against generalizing findings rendered herein regarding the NED to overall U.S. foreign policies.

But what *specifically* characterizes the current form of U.S. democracy elevated to the level of foreign policy, and how does it differ from previous U.S. attempts to export democracy abroad? And how is this current form of democracy being exported and *for what purposes*? Does democracy in this form contain sufficient contradictions to forestall or even counteract the United States' quest for world hegemony? And what is it about the export of American democracy that allows the Chamber of Commerce, the AFL-CIO, and the Republican and Democratic parties—organizations with seemingly diverse interests, to agree on the meaning of democracy in order to work in tandem and promote it abroad? These questions lend purpose to, and stake out certain specific areas of focus for, this study.

It is important, to begin with, to note that the intersection of democracy and hegemony has been examined before (cf. Gramsci, 1955; Laclau and Mouffe, 1985; Doyle, 1986a, Robinson, 1996). The uniqueness of this study, however, lies first in its understanding that these two concepts, democracy and hegemony, now occupy a central role in U.S. foreign policy (though the latter concept of hegemony is more an unspoken practice than a fully articulated policy).[7] And they have been conjoined by American foreign policymakers to take advantage of the new conditions provided by the post-Cold War world and the collapse of the former Soviet Union in an explicitly overt attempt to replace the anarchical nature of international politics with a "new world order" under U.S. leadership. And though R obinson argues t hat "a t ransnational elite w hich is t he agent of transnational capital" has already superceded ruling class direction from any particular national state, what is being argued by others is that the U.S., acting as a traditional sovereign state, is pursuing nothing less than a policy of world hegemony (Robinson, 1996, p. 4; Tyler, 1992, pp. 1, 14). One of the main fronts of this battle is in the realm of politics, the orienting of governments around the world to the structures of a capitalist market economy, a subordinate and apolitical trade union movement, institutions of civil society, and western liberal democratic forms of governance (competitive elections, individual procedural rights, an active role for private-sector organizations, etc.). Thus, there is a move to process or procedural democracy as opposed to s ubstantive democracy. In t his respect, procedural democracy is limited to the political and legal world of voting, due process, and fair procedures while substantive democracy expands the concept of democracy to include the former provisions in addition to equalizing social and economic conditions. Substantive democracy can thus be referred to as "results-oriented" democracy, in that the end result of the democratic process should produce a society approaching material equality. U.S. efforts at promoting procedural democracy abroad, to the contrary, are understood herein as encouraging form at the expense of substance, exacerbating material inequality in the process.

My hypothesis is that the type of democracy the U.S. wishes to export abroad is narrowly constructed and essentializes an unalterable tie to capitalist economics and, in particular, is supported abroad only insofar as it benefits U.S. national and economic interests as the predominant world capitalist power.[8] Such a conception of democracy does not allow for particular historical traditions and customs in any given country nor for the possibility of each state's objective conditions to influence its own democratic development; consequently, the U.S. promotion of democracy abroad will continue to engender resentment toward this foreign export because it is meant to serve U.S. goals and not indigenous needs, as has been witnessed most recently in the '90s in Haiti, Somalia, and Russia.[9] Also, I will show that because "democracy promotion" is often merely a mask for establishing and continuing U.S. hegemony abroad, contradictions are likely to emerge between the rhetoric and practice of this policy thus raising generalized doubts amongst the populations having this "democracy" forced on them. For example, multi-million dollar U.S. aid for the United Nicaraguan Opposition (UNO) in the 1990 presidential election in Nicaragua in addition to a simultaneous U.S. support for a brutal counterrevolutionary war against the governing Sandinistas found many Nicaraguans skeptical of U.S. efforts at promoting democracy.[10] And such doubts are not only about the nature of this brand of democracy but also about its subversion and challenge of the notion of state sovereignty which forms the basis of current international law. Moreover, to the extent that the demands of capital accumulation fail to reach their desired targets and social conflicts threaten to spill over from established institutions into the political arena in other countries, it is unlikely that the U.S. will be able to pursue its newfound evangelism of promoting democracy with as much fervor as it currently exudes. Should this crusade degenerate, however, it is doubtful that the U.S. will return to its idealized tradition of isolationism, as the logic of global capitalism now prohibits that luxury, lest the US yield its hegemony to another aspirant.[11] Indeed, if the use of force replaces or overshadows the weapon of democratic propaganda, the resulting visage of iron-fisted politics will cast into doubt whatever democratic intentions may have existed. Consequently, selective support for democracy abroad will expose U.S. interest in democratic development as merely self-serving, thus characterizing its commitment to democratic principles as primarily—though not merely—rhetorical and pretentious, as process democracy is exposed as merely a hollow shell without material content.

In order to begin our examination of the U.S. export of democracy, it is first necessary to inquire into the specificity of the concepts of democracy and hegemony. In Chapter 1, both concepts are defined according to past and present usages. In particular, it is argued that the term "democracy" has undergone an historical transition by which, under conditions of capitalism, its legitimacy as a valid theory of political obligation is being undermined. The work of C.B. Macpherson will be examined to bring out the key contradiction which emerges when democracy is mixed with capitalism; specifically, it is one that pits an owning class which must maintain a possessive market society in order to ensure its ruling position against a dispossessed working class which finds it increasingly difficult to remain politically obligated to a system that keeps it subordinated. In order to forestall any further damage to its legitimacy, attempts to mask this contradiction are continuously undertaken by those holding sovereign power while continuing to insist that the form of government by which they rule be classified as a democracy. And though ruling classes will always appeal to its citizens' sense of patriotism—that political sentiment which Hegel defined as "assured conviction with truth as its basis" which results from the citizens' belief that "rationality is *actually* present in the state"—to ward off challenges to its legitimacy, one is reminded of Marx's statement that the "state is too serious a business to be subjected to such buffoonery" [such as a despotism which relies on patriotism for its salvation]. "A Ship of Fools can perhaps be allowed to drift before the wind for a good while," he writes, "but it will still drift to its doom [i.e. the approaching revolution] precisely because the fools refuse to believe it possible" (Hegel, 1821/1967, pp. 163-4; Marx, 1943).

With regard to the concept of hegemony, various perspectives are laid out from that of Hedley Bull and Martin Wight to that of Michael Doyle and Antonio Gramsci. Gramsci's understanding of hegemony, which is rooted in the formation of the state itself, and which focuses on the interrelations between ruling classes and subaltern groups in the interplay between political society and civil society, is chosen as the methodological tool by which to examine the current U.S. export of democracy, for it is the only approach to hegemony, of those examined herein, which is based in a solidly class analytical framework.

In Chapter 2, an historical examination of the modern states system is undertaken so as to provide some background to contemporary international relations. In particular, an examination of the origins of the modern states-system is undertaken beginning with the Realist perspective of Martin Wight and Hedley Bull. This is followed by a delineation of various theoretical approaches within the discipline of international relations (IR). Some of these approaches take the sovereign state as their basic unit of analysis but others, since the rapid development of globalizing forces in the latter twentieth century, have yielded to analyses that are global in orientation and take the world capitalist system as their primary level of theorization. These later systems theorists provide the theoretical tools which lend guidance to this dissertation and help orient the reader to the complex processes which set the stage for the diplomatic practice of democracy promotion undertaken by the NED, understanding such democracy promotion as a necessary behavior on the road to globalization under U.S. hegemonic dominance.

In recognizing that post-Cold War U.S. foreign policy has a unity of purpose built around a specific theme, *viz.* "democracy," "democracy-building," and "democracy promotion," a genealogical exposition of prior attempts by the U.S. to promote democracy abroad is necessary to show that this is not a wholly new policy embarked upon by the U.S. Specifically, in Chapter 3, I will focus on the example of the long history of U.S. relations with Latin America and the Caribbean and the persistent U.S. interventionist behavior in those regions under the guise of promoting "freedom and democracy." This history will demonstrate that the U.S. has much practical experience by which to guide its current efforts to promote democracy throughout the world.

In Chapter 4, I focus on the origin, structure, and grant-funding practices of the NED itself and analyze the specific nature of the form of democracy being exported, how and for what purposes it is exported, and examine particular instances of NED funding in order to assess its impact on building democracy abroad. Because of the focused activities of the NED in many areas of the world, in particular in funding activist intellectuals who otherwise might be inclined to acquiesce to local anti-U.S. and/or anti-capitalist oppositional forces, it is implicit that the NED is succeeding in pacifying many foreign populations through its direct involvement in the internal political affairs of other countries. For example, despite the highly publicized open admission by U.S. officials of millions of dollars in NED aid, the Serbian opposition leader, Vojislav Kostunica, supported by many thousands of citizens claimed victory against incumbent President Slobodan Milosevic in the rump state of Yugoslavia in the September 2000 elections, eventually forcing Milosevic from office on October 6 with Kostunica ascending to the Presidency (Lancaster, September 19, 2000, p. A1; Erlanger, September 20, 2000; Dobbs, December 11, 2000, p. A1).

In Chapter 5, I critique this latest attempt by the U.S. to maintain its hegemony through the export of democracy abroad. I question whether the western liberal democratic state is the best form for the realization of continued capitalist accumulation under U.S. hegemony in the rest of the world or whether this form of state produces its own contradictions that could upset its hegemony. In this concluding chapter, I examine certain aspects of global capitalist development since WWII and the effect this development is having on the relations between the so-called "developing nations" *vis-à-vis* the so-called "developed nations." As well, with the accelerated globalization of the world market in the 1990s, I examine established international economic bodies assessing their role as regards the objective of supporting and/or maintaining U.S. hegemony. Utilizing a Marxian class analysis, I then construct a basic theoretical model of capitalist production as it operates within the current global market and analyze, on the basis of this model, the likely concomitant effect on the U.S. export of democracy in general within the ever-developing contradictory influences that are both bringing the world together in a web of economic ties while simultaneously exacerbating economic cleavages in the process.

I. Democracy and Hegemony

Democracy Conceptualized

To conjoin in one sentence the concepts democracy and hegemony is a contradiction, for while notions of freedom are conjured by the first concept (at least in our own historical epoch), its negation emanates from the second. And while both concepts refer to a specific type of political order, hegemony has more often been associated with a state's external relations, while democracy has been conceived historically as an endogenous state practice, a fact which heretofore has both facilitated and circumscribed the nature of "democratic" states' interactions.[12] To the degree that states interact either violently or through diplomatic means, the stronger—determined primarily by battlefield strength, though economic might and intellectual capacities have necessarily effected the form in which victories resulted—has usually dominated the relationship and thereby established a relationship of hegemony.[13] Democracy, on the other hand, is said to exist in so far as political authority arises from an uncoerced affirmation by a majority of citizens—at least of all those considered to be citizens.

Previous writers have postulated a similar dichotomy as the one stated above—*viz.*, the relationship between freedom and order (Lowe, 1988; Forsey, 1974; Gorovitz, 1967; Commager, 1966; Heimann, 1947; and Eden, 1948).[14] Indeed, students of politics will most assuredly be confronted with this latter dichotomy, as it is said that all of politics is a reconciliation of these two in one form or another (though some would claim, as do certain religions and philosophies, that both are unattainable without justice).[15] But to say that democracy and hegemony are analagous to freedom and order is to mistake the undelineated abstraction of the latter *concepts* with the specificity of the former when they, i.e. democracy and hegemony, are conceived as *practices*. Various kinds of states through-out history have claimed to serve the goals of freedom and order as does nearly every state today. But the particular political practices undertaken by different kinds of states to achieve these goals not only vary in their approaches but likewise in their specific conceptualizations of these goals, hence the specificity of democratic or hegemonic state politics as op-posed to, for example, aristocratic or confederation state politics—each of which seeks freedom and order in the abstract through different defini-tively ordered practices.

Both democracy and hegemony when conceived as ordered prac-tices thus relate to certain specified relationships that give cogency to their particularity. For example, a notion of *equality* characteristically sets off the concept of democracy from its alternatives, including—as p er Aristotle's constitutional schema—monarchy, aristocracy, polity, tyranny or oligarchy.[16] In fact, as far as Aristotle was concerned, democracy, along with tyranny and oligarchy, was a deviant form of governance. Democracy was a deviation from *polity*, for the *demos* or masses ruled not in the interest of the common good, i.e. for rich and poor alike, but only for their o wn advantage, i .e. "for the benefit of the m en without m eans" (Aristotle, 335-322 B.C.E./1984, Bk. III, Ch. vii, para. 1279a32-1279b4, p. 190).[17] Indeed, for the Greeks in general, democracy was literally taken to mean rule by a particular social class, the poor masses. The etymology of *democracy* comes from a combination of the Greek words *demos* (the people) and *kratia* (authority) and literally translates as 'power of the people.'[18] "Democracy," stated Aristotle in his *Politics*, exists w here sovereign power "is in the hands of those who have no stock of posses-sions and are without means" (Aristotle, 335- 322 B.C.E./1984, Bk. III, Ch. viii, para. 1279b16, p. 191).[19] That such a conception of democracy does not hold true in our own day—at least not officially admitted by the world's most self-identified democracy, the U.S., except on rare occasions—dem-onstrates the historical a lteration the concept has g one through, espe-cially under the conditions of capitalism.[20] The merger of democracy with capitalism must therefore be examined, since the shift away from the his-torical Greek origins of democracy has particular implications for the present study.

The Crisis of Political Obligation

In his book, *The P olitical T heory of Possessive I ndividualism: Hobbes to Locke*, C.B. Macpherson examines the foundations of liberal-democratic theory as found in the works of Hobbes, Harrington, Locke and the Levellers, all writing within the context of two seventeenth-century English revolutions.[21] Locating the "essential ingredient" of both the practical struggle and the theoretical justification of the seventeenth-century European revolutionary upheaval in the new belief in the value and "rights" of the individual (who, to the major theorists of the time, was chiefly the white European propertied male), a belief most clearly emphasized in Hobbes and Locke, Macpherson detects in their conceptions of the individual a central problem which, while corresponding substantially to the actual relations of a market society, has nonetheless come to undermine the legitimacy of liberal-democratic theory. The difficulty lies in the "possessive quality" which conceptualizes the individual "as essentially the proprietor of his own person or capacities, owing nothing to society for them." Freedom, as "the" human essence, was conceptualized in the negative sense as "freedom from dependence on the will of others"—freedom being a function of possession. Society was seen as constituted on a contractual basis and consisted of relations of exchange between proprietors. Political society, thus "became a calculated device for the protection of this property and for the maintenance of an orderly relation of exchange" (Macpherson, 1962/1988, p. 3). Seventeenth-century concepts of freedom, right, obligation, and justice were consequently shaped by this overriding concept of "possessive individualism." And while this concept of possession gave liberal theory its strength in the seventeenth century, it became its source of weakness in the nineteenth, and, has failed, according to Macpherson, as a foundation of liberal-democratic theory in the twentieth century. This transformation, states Macpherson, is *not* that the basic assumptions of possessive individualism no longer correspond to the conditions of market society; they still do—even though some liberal theorists do not recognize this and try to discard these assumptions. No, the real trouble, Macpherson argues, is that the social context changed with the emergence of "working-class political articulacy" in the nineteenth century, which is politically expressed today in the right of universal suffrage—a concession won by the dispossessed from the possessing class through the organization and mass mobilization of the working class.[22] Reflecting this political change in order to maintain their rule, the possessing class adopted the rhetoric and, at times, the symbolism, of equality, which democracy presupposes, while effectively denying it of substantive content, though concessions, however temporary, have also been won by the dispossessed, e.g. social security benefits. And though (as of 1962 when Macpherson's book was first published) the possessing (capitalist) class has still been able to maintain effective control over political power in much of the world, the increasing necessity to rely on deception to maintain its control is effectively undermining any adequate basis for a moral justification of liberal democracy.[23] The key contradiction which emerges when democracy is mixed with capitalism, therefore, is that between a possessing class, which must maintain the existence of a possessive market society to preserve its position, and a dispossessed working class, which, with the acquisition of the democratic franchise and hence a political voice, is increasingly skeptical of the liberal-democratic theory of political obligation.[24] Essentially, Macpherson foresaw in 1962 a continuous crisis of legitimacy on the political horizon for the liberal-capitalist state.

To unravel this contradiction, Macpherson examines the social basis of liberal theory which its founders, including Hobbes, Harrington, Locke and the Levellers, took for granted, and notes that all shared the recognition that each person's capacity to labor is his/her own property, is alienable, and is a market commodity which each man is freely able to hand over to others for a price (thus distinguishing the worker from the slave).[25] It is this characteristic of labor as alienable that prompts Macpherson to label this kind of society a "possessive market society" (Macpherson, 1962/1988, p. 48). Furthermore, once one's capacity to labor becomes a generalized commodity, then market relations begin to permeate all social relations. This form of society came into being in seventeenth-century England, and the acceptance of this society, rooted in the notion of possessive (white male) individualism, by the main political theories of the time is due to their shared recognition of the following basic assumptions:

> (i) What makes a man human is freedom from dependence on the wills of others.
> (ii) Freedom from dependence on others means freedom from any relations with others except those relations which the individual enters voluntarily with a view to his own interest.
> (iii) The individual is essentially the proprietor of his own person and capacities, for which he owes nothing to society.
> (iv) Although the individual cannot alienate the whole of his property in his own person, he may alienate his capacity to labour.
> (v) Human society consists of a series of market relations.
> (vi) Since freedom from the wills of others is what makes a man human, each individual's freedom can rightfully be limited only by such obligations and rules as are necessary to secure the same freedom of others.
> (vii) Political society is a human contrivance for the protection of the individual's property in his person and goods, and (therefore) for the maintenance of orderly relations of exchange between individuals regarded as proprietors of themselves (Macpherson, 1962/1988, pp. 263-64).

These seven assumptions, argues Macpherson, remain indispensable to liberal theory, but no sufficient principles of obligation can be derived from them today because there are two conditions of a valid theory of political obligation that can no longer be fulfilled by the current state of possessive market societies. First, Macpherson argues, a valid theory of political obligation (without relying on Nature or the will of God) "must be able to postulate that the individuals of whom the society is composed see themselves, or are capable of seeing themselves, as equal in some respect more fundamental than all the respects in which they are unequal." In the seventeenth and eighteenth centuries, this fundamental notion of equality consisted of the equal subordination of everyone to the determination of the market and its acceptance as rightful or inevitable by virtually everybody until the nineteenth century.[26] Under these conditions, argues Macpherson, "there was a sufficient basis for rational obligation of all men to a political authority which could maintain and enforce the only possible orderly human relations, namely, market relations" (Macpherson, 1962/1988, pp. 272-73).

The second condition of a valid theory of political obligation is that "there be a cohesion of self-interests, among all those who have a voice in choosing the government, sufficient to offset the centrifugal forces of a possessive market society" (Macpherson, 1962/1988, p. 273). By restricting political voice to a possessing class in the zenith of market society in the seventeenth century, an adequate cohesion of centripetal forces existed to decide periodically, without anarchy, who should have the sovereign power, thus providing a sufficient basis for an autonomous theory of obligation of the individual to a constitutional liberal state.

This condition, like the first, was fulfilled until the nineteenth century when the industrial working class (first in Europe and the U.S., though later replicated wherever capitalist relations became the dominant mode of production) developed an autonomous class consciousness and became, in Macpherson's words, "politically articulate." At that point, working "[m]en no longer saw themselves fundamentally equal in an inevitable subjection to the determination of the market," for the market was seen as overwhelmingly benefitting the possessing class. The evolution of market society thus had produced a class which by the nineteenth century "could envisage alternatives to the system" (Macpherson, 1962/ 1988, p. 273). As such, the first condition for an autonomous theory of political obligation was no longer fulfilled, for the working class did not see themselves as fundamentally equal to the possessing class. The inequality of the system in fact relegated the working class to a subordinate position in society. Similarly, the second condition of a cohesion of interests could no longer apply once the working class claimed the democratic franchise for itself, thus forcing the possessing class to yield on its monopoly of power. With two classes in opposition, both now with a political voice, the previous assurance of a cohesion of self-interests such as to periodically decide, without anarchy, who should have sovereign power was no longer tenable.[27]

As a result, the possessing or capitalist class, since the nineteenth century, has, by implication, had to deceive subject populations— or at least their working class components—about the true nature of capitalist democracy in order to maintain control over political power at home and colonialism abroad so as to generate possessing class cohesion on the international level in the advanced market societies. Indeed, the failed combination of monarchy with democracy was not lost on the Americans as they wrested paramount control over western capitalist relations from Britain during and following WWII.[28] The search for countless "enemies" to U.S. democracy, both internally and externally, has since gone on unabated as does numerous military interventions, assassinations, coups d'état, wars, drug smuggling, etc. (cf. Cockburn & St. Clair, 1998; LaFeber, 1993; Blum, 1986, 1995; Colby and Dennett, 1994; Gelbspan, 1991; Kwitney, 1984; Stockwell, 1978; and Agee, 1975). In the twentieth century, deception at home (e.g. the Tonkin Gulf "attacks", the Pentagon Papers, Watergate, Iran-Contra) continues to undermine the moral justification of liberal democracy.[29] Meanwhile, the success of national independence movements abroad (e.g. in Africa and Asia) undermines possessing class cohesion on the international level. Consequently, the domestic possessing class in the advanced market societies has acted to further increase its use of deception, or at the very least, obfuscation.[30] The goal, of course, is to effectively keep power out of working-class hands.[31]

Thus, the dilemma we are faced with today, argues Macpherson, is that "the maturing of market society has cancelled that cohesion, among all those with a political voice, which is a prerequisite for the deduction of obligation to a liberal state from possessive individualist assumptions" [McPherson's seven (see above)]. And yet, he states, we cannot simply reject these assumptions without at the same time rejecting market society itself. Thus, "[e]ither we reject possessive individualist assumptions, in which case our theory is unrealistic, or we retain them, in which case we cannot get a valid theory of obligation" (Macpherson, 1962/1988, p. 275). As it is today, he says, we have stuck with the possessive individualist assumptions and thus have remained without a valid theory of political obligation. If Macpherson is right about an increasing nonacceptance of the liberal theory of political obligation by the working classes of advanced market societies, and particularly the U.S., then on what basis can and should populations in other countries accept this form of capitalist-democracy or, as the Clinton Administration refers to it, market democracy?[32] By what means can the U.S. hope to convince other populations of the vitality of "made-in-America" democracy? To attempt to answer these questions, we will next need to focus on the concept of hegemony.

Hegemony Conceptualized

The specific form in which order manifests itself as hegemony (as distinct, for example, from confederation or union) is through *predominance*. In its Macedonian origins, the word *hegemony* stood for "leader" and meant preponderant influence or authority, especially of one nation over others. Hedley Bull prefers the term of *preponderance* to describe the unilateral behavior of great powers in particular areas of the world or among particular groups o f states; moreover, he recognizes that s uch behavior contributes to international order. Yet, not all forms of preponderance constitute hegemony for Bull. Instead, the unilateral exploitation of preponderance takes three forms for Bull: dominance, primacy, and hegemony. *Dominance*, Bull argues, applies to the relationship in which a great power—without exercising imperial sovereignty—treats smaller states within its domain as second-class members of international society. Specifically, it "is characterized by the habitual use of force by a great power against the lesser states comprising its hinterland, and by habitual disregard of the universal norms of interstate behaviour that confer rights of sovereignty, equality and independence upon these states" (Bull, 1977, p. 214). Military intervention and occupation are prominent aspects of this sort of behavior. At the opposite extreme to dominance is what Bull refers to as *primacy*. Primacy is exercised by a great power over lesser states "without any resort to force or threat of force and with no more than the ordinary degree of disregard for norms of sovereignty, equality and independence." Though not specific on what constitutes "the ordinary degree of disregard" of international norms, Bull does note that "some degree of disregard of these norms is characteristic of all international relationships" (Bull, 1977, p. 214). As regards the specificity of a relationship of primacy, Bull equates the position of the great power to one of "leadership", arguing that it "is freely conceded by the lesser states within the group concerned, and often expresses the recognition by the latter of the disproportionately large contribution which the great power is able to make to the achievement of common purposes" (Bull, 1977, p. 215). Between the extremes of dominance and primacy which characterizes the relations of great powers over lesser states is *hegemony*. As is characteristic of dominance, so too in hegemony is there a resort to force and the threat of force, but unlike with the former, this exercise of force "is not habitual and uninhibited but occasional and reluctant." Instruments other than force are preferred by the great power in this hegemonic relationship, and the great power resorts to force "only in situations of extremity and with a sense that in doing so it is incurring a political cost" (Bull, 1977, p. 215). Thus, although the great power is ready to violate norms of sovereignty, equality and independence of lesser states, it nonetheless recognizes that such norms or rights exists and hence is forced to justify its violations of them by "some specific overriding principle." Quoting Georg Schwarzenberger, Bull concludes that "hegemony is 'imperialism with good manners'" (quoted in Bull, 1977, p. 216).

Martin Wight writes of hegemony in a manner similar to Bull's though without the distinctions in reference to the ancient states-system of Hellas. "From the sixth century [B.C.E.] [the Greeks] seem to have thought of [the Hellenic city-states system] as having a natural leader or 'president', and they had several terms for this concept—*prostates tes Hellados, hegemon*" (Wight, 1977, p. 65). But with the unparalleled stress of the Persian invasions at the beginning of the fifth century, "a more collective conception appeared," notes Wight, such that Greek "hegemonial theory was linked with a generally egalitarian assumption about the members of the states-system." This egalitarianism, he argues, was shown not only by the survival of the archaic Amphictyonic constitution—a constitution which pledged a mutual respect of each member polis and a duty of defense against violators—but also by "the absence of a *hierarchic* conception of international society" (Wight, 1977, p. 65).[33] That the Greeks did not have any term corresponding to 'great power' sets off ancient Hellas from the modern states-system. Likewise, argues Wight, the apparent inability of the Greeks to develop a theory of the balance of power, a system of diplomacy, and public international law accounts for the absence of a sense of an equilibrium of power to act as a foundation or constitution of international society in ancient Hellas (Wight, 1977, p. 66).

In his work on *Empires* (1986a), Michael Doyle distinguishes hegemony from imperialism and, like Bull and Wight above, restricts hegemony primarily to the domain of control over a state's external relations. "Control of both foreign and domestic policy characterizes empire; control of only foreign policy, hegemony" (Doyle, 1986a, p. 40). The reason for this distinction is attributed by Doyle to Thucydides who, he argues,

> first drew this distinction, noting Sparta's "allies," despite their subjection to Spartan hegemony during the Peloponnesian War, exercised a considerable degree of domestic autonomy—unlike the imperialized "allies" subject to Athens (Doyle, 1986a, p. 40).

The distinction Doyle makes between the two concepts helps him to demarcate the different spheres of control while giving intrusive primacy to imperial over hegemonic control. In this regard, imperial control involves both the process of control and its outcomes. Control is achieved either formally (directly or indirectly) or informally through influence over the periphery's environment, political articulation, aggregation, decision making, adjudication, and implementation, and usually with the collaboration of local peripheral elites. The scope of the outcomes covers both internal and external issues—who rules and what rules (Doyle, 1986a, p. 40).

The intimate involvement of the great power in the domestic—as well as foreign—affairs of the subordinate states as denoted above by the great power's control over interest articulation and aggregation, decision making, adjudication, and implementation contrasts sharply with Doyle's notion of hegemony which denotes control over external policy alone.[34] He demonstrates the differences in the purview of each concept with reference to the fifth-century conflict between Sparta and Athens, which I will explore in some detail since it relates to the present focus on the export of democracy to enhance U.S. hegemony.

In the case of Athens, Doyle notes that its empire developed, first, by enslaving the populations and colonizing the land of captured cities; second, coercion and force were utilized to keep rebellious states within the Delian League and; third, Athenian emissaries supervised the payment of tribute and the policies of the weakest cities. And though force and the threat of force characterized this imperial rule, Athens nonetheless allowed its allies to have legally independent, formally sovereign governments, though generally requiring democratic assemblies. As such, Athens ruled the Delian League members by informal imperial means. Still, it "nonetheless determined both their foreign relations and their significant domestic policies" (Doyle, 1986a, p. 56).

Two primary means sustained Athens' informal empire including, firstly, military intervention and, secondly, "the mixture of popularity and unpopularity which Athenian democratic imperialism evoked among subordinate citizens." Though economic exploitation and imperial political restrictions provoked hatred, Doyle argues that Athenian imperial control was "preferable to the external threat of Persia and the internal threat of oligarchy." Moreover, though Athens benefitted from naval tribute, seizures of land, and restrictions on trade, the members of the Delian League received in exchange several benefits, including "integration into the Athenian market, Athens' suppression of piracy, and other imperially provided, international 'collective goods'" (Doyle, 1986a, p. 57). Still, the fact of political dependence on Athens was ever present in "the local *proxenoi*, the informal leaders of the democratic faction and the appointed representatives of Athenian interests" (Doyle, 1986a, p. 58).

In contrast to Athenian imperial control, Sparta's dominance over the Peloponnesian League did not require the payment of tribute by subordinate states nor did Sparta impose the jurisdiction of its courts over its allies affairs or regulate the commerce of its allies—activities which characterized Athenian rule. Doyle does note Thucydides' comment that Sparta made sure its allies were oligarchies—which does imply a certain degree of control over domestic affairs—but Doyle downplays this aspect of Spartan control claiming that it "had no effect on its allies' domestic societies other than to guarantee their preexisting oligarchic constitutions." Moreover, he implies that this Spartan requirement over the internal form of government of its allies was not so unusual, for "oligarchy was the traditional form of society in early fifth-century Greece, particularly among the cities that were members of the Peloponnesian League" (Doyle, 1986a, p. 59). As regards this last point, Doyle appears to be reaching here in order to support his distinction between Athenian imperialism and Spartan hegemony, for the fact that oligarchy was the traditional form of government of the Peloponnesian League carries no more supportive weight than to note that democracy characterized the form of government of the Delian League members. Still, the fact that Sparta's allies retained a right to participate in all decisions of the Peloponnesian League and to keep their own military forces does indicate a significant degree of Spartan noninvolvement when compared to Athenian control over its Delian League members.

More specific to Doyle's distinction of Athenian imperialism from Spartan hegemony lies n ot in Thucydides' observation t hat the three motives of security, honor, and self-interest drew the Athenians out from their city to expand and protect their empire, for Sparta too possessed these same motives, though not the same opportunities. What was particularly unique to the Athenian empire, however, was what Thucydides described as the Athenians' "adventurous spirit", which Doyle attributes to both the democratic constitution of Athens and to the socioeconomic fact that Athenian imperialism benefitted the citizens of Athens.[35] The Athenian state drew strength from its "[h]ighly participatory democracy" argues Doyle. This system, he writes,

> in which each [free propertied male] citizen is both statesman and soldier, produces an ideology of action, a ferment of policies, an attitude of aggressive problem solving—the spirit o f adventure t hat Thucydides described as being behind Athenian expansion. Since there is no mediation between the state and the citizen, the state being the people assembled, what each citizen proposes or votes for in the assembly is both for himself and for the public (Doyle, 1986a, p. 66).

Private [free propertied male] passions, reflecting both material and ideal interests, not only inspired Athenian imperialism but were also, in turn, shaped by the public honor conferred on these undertakings. Consequently, Doyle concludes, the Athenian empire was not only of and by the people, but also for the people [i.e. the free propertied male citizens] (Doyle, 1986a, p. 66).[36]

In this description of the Greek state, we should note the absence made by many observers, including Doyle, of the large number of slaves which provided the backbone of ancient Greek society. Whereas Wood & Wood note the dispute among contemporary historians of the actual size of the slave population and their significance to the economy of democratic Athens (Wood & Wood, 1978, pp. 36-7), de Ste. Croix—by combining the labor from slavery, serfdom, and debt bondage—makes a convincing argument that such "unfree labour" "was the main way in which the dominant propertied classes of the ancient [Graeco-Roman] world derived their surplus, whether or not the greater share in total production was due to unfree labour" (de Ste. Croix, 1981, pp. 52, 135, 173). As such, it is still correct to say that a large part of the ancient Greek state, the democratic polis, was comprised of non-citizens, albeit perhaps not all non-citizens were slaves. As to the significance of slavery and other forms of unfree labor to the ancient democratic polis, one must note M. I. Finley's argument linking the first articulation of the concept of personal freedom to the rise of slavery as the main dependent labor force in classical Greece. It is only after this fact, he tells us, that "words were then created or adopted to express that idea" (Finley, 1968/1972, p. 308). Alternatively, the Woods suggest that the concept of personal freedom may have "followed upon the liberation of native labour" and hence "was born among the Greeks out of their own experience of dependence and liberation, not simply in contrasts to the dependence of others." Still, the latter do admit the likelihood that "the idea of individual freedom was invented in reference to the condition of labour." However, though recognizing that the democratic polis, like other states, "was created and shaped by the relations between appropriators and producers and served as a means of dealing with the problems generated by the social division of labour," the Woods nonetheless go on to argue that "it is far too simple" to view the polis as merely an instrument of the ruling class designed to extract labor and protect the property of the ruling minority. On the contrary, they argue, the democratic polis "was as much—if not more—a weapon for the subject classes in their struggle against their rulers, and that it was the rulers who had reason to resist the political principle" (Wood & Wood, 1978, pp. 39-40). de Ste. Croix echoes this conclusion as regards the Greek democratic experience which, he writes, "gives the whole citizen population extensive and enforceable legal rights, and so gives the humbler and poorer citizen an opportunity of protecting himself against at any rate the more extreme forms of ill-treatment by the powerful" (de Ste. Croix, 1981, p. 141). It is perhaps this realm of enforceable legal rights, however limited and restricted, which earned for Athens a degree of popular legitimacy and recognition of its vitality.

Note should be made here of the similar exclusion of women from many scholarly accounts of the social basis of the ancient Greek state and particularly women's exclusion from the affairs of the polis. Spelman (1988) also points out the necessity to recognize the distinction between a "free" female—considered as such due to the status of "citizen" conferred on her husband—whom Aristotle referred to as "woman" as opposed to those females whom he failed to designate as such due to their slave status. This distinction is important for understanding Aristotle's conception of the well-ordered state, as "the distinction between male and female is important only for citizens; for slaves it is irrelevant" (Spelman, 1988, p. 42). This distinction further supports Spelman's argument that "it can never be the case that the treatment of a woman has only to do with her gender and nothing to do with her class or race. That she is subject only to sexism tells us a lot about her race and class identity, her being free or slave, and so on. For her, being subject only to sexism is made possible by these other facts about her identity" (Spelman, 1988, p. 53). Spelman also points out that Aristotle's exclusion of the female slave from the status of woman did not likewise translate into any superiority of her male counterpart, as the male slave was deprived of any authority over the female slave, for as Aristotle uses the term "male" in his *Politics*, "maleness signals the superiority a man has over a woman only if the male in question is a natural ruler. This means that one of the marks of inferiority of a male slave is that he is not a better specimen of humanity than his wife" (Spelman, 1988, p. 43).

Given the foregoing discussion of the limited extent of exactly who constituted "the people" in ancient Greek society, it is thus with some reticence that the contemporary reader is asked to believe in its "adventurous spirit" which is perchance simply the spirit of imperialism, which imbued the propertied classes of ancient Greece. And, likewise, in our own times, imperialism does benefit those in the metropole who, in turn, cast a blind eye to the needs of those in the periphery whose labor surplus daily fills the coffers of the imperial treasury. Writers like Thucydides and Doyle appear to be drawn by this apparent dynamism of the Athenian city-states, which reflects more the class position of both men than the objective nature of the system in question. Nevertheless, this writer will concede that indeed there was a desire for expansion on the part of many Athenian citizens, as many of the ancient writings tell us, though I do not share Doyle's judgement on its beneficent nature and will reserve comment on its etiology. The consequences of such exclusions of large segments of the population from political participation, however, are devastating to a modern theory of participatory democracy and contrary to any discussion of political obligation which depends on factors other than brute force and enslavement. Still, there remains the fact that ruling classes of the Athenian settler-states possessed a degree of freedom which distinguished them from their contemporaries.

On the contrary, Sparta's domestic society resembled a military camp. Below the two figurehead kings, real political power rested with the aristocratically-controlled senate (*gerousia*) which directed the assembly of citizen-soldiers and played a role in electing the *ephors*, the ruling public officials of the Spartan state. Below this were the *perioeici*, the conquered peoples of the Peloponnese and foreigners who had settled in the Peloponnese, all of whom lacked political rights of participation in Spartan policy. At the base of the Spartan state lay the previous Greek inhabitants of Messenia, the helots, who were conquered by Sparta in the seventh century B.C.E. (Doyle, 1986a, p. 69).

These distinctions in the respective domestic societies produced what, for Doyle, is the crucial difference distinguishing Athens from Sparta and Athenian imperialism from Spartan hegemony, namely:

> the difference in "spirit" between the two rivals. Athens was aggressive, innovative; Sparta passive, isolationist. Athens was capable of extending her civilization, Sparta was not (Doyle, 1986a, p. 70).[37]

With reference to imperialism and hegemony in general, Doyle concludes that imperial metropoles can be distinguished from merely large, populous, or rich countries by virtue of two features, first, transnational extension and, second, political unity. Furthermore, such metropoles must have peripheries under their rule. On the contrary, "[p]olitically unified states that possess superior quantities (relative to their neighbors) of the conventional resources of power—large populations, substantial armies, wealth—but lack the differentiated society needed as a foundation for transnational extension can, nonetheless, establish hegemonies" (Doyle, 1986a, p. 75).[38] Doyle is unclear as to what he means by a "differentiated society", though one presumes it to be a class-stratified society like the Greek city-states he admires.

More pointedly, as regards the Greek experiment in democratic imperialism, one should note its relatively short duration. From the rise of Athenian power between 480 and 475 B.C.E., as Persia was defeated in Europe and the Delian League was established in 477, to the imposition of Athenian hegemony in 457 with the incorporation of Boetia, Locris and Phocis into the Athenian alliance system and the uniform introduction of Athenian coins, weights and measures on top of the previously established tribute payments which continued to be exacted, to the full implantation of its empire between 448-445 B.C.E. following the Peace of Kallias which decisively thrust Persia "out of the Hellenic states-system" (Wight, 1977, p. 88), to the empire's expansion to include up to 400 cities by 425, ending in the eventual collapse of Athenian power in 404 B.C.E. after the Spartan defeat of the Athenian fleet the year before at the battle of Aegospotami which ended the Peloponnesian War, only a mere 76 years had passed, and of those, stability characterized the export of Athenian democracy for, at most, only 41 years. But even here, as Doyle notes, "[r]ebellions and defections were frequent—Naxos, Samos, and Mitylene are only the major revolts discussed by Thucydides"—to which we must add "the horrifying repression of Melos" (Doyle, 1986a, p. 58) and, not to forget, the two temporary oligarchies which took over Athens itself in 411 and 404.[39]

As to the causes of Athenian instability which led to an increase in defection and violence and ended with the dissolution of the empire, it is interesting to note that Doyle attributes these developments to "the near-equality" in material culture of Athens and its allied subordinates. This "near-equality" in material culture, Doyle argues, led to a perception of social and economic equality among the Greek islanders of the Aegean and the Greek settlers of Ionia, Sicily, and Thessaly to the effect that a feeling persisted that

> Athenian rule reflected no natural (or technical) superiority but was a control exercised by those who "should" have been equal (Doyle, 1986a, p. 58).

That this feeling of alienation between the Athenians and their subject populations may have stimulated the subsequent turmoil is not to be downplayed; indeed, one should not forget the actual policies which produced such estrangement, such as the heavy toll of Athenian taxes which engendered resentment so strong that, as Doyle notes, it often ended in the slaughter of the Athenian settler-garrisons.

Doyle's conclusion on Athenian instability is similar to that of Plato who in *The Laws* criticized the "excessive democracy" of Athens. This excess, Plato tells us, first began with the mixing of different styles of music which then led to the claim that there were no standards of right and wrong. As a consequence, argues Plato, the judgement of what constituted good and bad music was left up to the subjective taste of "the ordinary man" who had "the arrogance to set himself up as a capable judge." And music, Plato argues, only

> proved to be the starting-point of everyone's conviction that he was

an authority on everything, and of a general disregard for the law. Complete licence was not far behind. The conviction that they *knew* made them unafraid, and assurance engendered effrontery (Plato, 427-347 B.C.E./1970/1988, Bk. III, secs. 700-1, pp. 153-4).

To the degree that a general feeling of equality—or "near-equality" in "the material culture" as Doyle puts it—develops in societies, a state is thus faced with the choice of either attempting to arrest this development or, to the best extent possible, make the reality conform to the ideal. The Athenians chose the former course of action—and lost.

In contrast to Doyle, Wight, and Bull, Gramsci's conception of hegemony—which will be utilized in the present study because of its explanatory utility, in that it is the only approach to hegemony which is based in a solidly class analytical framework—is not limited either to (1) state-to-state behavior or (2) to control over a state's external behavior. On the contrary, Gramsci's concept of hegemony is rooted in the formation of the state itself and, hence, is a necessary strategm of any ruling group. In his "Notes on Italian History" (1929-35), Gramsci distinguishes between ruling classes and subaltern groups.[40] Ruling classes, he argues, maintain their historical unity not simply on juridical or political bases—though these are important—but, more fundamentally, it "results from the organic relations between [1] State or political society and [2] 'civil society'" (*PN*, p. 52). As regards this latter distinction, Gramsci at one point provides a formula for the state as "political society + civil society, in other words hegemony protected by the armour of coercion" (*PN*, p. 263). But elsewhere he deliberately distinguishes between the two concepts of state and civil society, reserving for the state a role as representing "the coercive and punitive force of juridical regulation of a country" (*PN*, p. 267). In this sense, the state is an "'educator'", "an instrument of 'rationalisation'" (*PN*, p. 247), with "organisational and connective" functions (*PN*, p. 12) to conform civil society to the economic structure. The state, therefore

> is the entire complex of practical and theoretical activities with which the ruling class not only justifies and maintains its dominance, but manages to win the active consent of those over whom it rules (*PN*, p. 244).

Civil society, on the other hand, "is the ensemble of organisms commonly called 'private'"; it is the ethical content of the state based in moral relations resulting from the cultural hegemony "which the dominant group exercises throughout society" (*PN*, p. 12). It is within civil society that subaltern groups reside.

And, subaltern classes, if they are to become the ruling classes—i.e. to form a state of their own—must subordinate or eliminate the established ruling classes while simultaneously winning the active or passive assent of other subaltern groups or allies. This process is thus one of a transformation from subaltern to hegemonic/dominant groups and involves the two phases of, first, establishing autonomy in relation to the enemies which are to be defeated and, secondly, receiving active or passive support from other subaltern groups. This struggle is played out in the field of civil society but eventually involves direct conflict with the state itself and its vast repository of juridical and coercive instruments. In the case of the nascent Italian bourgeoisie in the era of the mediæval communes, Gramsci notes the Italian bourgeoisie's failure "of uniting the people around itself" (*PN*, 53). Likewise, the bourgeoisie's failure to solicit widespread support in the national Risorgimento in Italy both delayed and moderated the outcome of the subsequent revolution.

The key to Gramsci's analyses and the methodological criterion on which he bases much of his own study is his understanding

> that the supremacy of a social group manifest(s) itself in two ways, as "domination" and as "intellectual and moral leadership". A social group dominates antagonistic groups which it tends to "liquidate", or to subjugate perhaps even by armed force; it leads kindred and allied groups (*PN*, p. 57).

It is with regard to this second aspect of "leading" kindred and allied groups with "'intellectual and moral leadership'" that Gramsci's use of the term hegemony is to be understood. His focus rests, in large measure, on the question of political obligation which concerns Macpherson above. Gramsci's debt to Lenin for this understanding of "leadership" is duly noted (cf. *PN*, pp. 357, 365, 380), yet I would argue, with Augelli and Murphy (1988), that Lenin's focus was restricted more to the task at hand, *viz.* "dominance in a revolutionary alliance" (p. 118). The context of Lenin's argument about leadership was a polemic written against the Menshiviks who, he argued, would abandon the peasantry and leave the task of the bourgeois revolution solely to the bourgeoisie itself.[41] Such tactics, Lenin argued, would result in the working-class party finding itself "'dissolved' in bourgeois democracy in the sense that the proletariat will not succeed in placing its imprint on the revolution" (Lenin, 1905/1972, p. 58).[42] More pointedly, Lenin stressed the arming of the proletariat to accomplish this revolutionary task, for, he noted: "In the final analysis force alone settles the great problems of political liberty and the class struggle" (Lenin, 1905/1972, p. 30). As such, Lenin "continued to assume that the consolidation of power was ultimately a matter of armed force" which places his concept of hegemony in "a very restricted historical phase, during a revolution" (Augelli & Murphy, 1988, p. 118). The significance of Gramsci's contribution, however, lies in his understanding that the necessity for leadership does not end with the taking of state power. He writes:

> A social group can, and indeed must, already exercise "leadership" before winning governmental power (this indeed is one of the principal conditions for the winning of such power); it subsequently becomes dominant when it exercises power, but even if it holds it firmly in its grasp, it must continue to "lead" as well (*PN*, pp. 57-8).

As Gramsci points out in his "Study of Philosophy" (*PN*), this concept of hegemony represents a great philosophical advance as well as a politico-practical one, for "it necessarily supposes an intellectual unity and an ethic in conformity with a conception of reality that has gone beyond common sense and has become, if only within narrow limits, a critical conception" (*PN*, pp. 333-4). Intellectual unity and political ethics are thus the two poles around which hegemony is to be constructed and expanded.

Such intellectual unity of a particular social class is the specific task of intellectuals who perform an essential mediating function in the struggle between the various subaltern groups and the ruling classes. Gramsci is not saying here that some humans are not intellectuals, rather he is referring to those who perform this immediate social function and hence form a professional category in that their task is that of intellectual elaboration. Intellectuals are thus "organizers and leaders", "'specialised' in conceptual and philosophical elaboration of ideas" who are able to distinguish concretely "the theoretical aspect of the theory-practice nexus" (*PN*, p. 334). For Gramsci, every social group which has an essential function in economic production creates organically one or more strata of intellectuals attached to it. And though he recognizes that certain "traditional" professional intellectuals tend to portray themselves as above class interests and thus as having an inter-class aura about them, it is the *organic intellectuals* who truly unite a social group by giving it "an awareness of its own function not only in the economic but also in the social and political fields" (*PN*, pp. 3-5). Writing in the 1930s, he argues that in the context of the existing state, "the intellectuals are the dominant group's 'deputies' exercising the subaltern functions of social hegemony and political government." Their task involves the generation of a "'spontaneous' consent given by the great masses of the population to the general direction imposed on social life by the dominant fundamental group" and the use of the coercive power of the state "which 'legally' enforces discipline on those groups who do not 'consent' either actively or passively" (*PN*, p. 12). This equation of "force and consent," the "'double perspective' in political action and state life....corresponding to the double nature of the Machiavellian Centaur"—the two essential elements in the maintenance of state power—are taken by Gramsci from Machiavelli who instructed the Prince to use both law and force, for though the former was natural for the control of men, it often proved inadequate, and hence the latter, which was necessary for beasts, should likewise be at the Prince's disposal (Gramsci, 1926-37/1957/1983, p. 161).[43]

A would-be ruling class must develop beyond an economic-corporate state through an ethical-political hegemony in civil society before it can achieve domination of the state. In this regard, a social group must first consolidate itself around its own immediate and narrowly selfish "corporate" interests before it can move on. Thus in addition to championing the ideas and aspirations of the particular social group and would-be ruling class,

> hegemony also presupposes account be taken of the interests and the tendencies of the groups over which hegemony is to be exercised, and that a certain equilibrium should be formed—in other words, that the leading group should make sacrifices of an economic-corporate kind (*PN*, p. 161).

Thus, as with the Jacobins in the French Revolution, the fundamental group must represent "the revolutionary movement as a whole, as an integral historical development."[44] This leading group must represent "future needs as well, and, once again, not only the needs of those particular physical individuals, but also of all the national groups which had to be assimilated to the existing fundamental group" (*PN*, p. 78). Sacrifices and compromises, however, have their limits which must be strictly observed, "for though hegemony is ethical-political, it must also be economic, must necessarily be based on the decisive function exercised by the leading group in the decisive nucleus of economic activity" (*PN*, p. 161).

But while protecting its fundamental economic basis, it is the duty of the ruling class [that social group which has achieved domination of the state apparatus] to push for its own expansion, i.e. an ever more extensive ruling class. In the case of the Moderate Party in Italy after 1848, Gramsci notes that their policy of "transformism"

> involved the gradual but continuous absorption, achieved by methods which varied in their effectiveness, of the active elements produced by allied groups—and even of those which came from antagonistic groups and seemed irreconcilably hostile. In this sense political lead-

ership became merely an aspect of the function of domination—decapitation, and annihilation often for a very long time (*PN*, pp. 58-9).

Gramsci attributes this policy of the Moderates to the making of the Risorgimento (i.e. the 19th century movement for Italian political unity) possible in the form in which it occurred, "as 'revolution' without a 'revolution', or as 'passive revolution'" (*PN*, p. 59). Furthermore, this policy indicates how ineffective leadership is based on force alone. The term "passive revolution" was taken by Gramsci from the early nineteenth-century conservative thinker Vincenzo Cuoco who argued that revolution "must at all costs be avoided, since it was a destroyer of the 'traditions' on which civilisation is based." The central aspect of passive revolution was therefore the implementation of "reforms in order to prevent revolution on the French model" (see footnote #11 in PN, p. 59).

In the case of the Italian Risorgimento, the north Italian state of Piedmont—led by a monarch—played the function of a ruling class. The fact that leadership was left up to a state and not a social group, Gramsci writes, was because the nuclei of several groups in favor of the new liberal order, who were heavily nationalistic, merely wanted their interests to dominate but not their persons; more importantly, none of them took it upon themselves to in fact lead. This fact is significant, noted Gramsci, for it was not a unified social group which led other groups, but rather a state which "'led' the group which should have been leading"—i.e. the Moderate Party—"and was able to put at the latter's disposal an army and a politico-diplomatic strength" (*PN*, p. 105). In effect, passive revolution in Italy from 1860 to 1900 involved first the incorporation of individual political figures from democratic opposition parties into the conservative-moderate 'political class', which was against any intervention of the masses in state life. After 1900, whole groups of leftists passed over into the moderate camp. What is key for the present study, however, is the fact that a state led a struggle for renewal. As Gramsci notes,

> it is one of the cases in which these groups have the function of "domination" without that of "leadership": dictatorship without hegemony. The hegemony will be exercised by a part of the social group over the entire group, and not by the latter over other forces in order to give power to the movement, radicalise it, etc. on the "Jacobin" model (*PN*, p. 106).

The liberals of nineteenth century Italy are thus embryonic of the psychological disposition of most NED-supported pro-capitalists today, in that most would be reluctant to act—as many failed to act during the Cold War—were it not for the monetary, military and political backing of a strong state which can bring power and resources to bear against any would-be opponents.

In the present case of examining the export of U.S. democracy abroad, reformist individuals and groups within targeted countries, contemporaneously referred to as "comprador elites" amongst many marxist and dependency theorists or, in the decade of the 1990s with the U.S. leading a worldwide movement for capitalist democracy, as "democrats", play the role of the Italian Moderate Party in that they seek the imposition of liberal democracy in their own countries.[45] The role of leadership or hegemony, however, is reserved for the U.S. which—through organizations like the NED—will provide the direction, the means, and provide the watchdog or enforcement function to see that such transitions occur as planned, are stabilized, and are not temporary phenomena. Consequently, democracy promotion as a practice becomes, in effect, the ethical-political basis upon which the extension of U.S. hegemony is this era of globalization rests.

In a 1994 report, the GAO noted that "there is no central U.S. policy regarding U.S. governmentwide democracy program, no overall statement of U.S. policy regarding U.S. objectives and strategy for democratic development, no specific and common definition of what constitutes a democracy program, and no specificity regarding the roles of the foreign affairs and defense agencies in promoting democratic processes" (GAO/NSIAD-94-83, 1994, p. 1). However, in that same report, the following policies, programs, and area-specific activities instituted by different U.S. foreign policy agencies to promote democracy abroad were detailed and indicated that the USIA, AID, DOD, and the State Department each had implemented such programs and were in the process of shifting resources and organizational support towards these efforts.

U.S. public diplomacy programs funded through the U.S. Information Agency (USIA) consists of foreign information programs, international broadcasting, a nd publicly funded educational and cultural exchanges including the Fulbright Exchange Program, the Edmund S. Muskie Program, the Mike Mansfield Program, Voice of America, Radio Free Europe/Radio Liberty, Radio and TV Marti, Worldnet TV, the East-West Center, the North/South Center, and the National Endowment for Democracy (GAO/NSIAD-96-179, 1996, pp. 14-19). Estimated expenditures on USIA democracy-promotion activities between 1991 and 1993 amount to $936 million.

"Democratic development" constitutes, since 1993, one of the four main areas where the U.S. Agency for International Development (AID) now concentrates its programs, with direct support of activities ranging from "the conduct of elections to the administration of justice, enhanced participation of beneficiaries in development programs, and the management of municipal government." Between 1991 and 1993, AID spend $703 million to promote "democratic development" abroad (GAO/NSIAD-94-83, 1993, pp. 11-13).

The U.S. Department of Defense (DOD) established its Office of the Assistant Secretary of Defense for Democracy and Peacekeeping in July of 1993 with the purpose "to develop, coordinate, and oversee the implementation of policy and plans for matters related to the promotion of democracy and democratic values." As of 1994, the DOD's Office of Democracy identified the following programs and activities as having "democratic development elements": Military-to-Military Initiatives in Africa, including the African Regional Military Assistance Program and the African Democracy Support Program; CINC and Nunn-Lugar initiatives, including humanitarian/civic assistance; Expanded International Military Education and Training Programs; George C. Marshall Center for Security Studies at Garmisch, Germany; Military-to-Military/joint contact teams; and Professional military education exchanges. Between 1991 and 1993, the DOD spent $166 million on its activities of "promoting democracy and democratic values" (GAO/NSIAD-94-83, 1994, pp. 14-19).

The U.S. Department of State's democracy promotion activities include "conducting diplomatic initiatives and exercising statuatory authority for program direction or for assisting in administering programs funded by other agencies. Its initiatives also include contributions to The Asia Foundation." In 1996, the State Department redesignated its Bureau of Human Rights and Humanitarian Affairs as the Bureau of Democracy, Human Rights, and Labor and charged the new bureau with coordination of U.S. government policy and programs for democracy promotion abroad. State Department officials estimated that between 1991 and 1993, State spent $431 million on "democracy promotion " abroad. State officials point out that these figures do not include the U.S. contribution to the United Nations or for its peacekeeping activities. State officials also indicate that its expenditures on international narcotics matters and on anti-terrorism activities "could arguably be attributed to democracy promotion" (GAO/NSIAD-94-83, 1994, pp. 19-21).

Specific legislation authorizing U.S. assistance for democratic development is contained in the following legislative Acts:

- United States Information and Educational Exchange Act of 1948, as amended;
- Mutual Educational and Cultural Exchange Act of 1961, as amended;
- Foreign Assistance Act of 1961, as amended;
- National Endowment for Democracy Act (1983);
- The Asia Foundation Act (1983);
- International Security and Development Cooperation Act of 1985;
- Support for East European Democracy (SEED) Act of 1989;
- Urgent Assistance for Democracy in Panama Act of 1990;
- National and Community Service Act of 1990; and
  FREEDOM Support Act (1992).

Why such a practice of promoting capitalist democracy abroad should come about under present historical conditions and exhibit a certain degree of success requires an examination of the historical development of the modern states-system as it has evolved from its genesis in the development of the nation state to the currently unfolding global capitalist system complete with supporting practices and institutions, which likewise have generated their own antisystemic tensions.

II. From Westphalia to Globalization

Globalization and the current backlash against its corporate-dominated form is the context in which the U.S. attempts to export its brand of democracy abroad in the 1990s and into the twenty-first century.[46] It is true that the NED predates the current focus on globalization and, indeed, the end of the Cold War was a necessary condition for the forces of globalizing the rule of capital to ensue. But the political program of the NED and the economic goals of capitalist globalization are closely intertwined. Operating under the catchword of "liberalization", the forces of organized capital seek to dismantle national controls to trade so as to allow for the free and unhindered movement of capital. While uniting peoples from all over the world in one giant marketplace for the relatively easy extraction of profits and movement of goods, this capitalist-oriented globalization is simultaneously causing growing disparities in income, wealth, and living conditions which have created firestorms of protests against those implementing it.[47] From the staggering leap in U.S. foreign direct investment to over two trillion dollars at market value in 1998 from over $51 ½ billion in 1966 (Scholl, July 1999, p. 40; "U.S. Direct Investment Position Abroad...," March 12, 1999), to the spread of electronic and fiber-optic technology and satellite transmission systems and the proliferation of increasingly inexpensive personal computers linking up into a web of global communication networks, to the expansion of world exports of merchandise and commercial services to nearly seven trillion dollars by 1997 ("World trade growth accelerated in 1997...," March 19, 1998), globalization—or the tying together of the national economies of the world—is causing many to wonder if the days of the nation-state are numbered.[48] Thus, globalization, in contrast to traditional international relations (IR) theory, incorporates the political, economic, social, and other international domains in a system which violates the traditional demarcation between internal and external units, where those units are understood to be independent sovereign states. Indeed, where theory assumes a priori this basic internal/external demarcation (cf. Waltz 1979), then whatever can be said of the international system usually excludes national or internal forces and developments and the impact of these internal forces on the system itself. Once the state is taken as the basic unit of the international system, then a condition of anarchy—where "the units are functionally similar and tend to remain so" (Waltz, 1979, p. 104)—is postulated as the characteristic nature of the international environment. "Self-help" and "balance-of-power", taking into account the differences in capabilities amongst states, become the defining actions of the international system. With this basic, so-called "Realist", understanding, it becomes characteristic to assert that the "enduring anarchic character of international politics accounts for the striking sameness in the quality of international life through the millenia" (Waltz, 1986, p. 53) or to suggest that "the nature of international relations has not changed fundamentally over the millennia" (Gilpin, 1981, p. 211) or to claim that "[i]nternational politics is the realm of recurrence and repetition" (Wight, 1966a, p. 26).

But the existence and effects of globalization continue to transform the international system at the dawn of the twenty-first century and thus call into question long-held beliefs in IR theory which either deny such a transformation of the states-system (cf. Waltz, 1979, p. 95) or fail to account adequately for change within the system. The persistence of the realist perspective of international relations is understandable given that international theory as taught in the United States and Western Europe for most of the last century located its origins in the European states-system which arose out of the 1648 Peace of Westphalia following the Thirty Years War.[49] An alternative view marks the origin of the states-system with the 1454 Peace of Lodi and the Most Holy League of Venice which "founded the Italian Concert and the first system of collective security" (Wight, 1977, p. 111). However, as Martin Wight notes, it was the 1648 Peace of Westphalia which denotes "the legal basis of the states-system" (Wight, 1977, p. 113). The states of this new political system were qualified by the establishment of standing armies, the use of conscription, the professionalization of diplomacy with the establishment of foreign offices and the systematic arrangement of means to finance war. "In retrospect," states Wight

> Westphalia was believed to mark the transition from religious to secular politics, from 'Christendom' to 'Europe', the exclusion from international politics of the Holy See, the effective end of the Holy Roman Empire by the virtual recognition of the sovereignty of its members, the formal admission of the United Provinces [of the Netherlands]

and the Swiss Confederation to the family of independent nations, and the beginning of the system of the balance of power (Wight, 1977, p. 113).

The existence of "a multitude of sovereign states," writes Wight, marks the "minimum condition of a states-system" (Wight, 1977, p. 129). This condition, he asserts, is satisfied by the 1414-18 Council of Constance, which is why Wight chooses this 1414-18 date as the origin of the states-system rather than the conventional 1648 Peace of Westphalia. "At Westphalia," he writes, "the states-system does not come into existence: it comes of age" (Wight, 1977, p. 152). Specifically, as Wight notes, the "modern secular sovereign states-system arose from the ruins of the medieval international papal monarchy," which itself was the bridge between the Roman empire and modernity. Indeed, the prior framework out of which the present states-system arose was not "international" in nature, argues Wight, but rather "ecumenical," for the Church provided the anchor around which the Middle Ages, its peoples and their relations pivoted. The event which demarcates the alienation of several nations from the previous unity which Christendom provided "is clearly marked by the Council of Constance" [1414-18] whose "chief aim...was to heal the Great Schism" which "had divided Latin Christendom into two—and later three—obediences under rival popes" (Wight, 1977, pp. 131). With the dismantling of the universal government of the papacy, national churches arose (later to be replaced by kings) which henceforth conducted their relations with each other and the papacy on an equal basis through the diplomatic instrument of the concordat (Wight, 1977, p. 28). From its birth at Constance, the states-system developed, firstly, with the adoption of the principle of *cujus regio ejus religio* in the 1555 Treaty of Augsburg whereby each man was to adhere to the religion of his prince.[50] This principle not only promoted the idea of difference among the several principalities in Germany but, more importantly, stirred opposition to the dictates of the Church and the Holy Roman Empire throughout Europe. Construction of the states system was further consolidated at the Treaty of Westphalia in 1648 ending the Thirty Years' War.[51] Besides effectively excluding the papacy from future treaty-making, the Westphalian treaty also marked the beginning of an international society in that the practice of resident diplomacy appeared, rules of war were developed, along with rules of trade and commerce, ideas of a balance of power, and the idea of multilateral negotiations.[52] Yet it was not until the Congress of Utrecht in 1712-13 that the present states-system gets fully articulated, having the following characteristics: "first, sovereign states; second, their mutual recognition; third, their accepted hierarchy; fourth, their means of regular communication; fifth, their framework of law; [and] sixth, their means of defending their common interests" (Wight, 1977, p. 129).[53]

Taking issue with Wight, Rosenberg (1994) argues that Wight's periodization of the origin of the states-system in 1414 "is constructed not as a historical explanation of how the modern system arose but as a bare dating of when one of its descriptive attributes appears" (p. 44). Moreover, rather than an internal transformation, Rosenberg argues that the division of feudal Europe into discrete political entities is an external fact. Wight's theory, he argues, is "firmly locked inside the familiar realist straitjacket" such that it "sees only what appears to be the timeless mechanics of an anarchical states-system" (p. 44). Alternatively, writes Rosenberg, if we view the international system not as a separate, autonomous realm, and thus dispense with realist assumptions, then we must look precisely to the type of societies involved in this transformation, to their "core institutions and practices comprised in their material and political reproduction" (p. 45). Instead of taking a condition of anarchy as our starting point, we must instead look at "what is distinctive in the social forms of modernity" (p. 46). The "historically specific structures of social relationships involved in their stable reproduction over time" is, argues Rosenberg, how we must proceed to understand societies and their transformation. Moreover, we must "rehistoricize the study of international relations by identifying *continuities* between domestic social structures and geopolitical systems" so as to see the states-system as part of "a wider social totality" (p. 55). To accomplish this, Rosenberg elaborates a historical materialist explanation which focuses on the dominant capitalist relations of production which distinctively separates the modern states-system from its feudal predecessor. Marx's insight from the third volume of *Capital* regarding the relation of workers to the owner of the means of production provides the basis for Rosenberg's method. Quoting Marx, he notes:

> "*It is always the direct relationship of the owners of the conditions of production to the direct producers... which reveals the innermost secret, the hidden basis of the entire social structure*, and with it the political form of the relation of sovereignty and dependence, in short the corresponding specific form of the state" (Marx, Capital, Vol. III, Ch. 47, quoted in Rosenberg, 1994, p. 51).

If Marx is correct, he notes, then in conceiving of the modern international system, or any social formation for that matter, then "we need to understand how its political dimension—in this case, the sovereign states-system itself—is of a piece with the basic social structures which distinguish modern societies" (Rosenberg, 1994, p. 57). Rather than delving here into what a historical materialist perspective would look like—such an inquiry will be explored separately below—at present we must flesh out in greater detail the traditional realist understanding of IR before alternatives to it are presented.

In this regard, we return to Wight's sixth and last characteristic of the present states-system—"their means of defending their common interests", as it indicates that the novice states of Europe shared a foremost concern over their own stability. As Hedley Bull emphasizes in *The Anarchical Society*, "[t]he maintenance of order in international society has as its starting-point the development among states of a sense of common interests in the elementary goals of social life" (Bull, 1977, p. 67). Specifically, the modern states-system shares three principle goals which, Bull argues, include, first, the preference of a society of states over "such alternative ideas as that of a universal empire, a cosmopolitan community of individual human beings, or a Hobbesian state of nature or state of war, as the supreme normative principle of the political organization of mankind" (Bull, 1977, pp. 67-8). Secondly, states share certain minimum rules of coexistence which include the limiting of violence solely to sovereign states in the act of war, limitations on the causes, conduct and geographical spread of war, and rules governing the interaction of states—e.g. *pacta sunt servanda* (the keeping of agreements) or *rebis sic stantibus* (their annulment under changed conditions). Likewise rules of coexistence include those governing the control or jurisdiction of each state over its own persons and territory, including the central principles of respect for each state's sovereignty, nonintervention, and equality in enjoyment of the rights of sovereignty. Thirdly, a complex of rules exists which regulates cooperation among states beyond what is needed for mere coexistence. These include rules facilitating cooperation in political, strategic, economic and social areas, that is, rules of prescriptive behavior appropriate to "goals that are a feature of an international society in which a consensus has been reached about a wider range of objectives than mere coexistence" (Bull, 1977, pp. 67-70). To the degree that there was room for agreement on basics among the nascent states of Europe in the eighteenth century points to a certain shared identity in their composition.

In addition to these two Realist, and complementary, accounts of the origin of the states-system, several alternative traditions held sway in western IR scholarship which either essentialized the sovereign dominance of the state, argued against the limitations which its fundamental units—i.e. sovereign states—posed to transforming the system, or postulated the mutual interdependence of sovereign states within a system of recognized rules and norms.[54] "The primary questions of international theory," asserts Martin Wight, "concern the nature of international society and of international law" (Wight, 1966b, p. 92).[55] Addressing the then-prevailing perspectives on these questions, Wight (1966) and Bull (1966; 1977) delimited the range of thought in western international relations (IR) scholarship to three competing traditions. At the extremes are the Hobbesian and Kantian traditions which are irreconcilable on the questions of international society and international law such that the Hobbesian or realist tradition "describes international relations as a state of war of all against all" while the Kantian or universalist tradition "sees at work in international politics a potential community of mankind" (Bull, 1977, p. 24). On this Hobbesian view, international society is "a fiction or an illusion." It is "only the sum of the principles and rules which states—the *real* political units—have agreed to regard as obligatory; and the basis of international obligation is purely contractual. This is the doctrine," argues Wight, "of legal positivism" (Wight, 1966b, p. 93). Neither the desires nor passions of humanity are, in themselves, a sin, argues Hobbes, nor even their "Actions, that proceed from those Passions, till they know a Law that forbids them" which they cannot know "till they have agreed upon the Person that shall make it" (Hobbes, 1651/1980, Part I, Chapter XIII, p. 187). The Hobbesian tradition thus denies the existence of international society, proclaiming instead that within the international anarchy, the ultimate unit of political society—and hence the limit of any possible society—is the state. By contrast, the Kantian tradition claims that "the society of states is the *unreal* thing—a complex of legal fictions and obsolescent diplomatic forms which conceals, obstructs and oppresses the *real* society of individual men and women, the *civitas maxima*" (Wight, 1966b, p. 93). Hence, the essential nature of international politics from the Kantian perspective "lies not in conflict among states" but rather "in the transnational social bonds that link the individual human beings who are the subjects or citizens of states" (Bull, 1977, p. 25). And while the Hobbesian views peace as only "the period of recuperation from the last war and preparation for the next," the Kantian seeks perpetual peace in the ideas of world federalism, advocating that without a federated league of nations the unchecked right of nations will only lead to a "perpetual peace in the grave" (Bull, 1977, p. 25; Kant, 1795/1983, p. 117).

On the question of international law, the Hobbesian tradition sees this as constituted purely on a contractual basis which is obligatory only so long as adhering to international law is expedient to state interests. Free to pursue its goals in relation to other states without moral or legal restrictions and subject only to the rules of prudence and expediency, the Hobbesians assert that the sole basis for moral behavior in the international anarchy lies wholly within the realm of the state itself and in its own self-assertion in the international arena. Outside of the state lies a condition of anarchy, of "warre of everyman against every man." And in this external condition, writes Hobbes, "nothing can be Unjust." "The notions of Right and Wrong, Justice and Injustice have there no place. Where there is no common Power, there is no Law: where no Law, no

Injustice." Justice and injustice, writes Hobbes:

> are Qualities, that relate to men in Society, not in Solitude.   It is
> consequent also to the same condition, that there be no Propriety, no
> Dominion, no *Mine* and *Thine* distinct; but onely that to be every
> mans that he can get; and for so long, as he can keep it (Hobbes, 1651/
> 1980, Part I, Chapter XIII, p. 188).

The Kantian, however, is enjoined by moral imperatives to seek "the over-throw o f the system of s tates and i ts replacement b y a c osmopolitan society" (Bull, 1977, p. 26). Only in a cosmopolitan society, the Kantian holds, can the rights of individuals, and hence the rule of law, be fully guaranteed. In the "already established nations," Kant observed, "progress toward full development of man's natural capacities" is hampered by "expending all of the commonwealth's powers on arming itself against others, by the devastation caused by war, and, still more, by maintaining themselves in constant readiness for war" (Kant, 1784/1983, pp. 35-6). Hence, for the Kantian, not only is the community of humanity the central reality in international politics but, moreover, it is the object of the highest moral endeavor. The consequences of this position for international law, therefore, impose a duty on the Kantian to ignore any rule that seeks to sustain coexistence and social intercourse among states.

Existing between these two extremes, a third tradition of thought in international relations scholarship "describes international politics in terms of a society of states or international society" (Bull, 1977, p. 26). Known as the "father of international law," Hugo Grotius (1583-1645) divided law into two categories: natural law and volitional law, which, out of the latter, arose the subclassification of the law of nations (*jus gentium*). States Grotius:

> But just as the laws of each state have in view the advantage of that
> state, so by mutual consent it has become possible that certain laws
> should originate as between all states, or a great many states; and it is
> apparent that the laws thus originating had in view the advantage, not
> of particular states, but of the great society of states. And this is what
> is called the law of nations, whenever we distinguish that term from
> the law of nature (Grotius, 1625/1646/1957, p. 13).

The Grotian or internationalist, or rationalist (cf. Clark, 1996/1999, p. 5), tradition, as this perspective is known, "does not see international society as ready t o supersede domestic society; but it notes that international society actually exercises restraints upon its members" (Wight, 1966b, p. 95). Thus against the Hobbesian or realist tradition, "the Grotians contend that states are not engaged in simple struggle, ... but are limited in their conflicts with one another by common rules and institutions." In contrast to the Kantians or universalists, however, the Grotian tradition accepts "the Hobbesian premise that sovereigns or states are the principal reality in international politics"—rather than individual human beings (Bull, 1977, p. 26).

On the question of international law, the Grotians are closer to the Hobbesians than to the Kantians in their contractual view of international obligation; however, unlike the realists, they hold that states "are bound not only by rules of prudence or expediency but also by imperatives of morality and law" (Bull, 1977, p. 27). And because of their state-centric perspective, the Grotians disagree with the Kantian moral imperative on the necessity to overthrow the system of states and replace it with a federation of free states or cosmopolitan society, opting instead for "the requirements of coexistence and co-operation in a society of states" (Bull, 1977, p. 27).

The three approaches described above—the Hobbesian, the Kantian and the Grotian—were delineated as the prevailing traditions of thought in western international relations scholarship in the late 1960s to mid-1970s by the British IR theorists Martin Wight and Hedley Bull. These three approaches were developed partly in response to the need to counter the growing Marxist challenge to traditional IR theory in the West in the late 1960s and early '70s, but as well it was part of the behavioralist–traditionalist debate then raging at the time.[56] Indeed, "great debates" have been the conventional manner of retelling the history of international relations in the West. Neumann and Wæver, in fact, list a series of four such debates as follows:

1) realism versus idealism—1940s;
2) behavioralism versus traditionalism—1960s;
3) interparadigm debate between realism, dependence theory, and neo-Marxism—mid-70s; and the
4) confrontation between rationalists and reflectivists spurred on by the continental "postmodern" and "poststructuralist" philoso phies—late 1980s (1997, pp. 8-9).[57]

Since the 1980s, after the Foucaultian and Derridian critiques swept through western academia calling into question the centered subject while even, in some cases, killing off the author entirely (cf. Foucault, 1979/1984), some scholars prefer not to have their work attributed to any particular school of thought or, rather, prefer the nomenclature "postmodern" or "poststructuralist". As one survey of new "masters" of International Relations put it:

Usually, someone working in IR aims at some kind of coherence at the same time as striving to make complex and novel moves across established lines. All theorists make personal choices and the ability to retain an integrated academic persona(lity) is not secured once and for all by picking a 'position'. The traditional presentation of IR in terms of 'paradigms' or 'schools' obscures this since the writings of complex authors are often cut up and treated in separate sections. Only those who fit unequivocally into one box will be treated as whole persons—and most writers do not see themselves as operating within one of the boxes. As an academic *person* one would therefore learn more from tracing other unboxable persons in their trajectories through the discipline (Neumann and Wæver, eds., 1997, p. 2).

By focusing on "how meaning is constituted, how dominant ways of conceptualizing have been produced, and not least how the 'academic' writings of IR participate in the construction of what they [i.e. IR theorists] take as their independent object: 'international relations'," these reflectivist theorists seek not to gain a *better* perspective on international relations, for, indeed, it is exactly this quest for objectivity, control and security which they seek to jettison. In their attempt to avoid the ideological traps of traditional IR theory, these reflectivist writers opt out of the paradigmatic debate claiming that their debate is *not* one of incommensurability but rather that the important aspect to be studied is how the debate is "shaped by the self-understanding about its character" (Wæver, in Neumann and Wæver, 1997, p. 22). In this respect, reflectivists emphasize interpretation and intersubjectivity between institutions, norms, regimes, etc. and actors which both constitute such phenomena and, in turn, are constituted by them. Argues Devetak regarding the postmodern theorists, including Richard K. Ashley, Rob Walker, and James Der Derian, who arose in the mid-1980s to challenge traditional IR theories:

Instead of taking for granted issues of epistemology (knowledge claims) and ontology (claims about being or thinghood), it was now seen as essential to investigate how such issues had been dealt with by the competing 'traditions' of thought (Devetak, 1996, pp. 180-1).

That the formal western discipline of IR has been transformed since the first department of international relations was established at the University of Wales in Aberystwyth in 1919 is unquestioned, in a formal sense. Some, however, may argue that, substantially, IR still remains essentially dichotomized as it has been since 1916 following the publication of Lenin's *Imperialism: The Highest Stage of Capitalism*, between defenders of the capitalist order and their socialists and communists antagonists. Nevertheless, many strains of thought have developed on either side of the economic question during the ensuing years of the twentieth century with much overlap both in theory and practice amongst both practitioners and theorists. Indeed, the developing globalization of the capitalist economy has prompted many IR and International Political Economy (IPE) theorists to utilize theoretical methods from both capitalist and Marxist traditions. And whether we consider Lenin's New Economic Program, Keynes advocacy for the socialization of investment, FDR's stimulation of aggregate demand (itself based upon Keynes's theoretical insights), Gorbachev's perestroika, or Deng's reforms of Chinese agriculture, etc., the real world of politics is much more practical in its use of different theoretical models. The increasing adherence to dependency and Marxist theories in the mid-1970s certainly reflected the need for new explanatory paradigms to help make sense of changing world events, but by the late 1980s and early '90s, following the collapse of the Soviet Union and the socialist regimes in eastern Europe, much of the faddish interest in the radical theories of the '70s and early '80s waned while those who continued to adhere to these theories often deemphasized the Leninist or vanguard political aspects of these theories. Indeed, argue Burbach, Núñez, and Kagarlitsky (1997),

> Marxism-Leninism, erred fundamentally in asserting that a new order could be ushered in by taking control of the state, thus transforming the economy and society from above.

To the contrary, they argue:

> A new order cannot appear unless beliefs and values are changed in civil society—at the grassroots level—so that the state becomes a responsive apparatus rather than the principal agent of transformation (1997, p. 3).

Still, with the rapid pace of globalizing forces from telecommunications[58] and transport to the spread of the transnational as opposed to the multinational corporation and to the growth and relative autonomy of a multitude of international regimes from the International Monetary Fund (IMF) and International Bank for Reconstruction and Development (IRBD), otherwise known as the World Bank, to the World Trade Organization (WTO), many contemporary IR theorists argue that the state-centric focus either is in the process or has already been eclipsed by forces superordinate to the state (e.g. Robinson, 1996).[59] Thus, it is with a renewed relevance that one of the persistent questions in IR theory should focus on the level of analyis.

The Level of Analysis in International Relations Reconsidered

Existing as a subfield in the discipline of political science, international relations' underlying focus is the species homo sapiens and its members' interaction with their material environment and with each other. While sharing with other areas of political science a concern with human behavior predicated on interests defined in terms of power, IR has traditionally restricted itself to analyzing power as defined in military terms at the nation-state level of analysis. Domination in the military sphere was assumed to guarantee control over rules of behavior in other spheres. Thus, it was the use of diplomatic and military strategy to attain power which preoccupied many IR studies (cf. Kissinger, 1964). Such a view can be traced back to Thucydides and "The Melian Dialogue" where the operative principle, or "safe rule" as the Athenians referred to it, was "to stand up to one's equals, to behave with deference toward one's superiors, and to treat one's inferiors with moderation" (Thucydides, c. 460-404 B.C.E./1954/1985, p. 407). This principle need not apply only to the behavior between countries, however; indeed, the Athenians were "not so much frightened of being conquered by a power which rules over others,..., as of what would happen if a ruling power is attacked and defeated by its own subjects" (Thucydides, c. 460-404 B.C.E./1954/1985, p. 402). Hence, in our analysis of power in IR, the "level of analysis" is a significant factor which will affect both the type and the extent of the conclusions we reach.

In deciding on a level of analysis, one's underlying theoretical approach must be scrutinized for possible clues. In this respect, theory is a guide to study and hence to action, as well as a proposed explanation for the causal mechanisms responsible for a phenomenon or a set of facts. And as Hempel stated, "tentative hypotheses are needed to give direction to a scientific investigation" (Hempel, 1966, p. 13). Notes the *Internet Encyclopedia of Philosophy*, Hempel:

argues that it is impossible to derive observational statements from a scientific theory. For example, Newton's theory of gravitation cannot determine the position of planets, even if the initial conditions are known, for Newton's theory deals with the gravitational force, and thus the theory cannot forecast the influences exerted by other kinds of force. In other words, Newton's theory requires an explicit assumption—a provisoe, according to Hempel—which assures that the planets are subjected only to the gravitational force. Without such hypothesis it is impossible to apply the theory to the study of planetary motion. But this assumption does not belong to the theory. Therefore the position of planets is not determined by the theory, but it i s implied by the t heory plus a ppropriate assumptions <http://www.utm.edu/research/iep/h/hempel.htm>.

Our level of analysis in the study of IR is arguably thus a consequence of the theoretical assumptions we hold about how the world works. But whatever theory is chosen as a g uide to study, Singer p oints out t hat certain key elements must be present in the model if our subsequent level of analysis is to prove useful in correctly analyzing the reality one is dealing with. First, the theory must "offer a highly accurate *description* of the phenomena under consideration." Second, the theory must possess the "capacity to *explain* the relationships among the phenomena under investigation." And third, the theory should "offer the promise of reliable *prediction*" (Singer, 1961, pp. 78-9). As such, the methodological assumptions, constructs, terminology, experiences, etc. we utilize are variables which determine our epistemological and ontological conceptions of the world. That is, how we come to have knowledge of the world and what we can say is real or existing independently of the mind will affect our subsequent analytical approach and conclusions.

In this respect, we must first focus on the term "International Relations" or "International Politics," for these terms prejudge the field of inquiry to an extent by calling attention to only those aspects of human behavior which have "inter-*nation*-al" repercussions. As Young stated, "the very notion of *international* ... subsumes the postulate of the nation-state as the fundamental unit of world politics" (Young, 1972, p. 126). While states as legal entities are synonymous with ancient Roman and Greek empires in that they make decisions and enforce rules for their inhabitants, nation-states have become principle actors in world politics only within the last 300 years. As opposed to rulers of ancient empires or feudal nobles who claimed ownership of the state and its benefits for themselves either due to divine sanction, hereditary right, or conquest, the modern nation-state claims its authority from the consent of the governed, who likewise participate in the benefits derived from the operations of the state. The term "nation-state" itself "suggests a growing coincidence over time between states as legal entities and the psychological identification of people with particular pieces of territory" (Kegley, Jr. and Wittkopf, 1985, p. 74). Now whether this shared psychological identification rests primarily on the basis of ethnicity, a shared language, cultural homogeneity, territorially demarcated fixed boundaries, or simply collective subjugation by dominant classes is open to further study; what cannot be denied, however, is the fact that national entities continue to play a major role in the international arena as the collective representatives of statistically significant domestic populations who c ontrol state power. The study of IR, therefore, focuses the field of inquiry so that research concerns itself with relevant aspects of cross-national politics such that regularities and general tendencies of behavior can be observed. Nonetheless, if our level of analysis is fixated solely on the nation-state, and if we define nations as unitary and purposive actors, then we will tend to limit IR to the study of foreign policy.

From 1945 and up through the early 1960s, most of the texts published in IR qualified as studies in foreign policy, and specifically U.S. foreign policy. And in most of these texts, asserted Singer, "[n]ot only is the world often perceived through the prism of the American national interest, but an inordinate degree of attention (if not spleen) is directed toward the Soviet Union" (Singer, 1961, p. 84). Nonetheless, this state-centric level of analysis provided political scientists with various approaches to studying international behavior including historical description and analysis, especially the study of diplomatic history (e.g. Albrecht-Carrié, 1958); legal analysis concerned with analyzing various legislative provisions of countries, the treaties they entered into both with o ther countries and International Governmental Organizations (IGOs) (e.g. Sherr, 1986); numerous balance-of-power studies which examine the coalescence of countervailing coalitions to check countries embarking on hegemonistic policies (e.g. Newman, 1968); and analyses which focused on official decision-makers of countries as being of prime importance (e.g. Snyder, et al. 1962; or Janis, 1982/1983).

This preoccupation with the nation-state as the primary level of analysis in IR can be charted from its origins in the aftermath of the Thirty Years' War and the Peace of Westphalia in 1648 up to the present. Such an historical review of the development of IR is necessary, for, as Wightman stated:

> As all human societies are subject to change, they reveal their characteristics not simultaneously, but successively over time. To see them flat is not to see them at all. A snapshot view will miss the sense of direction and movement; it will fail to distinguish what is old from what is new, the elements of continuity from the appearance of change (Wightman, 1984, p. 23).

Prior to 1648, political unity in Europe consisted either of a universal empire, a monolithic state, or separate city-states whose rulers derived legitimacy as part of a divine order. Law in each of these forms was derivative from Roman imperial law which, while universal, had existed side by side with local jurisdictions. Due to the lack of centralization in the Roman Empire, interpretation and enforcement of law had varied from province to province. This practice of local jurisdiction continued with Rome's conquerors and dominated political thought in feudal Europe.

With the triumph of Christianity in medieval Europe, legitimacy of the universal order gained divine sanction with the Pope as God's representative on earth (Mansbach, et al., 1976, p. 9). It appeared as if knowledge of the Mayan or Incan Empires or universal empires in China, India, Africa, and the Arab World were largely unknown to the Europeans and hence posed no threat and presented no opportunities to their agricultural-based economies (Finlay & Hovet, 1975, p. 271).

However, as Abu-Lughod (1989) has recently demonstrated, there existed prior to the European world-economy which came to dominance by the sixteenth century, a number of world-economies or trade systems which, in the thirteenth century, joined the Middle East (including North Africa), India, and China. The interaction between these regions "stretched through the Mediterranean into the Red Sea and Persian Gulf on into the Indian Ocean and through the Strait of Malacca to reach China" (Abu-Lughod, 1989, p. 12). Without the existence of these various preexisting world economies, asserts Abu-Lughod, "when Europe gradually 'reached out,' it would have grasped empty space rather than riches" (Abu-Lughod, 1989, p. 12). In fact, she concludes, it was the "Fall of the East" which preceded the "Rise of the West." Rather than viewed as a simple takeover of a prior economic system or attributable solely to the internal characteristics of European culture, Abu-Lughod argues, Europe's subsequent predominance can be attributable to two paradoxical forces: 1) "pathways and routes developed by the thirteenth century were later 'conquered' and adopted by a succession of European powers," and 2) "the new European approach to trade-cum-plunder...caused a basic transformation in the world system" (Abu-Lughod, 1989, p. 361). More specifically, Abu-Lughod writes that it "was not so much the Portuguese takeover of the 'old world' but the Spanish incorporation of the 'new world' which had a decisive influence on why Europe's world economy became the center of world gravity in a decisive manner"; moreover, it provided "the windfall of wealth that e ventually were s pun into industrial gold" (Abu-Lughold, 1989, p. 363). In this sense, the wealth derived from the plunder of silver and gold from the Americas provided the primitive accumulation necessary for Europe's industrial revolution, and this, she says, "is why European scholars have in the last analysis been fixated on the sixteenth century" (Abu-Lughod, 1989, p. 363).

It is nonetheless true that following the Thirty Years' War in 1648, fairly well-defined nation-states resulted from the casting off of feudal traditions and their replacement with statist tendencies and administrative capabilities that emphasized territoriality and the centralization of legitimate authority and military power in the state. Legitimation was based on the doctrine of sovereignty which championed the right of each state to make and execute laws within its own territory. Beyond these borders, however, existed "an international system of shared authority and decentralized power" (Mansbach, et al., 1976, p. 17). The feudal economic base which had tied agricultural production in the countryside with the craft guilds organized in the feudal towns was replaced by the domination of mercantilism and the notion that the economic interests of the nation transcended individual or group interests. With the discovery of America by Europeans and the opening up of the world market, the context was set for the first wave of European imperialism with absolutist states seeking to increase their power through the acquisition of gold and silver. The related theoretical cataclysm resulting from the Protestant Reformation and the Enlightenment aided in this economic transformation by separating the political s ystem from the dominant i nfluence of the Roman Catholic Church. And as the closed guild system gave way to manufacturing in the realm of production, so too in the realm of thought did free competition gain expression in the forms of religious liberty and freedom of conscience, noticeable advances capitalism had over feudalism (Marx & Engels, 1848/1948/1998, p. 29). Legitimacy based in divine sanction thus gave way to political authority presented in the form of a social contract, and nationalism, or the doctrine of supreme loyalty to the state, became the unifying rallying call.

After the Peace of Westphalia, besides the Dutch and British who exercised hegemonic leadership over Europe in the seventeenth and nineteenth centuries respectively, no state politically, militarily, and culturally dominated Europe until the attempt by France under the leadership of Napoleon at the beginning of the eighteenth century. But his defeat at Waterloo enabled the 1815 Congress of Vienna to achieve a quasi-institutionalized acceptance of a "balance" of forces among the European powers. In this respect, states' internal politics became subject to international sanction if domestic policies encouraged hegemonistic threats to other European powers. It is in this regard that Britain's hegemony in the nineteenth century is said to have taken the form of a "balancer" to counter hegemonic threats to the European states-system. This arrangement provided stability for the European state system and held its principal actors together until 1914 and the outbreak of World War I. In the interim, however, the nineteenth century witnessed the creation of independent states in South America along with the colonization of Africa and Asia in the latter quarter of the century. The basis upon which power was constructed in both of these movements rested on the establishment of territorial borders formally represented by nation-states.[60] Thus, by the end of WWI, the recognized legitimacy of nation-states gave impetus to the organization of the League of Nations. Lacking enforcement power and credibility due to the refusal of the U.S. to join, however, the League was unable to halt the conflict which led to WWII. With the defeat of the Axis powers, the new correlation of forces after the second world war gave way to a bipolarity between the two great superpowers and their attempt to coalesce and control the former colonies who were now emerging formally as independent states. The establishment of the United Nations in 1945 constituted a significant symbol of this post-war paradigm, and, unlike its predecessor, the UN had the two major post-war powers as members (i.e. the United States and the Soviet Union). Though promoted as a community of sovereign nations, this multiplicity of states and their nominal independence were, it should be noted, more form than substance as they were subjected to the constant control and manipulation by their superpower sponsors. And from this history and within this modern framework, the still-prevalent orientation toward the state as the primary level of analysis remained fixed for a large part of the twentieth century.

The distinguishing characteristic of the post-WWII period, however, was, and continues to be, the overwhelming qualitative transition in military power associated with the development of nuclear weapons. As nuclear stockpiles proliferated, national boundaries become obscured and insufficient walls behind which to hide. The security provided by the territorially-inscribed boundaries of nation-states offer little protection in this new era characterized as a "balance of terror", a new concept mentioned by President John Kennedy in a 1958 speech and later expounded upon by his Secretary of Defense Robert S. McNamara and others (see, for example, an article by Albert Wohlstetter entitled "The Delicate Balance of Terror" from *Foreign Affairs*, January 1959). Hence, reliance on military power is increasingly rendering irrelevant that which it was meant to defend, *viz.* the nation-state. Similarly, while diseases from Acquired Immunodeficiency Syndrome (AIDS) and the West Nile and Ebola viruses know no state boundaries to which they are restricted, environmental destruction from pollution and depletion of non-replenishable resources cuts across national boundaries and national concerns. As such, the tragedy of the commons becomes the common tragedy of all.[61]

With perhaps less disastrous consequences albeit more far-reaching effects, however, technological revolutions in areas of communications, production, transportation, and most especially the development and refinement of computational tools—specifically the computer, the Internet, and the World Wide Web—render the geographical and cultural differences in the world increasingly more manageable. Construction of large centralized production facilities have been rendered unnecessary with increased efficiency and advances in transport, the latter which can not only quickly supply a company's or an individual's needs but, moreover, such products can accurately be tracked via the internet while they are in route. Diffusion of production facilities along with rapid and reliable means of communications and transport thus establishes a web of resources able to meet the needs of a global market. Global diversity there-fore, in theory, becomes less a tool for jingoistic manipulation as peoples come to identify with and relate their interests with the well-being of oth-ers in different areas of the globe. Human exchanges and concerns begin to cut across national and cultural boundaries on a scale unprecedented in human history. And the necessity for unified action to address global concerns becomes more pronounced and possible.

To analyze and understand the development of these new fac-tors which were only then in their infancy, a new paradigm arose in the 1950s-1960s seeking to place the level of analysis at the global level. This change in analytical approach reflected the change in world politics which saw t he ascendancy o f a g lobal international s ystem in p lace of t he Eurocentric system which had lasted from the Peace of Westphalia until WWII. And the primary determinant of this change was the global diffu-sion of technology (Dougherty and Pfaltzgraff, Jr., 1981, p. 137). The practitioners of *general systems theory* argued that the observer is always confronted b y a sy stem or i ts sub-systems a nd though t he cluster o f phenomena to be observed can range from the minute to the universe itself, the choice of which phenomena to focus on cannot be a function of whim or caprice. Systems theory, therefore, "assumes the interdepen-dence of parts in determinate relationships, which impose order upon the components of the system" (Dougherty & Pfaltzgraff, Jr., 1981, p. 141). Systems, Holsti pointed out, are distinguished by: a) boundaries which designate the line between interaction and environment beyond which political units have no environmental affect and environmental conditions pose no political affect; b) the main characteristics of the political units in the system; c) structures of power and influence or persisting forms of dominant and subordinate relationships within the system; d) common forms of interaction (e.g. diplomatic, trade, types of rivalries, and orga-nized violence or warfare); and e) explicit or implicit rules, customs, and values which govern relations (Holsti, 1967, pp. 28-29). Inputs and out-puts are the key components of systems theory which interact in a con-tinuous feedback loop which allows for self-adjustment by the system. Some of the initial approaches which developed from this systems-ori-ented perspective included Parson's Action System (cf. Parsons and Shils, 1951), Structural-Functional Analysis (Levy, Jr., 1952), Input-Output Analy-sis (Easton, 1953, p. 129), and an ecological systems approach (e.g. Sprout & Sprout, 1971).

The systems level of analysis permits the examination of IR as a whole. But, in practice, stated Singer, it tends to "lead the observer into a position which exaggerates the impact of the system upon the national actors and, conversely, discounts the impact of the actors on the system" (Singer, 1961, p. 80). Autonomy and choice are thus downplayed among systems level theorists who tend to gravitate toward a more deterministic orientation which emphasizes structure over its internal units (cf. Waltz, 1979). Moreover, if we postulate a high degree of uniformity in the foreign policies of national actors, then the scant room we allow for divergence amongst state actors may lead us to assume that "statesmen think and act in terms of interest defined as power" (Morgenthau, 1960, p. 5). The systems-oriented approach thus often discounts o r denies differences among states or in their internal workings and "concludes with a highly homogenized image of our nations in the international system" (Singer, 1961, p. 82). Structural approaches alone, therefore, tend to be static and empty and provide little understanding of how change occurs in the international system. To the extent that they do explain change, they tend largely to be wholly deterministic.

Thus faced w ith the functionalist constraints o f the s ystemic level of analysis which leads to determinism and the reductionist tendency inherent in the dominant view of the state as the primary level of analysis, IR theorists continued to seek out new paradigms which can unite both structures with human practices, and hence choice, and still provide a coherent explanation of social relations at the international level. Three aspects are necessary for the validity and hence usefulness of such a framework. First, the general theory should be logically consistent with its parts and every part should be explainable in relation to the totality. Second, there must be some way to test and validate the knowledge claims of the theory. And third, any such general theory of IR must possess, as Maclean argues, "an adequate account of change" (Maclean, 1981, p. 47).

Two related and yet opposing globalist paradigms which became prominent in the 1970s in western IR scholarship are theories which have developed mainly outside of American academic thought. And both of these theories have reluctantly been accepted into the American field of IR owing only to the inadequacy of much of the previous analyses. These two alternatives, and often conflicting paradigms, are *Dependency Theory* and *Imperialism*, and both have historical roots which are much older than the current academic interest in them. Comparing and assessing the central tenets of these two theories' propositions will help elucidate their respective level of analysis.

Before venturing into a contrast between Dependency and Imperialist theories, however, some general remarks about globalist theories must be made. As Viotti and Kauppi (1987) point out, there are both Marxists and non-Marxists who work within the globalist paradigm. What unites them, however, is that these theorists "see the **world capitalist system** as their starting point or who focus on dependency relations within a global political economy" (p. 399). Moreover, they assert, globalists are guided by four key assumptions:

1) Global context—"Globalists argue that to explain behavior at any and all **levels of analysis**—the individual, bureaucratic, societal, and between states or between societies—one must first understand the overall structure of the global system within which such behavior takes place."

2) Historical analysis—"Only by tracing the historical evolution of the system is it possible to understand its current structure. The key historical factor and defining characteristic of the system as a whole is **capitalism**. This particular economic system works to the benefit of some individuals, states, and societies but at the expense of others."

3) Mechanisms of domination—"[G]lobalists assume that particular *mechanisms of domination* exist that keep Third World states from developing and that contribute to worldwide **uneven development**."

4) Economic factors—"[G]lobalists assume that *economic factors* are absolutely critical in explaining the evolution and functioning of the world capitalist system and the relegation of Third World states to a subordinate position" (pp. 399-400).

Bearing these four assumptions in mind, an examination will first be made between Dependency and Imperialist theories and, following this, an analysis of an alternative globalist paradigm, World Systems Theory, will be presented.

Dependency theory is sometimes referred to as the theory of underdevelopment, and, as one would expect, the underdevelopment refers to areas in Latin America, Africa, and Asia where traditional colonial ties have continued in different forms despite the formal independence of these previous colonial states. Most of the thought on dependency theory has been developed by Latin Americans with the original arguments for dependency theory originating with the chief economist, Raul Prebisch, of the United Nations Economic Commission for Latin America (ECLA) after WWII. Prebisch pictured a divided world consisting of a *center* of industrialized countries and a *periphery* of underdeveloped countries. Prebisch argued that underdevelopment was caused by unequal terms of trade which led to a decline in exchange earnings. To remedy these effects, Prebisch asserted that governments in the periphery needed to subsidize the development of their own infrastructures, enact protective tariff measures and gear domestic production toward import substitution (Chilcote, 1981, p. 12). At the same time, Prebisch called for external funding from the industrialized developed countries in order to buttress domestic capital formation needed for development. Prebisch's lament (1971) is still relevant today concerning the insufficiency of such financial resources and the heavy debt burden accompanying such transfers.

> The amount of financial resources transferred has been inadequate and the burden of the corresponding service payments excessive.... In combination with the deterioration of the terms of trade, they [i.e. heavy service payments] have had a highly prejudicial effect on the mobilization of domestic resources and on investment (Prebisch, 1971, pp. 234-5).

Central to Prebisch's and later dependency theorists' arguments, therefore, is that *desarrollo* or development in the periphery (the primary producing countries for food and raw materials) is stifled by control from the center (areas of industrialization consisting of both developed market economies and centrally planned economies). And by "development," dependency theorists mean capitalist development. What is needed, the dependency theorists argue, is state planning and reform to promote autonomous national development. This movement would take the form of a class alliance between the national bourgeoisie and the masses to oppose domination from the industrialized center while supporting capitalist development in the underdeveloped periphery (Sunkel, 1972; Furtado, 1963). Internal development is faced with similar problems, for the same conditions of uneven development and traditional colonialism are found within countries also. Hence the formation of a national bourgeoisie and domestic capitalist development is seen as a remedy to "internal colonialism" (Gonzalez Casanova, 1970) and "poles of development" (Perroux, 1968; Andrade, 1967). Thus, the central question of dependency theory is: "Is capitalism possible in the periphery?" (Blomstrom and Hettne, 1984, p. 75). The answer is affirmative if one believes in the neo-classical theory of trade which operates under the rubric of "comparative advantage" (cf. Rostow, 1960). Such a perspective argues for an international division of labor operating under the assumption that

> any two nations will benefit if each specializes in those goods that it can produce relatively cheaply and exchange for goods that it can produce only at a higher cost.... Thus, when trade is unfettered by nonmarket forces or politically imposed barriers, all nations stand to share in the benefits and to grow more rapidly than they would when faced with barriers to free trade (Kegley, Jr., and Wittkopf, 1985, p. 172).

The problem, however, claim the *dependentistas*, as the adherents of this school are sometimes known, is that the terms of trade and most of the profits benefit only the industrialized countries. This is due to technological progress in the center which reduces costs and hence increases profits, but this rarely leads to price reductions on goods sold in the periphery due to "the high degree of monopolization of the factor and goods market there" (Blomstrom and Hettne, 1984, p. 41). This in turn leads to the co-opting of labour unions in the center which could use their strength and hence bargaining power to claim their cut of the increased profits resulting from the technological progress. This uneven development continues because both capitalists and workers profit in the center, and the former can maintain the unequal terms of trade over the periphery as long as workers in the center receive their share of the spoils.

Some writers have emphasized a neo-Marxist interpretation of dependency such as Baran and Sweezy (1966) who argue that corporate capital controlled by multinational corporations has replaced finance capital controlled by banks as the dominant form of capital accumulation in the world today. Baran and Sweezy emphasize the division of rich and poor countries based on the extraction of a surplus by multinational corporations with profits repatriated to the rich countries. Frank echos this idea of commercial monopoly in his theory of the "capitalist development of underdevelopment" in which he argues that "underdevelopment is in large part the historical product of past and continuing economic and other relations between the satellite underdeveloped and the now developed metropolitan countries" (Frank, 1966, p. 18). The agents of penetration in the Third World in Frank's schema are multinational corporations who seek to satisfy capitalism's need for external sources of demand and profitable investment outlets. What results is technological dependence, cultural imperialism, and a transfer of profits from the periphery to the center. Thus, in contrast to the developed economies, "the development of the national and other subordinate metropoles is limited by their satellite status" within a capitalist world framework (Frank, 1966, p. 23). Cardoso contended with Frank's development of underdevelopment thesis which alleges that the national bourgeoisie is unable to accumulate capital and offers instead his view of "associated dependent development" which argues that bourgeois-democratic revolutions in the periphery are impossible due to the penetration of the international capitalist system in peripheral economies (Cardoso, 1973). Capital accumulation is unable to complete its cycle in the periphery, because industrialization in the Third World produces goods not for mass consumption but for consumption by the local bourgeoisie. Nonetheless, the structure of the international division of labour by multinational corporations allows part of dependent economies to benefit from productive investment. Thus, through this type of gradual development, Cardoso favored "reformist policies and an evolutionary rather than a revolutionary approach to development" (Chilcote, 1981, p. 47). Dos Santos offers an alternative to Frank's emphasis on surplus extraction and argues that international relationships after WWII created a new form of dependency characterized by "technological-industrial dependence" which conditions internal structures in the periphery.[62] Foreign capital controls the marketing of exported products which maintains the dominance of the traditional landed bourgeoisie in dependent countries. The conservation of agrarian or mining export structures generates a link between metropolitan areas and more advanced economic centers that extract surplus value from more backward sectors. Thus, the "unequal and combined character of capitalist development at the international level is reproduced internally in an acute form" (Dos Santos, May, 1970, p. 234).

What is suggested in these views, as in nearly all dependency theory, is that capitalism develops primarily on the basis of the exploitation of countries rather than on the exploitation of workers. Moreover, dependency theory understands industrial development to be dependent on export earnings. Industrial development in the periphery is thus undermined by balance of payment deficits due to developing countries' inability to compete in a monopolized international market, control the repatriation of foreign profits by multinational corporations, and break free of their dependence on foreign capital to finance development.

Dependency, therefore, promotes the idea of inferiority of the periphery by suggesting that Latin American, African, and Asian countries *depend* technologically and financially on centers of industrialization and finance. Hence, the level of analysis in dependency theory is at the point of the circulation of commodities, market relations, and the unequal exchange of surplus value. But as one critic writes:

> In this light capitalism always appears impossible to attain, for one is seeing things through the perspective of the underdog capitalist who can never seem to make it imperialistically big (Johnson, 1983, p. 84).

Regarding the current analysis of the NED, the dependency approach fails to provide a motive for the U.S. export of democracy, for if the countries of Asia, Africa, and Latin America are permanently dependent on what happens in the core industrialized countries and, hence, are permanently disabled and unable either to compete with the core countries either in the production and export of commodities or in completing the cycle of capital accumulation, then why should the U.S. even bother with promoting a populist sounding political system, namely "democracy", attuned to the demands of U.S. capital accumulation, if these countries are locked into a system from which they cannot escape?

The problem for the Dependency theorists, asserts Johnson, is that they question why the countries in the periphery aren't imperialist, and the answer they arrive at points to their domination by imperialism (Johnson, 1983, p. 85). Johnson, as a representative of the Imperialist school of thought, therefore, objects to an absence of a historical materialist explanation of social relations represented by the concept of dependency, and hence objects to the *dependentistas'* level of analysis. Analysis, the Imperialist paradigm holds, "must be maintained at the level and moment of production/appropriation" (Johnson, 1983, p. 86). It is the theory of Imperialism which rests its methodology on a historical materialist analysis which will be explored below.

Imperialism as an alternative paradigm in IR has its roots in the Greek and Roman empires, but its modern forms date from the period of mercantile capitalism, which corresponded with the establishment of colonies and the quest by European powers for gold and silver and other sources of raw materials, to the beginnings of industrial capitalism, a period which Magdoff (1978) divides into three phases:

> 1) end of fifteenth century to 1650—marked by Europe's overcoming of the shipping blockade of the Ottoman Empire, opening up of the Americas to plunder, particularly of gold and silver resources and the use of cannon power to take over trade routes previously dominated by Asians and Africans;
> 2) 1650-to late eighteenth century—emergence of British dominance on the seas with the "political triumph of commercial capital" resultant upon the class struggles which brought on the English revolution in addition to the establishment of plantation "white-settler colonies" which built up demand for British manufacturers "to meet the needs of the settlers" as well as the utilization of slave labor on sugar plantations in addition to "the boom of export markets…under monopoly conditions secured through war, control of the seas, and political domination" (Magdoff, 1978, pp. 103-4); and
> 3) late eighteenth century-1870s—transition of the colonial system from one based on merchant capital to one based on industrial capital, coupled with the Industrial Revolution and the rise of industrial capital whereby imperial European powers penetrated into colonial interiors to secure control over raw materials and food production and imposition of the capitalist mode of production in colonial areas including the "introduction of private property in land; extending the use of money and exchange; imposition of forced labor and recruitment of a labor force depending on wages; destroying competitive native industry; creating a new class structure, including fostering of new elite groups as political and economic junior partners of the imperial powers; imposition of the culture of the metropolitan centers, along with racism and other sociopsychological characteristics of minority foreign rule" (Magdoff, 1978, pp. 106-7).

It was in this third stage of imperialism, writes Magdoff, whereby "European nations spread their control…from 35 percent of the globe's land surface in 1800 to 67 percent in 1878" (p. 108). As such, argues Chilcote

(2000), this new imperialism in the eighteenth and nineteenth centuries which was advanced initially by Britain and then later by the United States:

> signified a shift from dominance over trade to control of industrial transformation associated with the industrial revolution and the push of Europe toward manufacturing which necessitated extraction of raw materials in the periphery and expansion of the world market (p. 14).

By WWI, notes Magdoff, the "near-completion of the territorial division of the world" was accomplished "among the leading capitalist nations (from the 67 percent of the earth controlled by the Europeans in 1878 to 84.4 percent in 1914" (p. 108). After WWII, it is the successful "challenge by the United States to the financial hegemony of Britain" which distinguishes this period (Magdoff, 1978, p. 109) although imperialism was continued anew by transnational and multinational corporations who exerted their influence "beyond the national borders of the dominant nations" (Chilcote, 2000, p. 14).

With the rise of manufacturing and the expansion into industrialization by the late nineteenth century new markets were needed for products, for overproduction and underconsumption in the domestic market were said to spur the movement of capital and hence imperial control to foreign markets (Hobson, 1902). Two Marxist writers, Hilferding (1910/1981) and Lenin (1916/1982), took exception to Hobson's claims of underconsumption as the cause of British imperial expansion in the nineteenth century to other parts of the world and instead argued that capitalism had reached a new stage of monopoly capitalism with finance capital, that is capital controlled by banks and employed by industrialists, as its basis. Lenin expanded this argument and saw the political implications of this monopoly stage of capitalism as *imperialism*, which he argued was the apex of capitalist development that would set the stage for the eventual transition to socialism.

The theory of Imperialism has its roots in Marxism and the subsequent development of this thought by Lenin and others. As Linklater notes, recent years have seen a "more balanced view of the strengths and weaknesses of Marxism" which "has replaced the stereotypical representations of the doctrine which once prevailed." Concerned with developing a critical theory of international relations, its "impact is also clearly evident in efforts to construct a political economy of international relations which analyses [sic] the interplay between states and markets, the states-system and the capitalist world economy, the spheres of power and production." Moreover, Linklater argues that Marxism's relevance for international relations has increased since the ending of "the age of bipolarity and with the heightened impact of globalization," for, he writes,

Marxism is "intrigued by the processes which are unifying the human race—by globalization in the common parlance—and rightly identifie[s] capitalism as the main driving force behind the unprecedented level of international interdependence" (1995/1996, pp. 119-120).[63]

The methodology behind Marx's understanding of s ocio-historical relations is dialectical in orientation while his epistemology combines dialectics with a materialist outlook.[64] Marx's whole purpose was to develop a theory of social change, for he sought to resolve the dualism between consciousness and reality while reserving the independence of consciousness from external being. In what Maclean refers to as the "empirico-analytic tradition," one sought to "distinguish between objective facts, and non-objective, evaluative statements" (Maclean, 1981, p. 54). The consequence of this view, asserts Maclean, is that it both disallows "the possibility of coping with significant change" on the one hand while positing the construction of social reality "as independent of persons activities within it" on the other (Maclean, 1981, p. 54). In this respect, the individual existed in the world but was not of the world, and while social reality was seen as natural and unchanging, practical questions of change were couched in mechanical and deterministic terms. The epistemological dilemma which Marx sought to correct, therefore, was the contradiction between idealism and mechanistic materialism.

Marx's starting point for the process of change and the means of change was his understanding that a ll societies must reproduce themselves and this requires that they engage in material production. The practical aim of this activity is thus to transform natural objects of little or no use in their original form into a condition where they can satisfy human needs. And these needs, like the abilities required to satisfy them, are themselves historically produced and transformed. Thus, by production, "what is meant is always production at a definite stage of social development—production by social individuals" (Marx, 1857/1953/1973, p. 85). Material production, or the "practical construction of an *objective world*, the *manipulation* of inorganic nature, is the confirmation of man [and woman] as a conscious species-being; i.e. a being who treats the species as his own being or himself as a species-being" (Marx, 1843a/1964, pp. 127-28). And humans, unlike animals, are not one with their life activity, for it is conscious life activity itself which "distinguishes man [and woman] from the life activity of animals.... Only for this reason is his [or her] activity free activity" and thus an object of his [or her] will and consciousness (Marx, 1843a/1964, p. 127). Reality, therefore, is "not merely objective datum, external to people, but is shaped by them through consciousness" (Maclean, 1981, p. 55). At the same time, Marx maintains that there does always exist a natural material sub-stratum to the activity of human consciousness. Cognitive action, therefore,

is practical and material itself—it is objective activity, and so epistemology itself is not merely a cognitive reflection upon an external
world, but becomes the means for shaping, and therefore changing,
reality (Maclean, 1981, p. 55)

Thus transformative activity or human practice in social life is what makes
human activity distinctive, for it is in recognizing the world that humans
continually create and change it and in this process change themselves.
Stated Marx,

> All social life is essentially *practical.* All mysteries which lead theory
> to mysticism find their rational solution in human practice and in the
> comprehension of this practice (Marx, *Theses on Feuerbach* [8th
> thesis], quoted in Bottomore, et al., 1983, p. 386).

The search for a deterministic causality based on the laws of nature itself
is thus abandoned for a perspective which sees causality as directly related to the actions of individuals upon nature (Chilcote, 1981, p. 184).

Historical change from this perspective is the result of conflict
between a society's *forces of production* and its *relations of production.*
While the former consist of the sum of the material conditions of production including the raw materials, tools, machines, etc., as well as the human
beings themselves, with their knowledge and experience, the latter are
understood as the relations between human beings during the process of
production and the exchange relations of the material products in a society. Together, the forces and relations of production form the *mode of
production* which constitutes a society's economic structure which is the
determining factor in historical development.

From a dialectical perspective, the forces and relations of production interact with each other and changes in the former require adjust-
ments in the latter. But, Marx argued, society heretofore has been organized into classes conforming to people's relationship to the means of
production, and those in a class society who benefit from obsolete production relations will not voluntarily relinquish their privileged positions.
The consequent struggle between the different classes in society thus
results either in the defeat of the contending class or the overthrow of the
previous ruling class. The state from this perspective acts in the interests
of the economically dominant ruling class and ensures that all other societal interests are subordinated to those of the ruling class. Under capitalism, Marx and Engels asserted, the "modern state is but a committee for
managing the common affairs of the whole bourgeoisie" (Marx & Engels,
1848/1948/1998, p. 11). In this respect, the state mediates the interests of

the bourgeoisie but in no way reconciles class conflict. As Lenin outlined Marx's idea of the state, he noted:

> The state is the product and the manifestation of the *irreconcilability* of class antagonisms. The state arises when, where, and to the extent that the class antagonisms *cannot* be objectively reconciled. And, conversely, the existence of the state proves that the class antagonisms *are* irreconcilable (Lenin, 1917/1971, p. 8).

Class, therefore, is the basic unit of analysis from a Marxist perspective and hence in the theory of imperialism, but its meaning is void unless one is familiar with the elements on which classes rest. For example, in the capitalist epoch, one must understand the relationship between wage-labour and capital. Capitalism, Marx stated, simplifies class relations pitting the bourgeoisie or owners of the means of production—or, more specifically, those who appropriate the surplus labor in the form of surplus value as well as those capitalists (merchants or moneylenders) who provide for conditions of existence for the fundamental class process—against the ranks of the proletariat or "a class of laborers, who live only so long as they find work, and who find work only so long as their labor increases capital" (Marx & Engels, 1848/1948/1998, p. 15).[65] Under capitalism, the value of a commodity produced exceeds the sum of the value of labour-power and means of production consumed in the process. This is possible only because the exchange value of labour-power is less than its use value in the means of production. Unless the use value of labour-power exceeds its exchange value, no surplus value is created. Thus labour-power is the only commodity whose use adds value to other commodities and, consequently, is the source of all value. The class confrontation in capitalism thus arises out of the fact that the proletariat is first forced to sell its labour-power to the bourgeois owners of production for a wage in order to subsist, and secondly, the workers must produce more value than they are paid in wages. Thus conflicts over the intensity and conditions of work characterize the antagonistic class conflict of capitalist production and structure the technical and social aspects of that production (Bottomore, et al., 1983, p. 266). The level of analysis from a Marxian perspective, as a result, must always concern itself with the mode of production.

　　To understand the political economy of capitalism, we must, therefore, begin with commodities from the moment products are exchanged one for another. These products exchanged are commodities in so far as they represent a relationship between two persons or communities. The thing or product thus represents the relation between producers and consumers who are no longer, as in feudalism, united in the same person.

Economics, therefore, deals not with things but with relations between persons and, in the last resort, between classes; yet these relations always are attached to things and appear as things. While c ommodity production b rought t ogether propertyless workers with property-owning capitalists, it possessed certain internal contradictions which Marx saw as the basis for its transformation. Capitalists engaged in commodity production in order to accumulate capital. As such, capitalists d o not s eek to raise the standard of living of the masses, for this would mean a lower rate of profit. Surplus capital, therefore, will always be used for the purpose of increasing profits. This process of accumulating capital, however, led toward the increasing concentration of the means of production and command over labour-power in the hands of a few capitalists, which in turn, as Marx pointed out, widened the basis for large-scale production. By the late 19th century, the tendencies to greater concentration of capital, and h ence larger-scale production, developed to the point where monopolies formed which subjugated free competition to capitalist monopoly. The results of this inherent contradiction between monopoly and the subjugation of the fundamental characteristic of capitalism of free competition were "cartels, syndicates and trusts, and merging with them," wrote Lenin, "the capital of a dozen or so banks manipulating thousands of millions" (Lenin, 1916/1982, p. 88). Monopoly, therefore, contradicts free competition, and by repressing the latter it sets the stage for the transition from capitalism to a higher system of production, turning *laissez-faire* capitalism into its opposite.

Capitalism must ever strive for the accumulation of capital, but the qualitative leap in large-scale production along with the tremendous concentration of capital erected a barrier to the continuation of capital accumulation on the national market alone. Surplus profits, therefore, had to be exported abroad to, what Lenin called, the "backward countries" (Lenin, 1916/1982, p. 63). Thus, it is monopoly which forms the basis for the qualitative leap in the socialization of production, and the focus of socialization now concentrates on integration of this process on a global scale. The tremendous significance of this socialization of production, wrote Lenin, is that:

> Capitalism in its imperialist stage arrives at the threshold of the most complete socialisation of production. In spite of themselves, t he capitalists are dragged, as it were, into a new social order, a transitional social order f rom c omplete free competition t o complete socialisation.
> Production becomes social, but appropriation remains private. The social means of production remain the private property of a few. The general framework of formally recognized free competition re-

mains, but the yoke of a few monopolists on the rest of the population becomes a hundred times heavier, more burdensome and intolerable (Lenin, 1916/1982, p. 25).

War, therefore, in the stage of imperialism is the only means to break through the obstacles of continued capitalist accumulation and export of capital and commodities and to set a new framework for accumulation.[66] War becomes a necessary and central element to the workings of the whole system more so than at the earlier stages of capital accumulation. Thus, the political divisions between countries become important in the sense that states, which represent the power and interests of different ruling classes, must mediate the potential conflict of ruling class interest. This conflict can take the form either of inter-capitalist rivalry or rivalry between a capitalist and a pre-capitalist state. Whatever form the rivalry takes, however, will result in the territorial division of the world among the great capitalist powers, and production and distribution will become centralized in internal capitalist monopolies, trusts or cartels.

It is thus in this fundamental historical materialist thesis where the Imperialist paradigm disagrees most with the Dependency theorists, for the Imperialist school asserts the parasitic nature of capital on labour in general and not merely between national capital. Thus imperialism refers not to the "oppression and 'exploitation' of weak, impoverished countries by powerful ones" but "to the process of capitalist ACCUMU-LATION on a world scale in the era of MONOPOLY CAPITALISM, and the theory of imperialism is the investigation of accumulation in the context of a world market created by that accumulation" (Bottomore, et al., 1983, p. 223). The Dependency school, by basing its entire theoretical argument on the technological and financial dependence of Latin America, Africa, and Asia on centers of industrialization like the United States or Great Britain, thus maintains the mystification of the power of capital and technology as the remedy to "development," while the class contradiction of production and appropriation is all but ignored. States Johnson,

> They distract attention from the essential Marxian concept (and materialist point) that labor power alone is the creative force of social history (and of technology and capital), while capital is but a mere form of social relations, a product itself of that labor power (Johnson, 1983, p. 89).

In this respect, the dependency perspective is criticized for its underemphasis on class analysis and its overemphasis on external determination to the neglect of offering materialist explanations of the sociohistorical relations which exists.

Underdevelopment, therefore, cannot be totally attributed to capitalism which forces a uniform mode of production on countries in the periphery. The historical-structural s truggle between c lasses must b e examined in particular. While the drive for accumulation on a world scale structures territorial classes into subordinate relationships, it must not be forgotten, as Marx pointed out, that people "make their own history but they do not make it just as they please" but rather "under circumstances directly found, given and transmitted from the past" (Marx, 1852/1978, p. 595). The historical imposition of capitalism on the Third World appropriated "other modes of production and/or division of labor, dominant classes, or religious beliefs to facilitate or guarantee its dominance and reproduction" (Chinchilla, 1983, p. 160). Hence, the pace and development of capitalism will vary according to other modes of production with which it interacts. The contradictions engendered by these conflicting modes of production and the process of change must be understood therefore not as a linear evolutionism but as dialectical and interactive. Thus in articulating modes of production as the basic level of analysis, it is first necessary to be cognizant of conflictual relationships between different modes of production and with their own internal contradictions emanating either in the forces or relations of production. And secondly, focusing on modes of production as the primary level of analysis is done in order to understand the material basis and workings of the basic unit of analysis in Marxian thought which is class or class alliances.

    In recognizing relations of dependency as a product of structural heirarchies beholden to monopoly capital, one understands the material basis for this situation as arising out of the struggle between the contradictions of social production and private appropriation which "one must be able to link up the ideological theses within the social sciences with specific class needs at particular moments in history" (Johnson, 1983, p. 91). Only from this material contradiction, asserts Johnson, "can one understand Marx's political conclusions about the historical need for socialist revolution" (Johnson, 1983, p. 93). Lacking this basic materialist understanding, the *dependentistas* propose ideas of socialism which tend to isolate the local dominant classes thereby isolating workers while encouraging "petty bourgeois intellectuals into isolated acts of guerilla violence" which have little short-term effects and "monopoly capital (imperialism) remains untouched in the end" (Johnson, 1983, pp. 95-96). And these conclusions are the d irect result o f the *d ependentistas* p ositing their level of analysis at the point of market and exchange relations and the circulation of commodities, capital, and labour. In analyzing nation to nation relations, therefore, the ideological theses of the dependency school concludes as follows:

First, the United States (monopoly capital) *depends* on Latin American countries (competitive capital) for the production and appropriation of surplus-value; second, Latin American countries *depend* on the United States for finance capital and technology, given the historical conditions of imperialism's control over the means of production and capital; and third, the United States and Latin American countries (inter)*depend* on one another, given the international division of labor and the system of capital production (Johnson, 1983, pp. 87-88).

Had they located their level of analysis in the mode of production, the dependency theorists would have recognized the determining contradiction of socialized production and private appropriation and thus of the parasitic nature of capital on labour in general and not merely between national capitals. From this materialist level of analysis, they would have been able to reverse their scientific theses, which justifies continued imperialist domination, and linked them with the historical needs of the proletariat, to read as follows:

First, the United States is *independent* of Latin American countries, given its control over the means of production, its own labor forces, and its control over capital accumulation; second Latin American countries are *independent* of the United States, given their productive, creative potential to construct their own historical process; and third, the United States and Latin American countries are *independent* of one another based on each other's relative position of autonomy within the international division of labor, and so on (Johnson, 1983, p. 88).

From this materialist understanding, derived by basing one's level of analysis in a society's mode of production and analyzing the contradictions which therein arise, Marxists claim to be able to posit a coherent theory of IR which understands the imperialist nature of monopoly capitalism thus avoiding the dependency theorists' fixation with surplus value exchange which has left them "unable to combat the very relations they explicitly hope to eliminate: the imperialist relations of production and appropriation of capital" (Johnson, 1983, p. 90).

Many of these debates between the Dependency school and the Imperialist school impacted upon the development of World-Systems theory which first arose out of Immanuel Wallerstein's *The Modern World System* (1974). World-Systems theory, as an alternative globalist paradigm, is primarily a response to the structural-functionalist approach dominant in the U.S. from the 1940s through the 1960s which postulated a universal model of societal development known as "modernization theory". Counterposing traditional "undifferentiated" societies with a limited number of institutions (oriented primarily around family and kinship) to modern industrial "differentiated" societies—with differentiated institutions, both public and private, being the key to development and societal survival—modernization theory held that all societies have already or will shortly develop through a similar developmental process. Lack of development in Third World societies was thus "simply the result of 'historical backwardness'." Once traditional societies overcame their backwardness by revamping their "social structures, cultural values, and political institutions," then "these societies would be in a position to take advantage of transfers of industrial technology from the West and to begin improving their economies" (Shannon, 1989, pp. 4-5). Key to modernization theory was the necessity to copy institutions of the advanced states in the West and, with Western educational and technical assistance and training, speed up the process of development. The motivation for Western industrial societies to actively participate in this program of assistance to developing countries was in part to counter communist influences in these "backward" countries. States Shannon:

> If modernization was not encouraged and shaped by Western efforts, the rising discontent that derived from the breakdown of traditional value systems and institutions and from increased expectations among the impoverished masses could lead to support for Communist-inspired revolutions and the creation of totalitarian dictatorships hostile to the West (1989, p. 6).

While criticism of modernization theory was varied and included castigation of its ahistorical approach, its lack of concern with the particularities of different societies, its assumptions of orderly change and preference for stability, the major criticism by World-Systems theorists dealt with modernization theory's attribution of the problems and lack of development in the so-called backward countries as an internal factor owing to these societies' preference for traditional institutions. To the contrary, argued modernization theory's critics:

> such a view ignored several centuries of cultural contact, trade, colonization, and political-military intervention by Europe and (later) by the United States. Hence, said the critics, these countries stopped being true traditional societies well before the twentieth century. Rather, they had been changed into new kinds of societies that fit neither the traditional nor modern categories of modernization theory (Shannon, 1989, pp. 6-7).

Historical backwardness in developing nations was thus the result of a system of exploitation emanating from the relatively developed industrialized societies in the world system.

Influenced by the work of Fernand Braudel (1981, 1982, 1984) and the concerns of French historical thought associated with the Annales school and its journal, Wallerstein was initially interested in the colonial structures as they applied to Africa but was unable to account for general attributes of this situation without focusing on the world-system itself. After jettisoning states as an appropriate unit of analysis in his research, he concluded that the world-system which had arisen out of Europe in the sixteenth century and spread across the globe was the only useful level of analysis for his purposes. He states: "I had one type of unit rather than units within units. I could explain changes in the sovereign states as consequent upon the evolution and interaction of the world-system" (Wallerstein, 1974, p. 7). This decision then led him to focus in on what he felt was a fundamental discontinuity or break in the historical process which produced this world-system. The "rupture" in the historical process, he concludes, occurred in Europe

> in the long sixteenth century and that involved the *transformation* of a particular redistributive or tributary mode of production, that of feudal Europe (Braudel's "economic *Ancien Régime*") into a qualitatively different social system (Wallerstein, 1980, pp. 7-8).

The significance of this historical watershed, states Wallerstein, is matched only by "the so-called neolithic or agricultural revolution" (Wallerstein, 1974, p. 3).[67] As opposed to the previously existing isolated world-empires or world-economies which perchance did trade with one another, Wallerstein postulated the development of a world economy which originated in sixteenth century Europe and was linked initially with South America but later expanded to incorporate most areas of the world thus forming the modern world-system. In this sense, a world-system

> is a social system, one that has boundaries, structures, member groups, rules of legitimation, and coherence. Its life is made up of the conflicting forces which hold it together by tension, and tear it apart as each group seeks eternally to remold it to its advantage. It has the characteristics of an organism, in that it has a life-span over which its characteristics change in some respects and remain stable in others. One can define its structures as being at different times strong or weak in terms of the internal logic of its functioning (Wallerstein, 1974, p. 347).

In addition, he adds, a world system has an "extensive division of labor" which "is not merely functional—that is, occupational—but geographical. That is to say, the range of economic tasks is not evenly distributed throughout the world-system" (Wallerstein, 1974, p. 349). Moreover, "the classical lines of division within social science are meaningless," he argues, when one studies a social system as opposed to a "liberal conception of the state and its relation to functional and geographical sectors of the social order." As a consequence, world-systems theory calls for a "unidisciplinary approach" as opposed to a "multidisciplinary approach", thus uniting the efforts of anthropology, economics, political science, sociology, and history (Wallerstein, 1974, p. 11).

Historically, the modern world-system is the only such world-system and incorporates a "set of relatively stable economic and political relationships that has characterized a major portion of the globe since the sixteenth century" (Shannon, 1989, pp. 20-21). This new type of social system which emerged is set apart from its historical antecedents by the particular nature of its political economy which is "a *capitalist* economy organized into an *interstate system*" (Shannon, 1989, p. 22). By this understanding, it is the particular way in which exploitation occurs which distinguishes the modern world-system from previous societal formations. Whereas accumulation of surplus previously had been extracted by political coercion through taxes, tribute, slavery, and other means usually by a hereditary aristocracy who controlled the state, by contrast accumulation of surplus under capitalism is undertaken by the private owners of the means of production. The role of the state under this new economic system

> consists of enforcing the social relations of production between owners and workers. It does so by protecting property rights and enforcing the terms of exchange among participants in the economy. The state also creates conditions favorable to operation of productive enterprises (Shannon, 1989, p. 22).

This new system is a capitalist system because it is based upon "(1) profit maximizing and the search for competitive advantage through efficiency, (2) the quest for continual capital accumulation, and (3) the exploitation of labor by the owners of the means of production" (Shannon, 1989, p. 23). Its fundamental imperative, however, "is capital accumulation for the owners of the means of production" (Shannon, 1989, p. 28). Moreover, as Hopkins explains, the most fundamental theoretical claim of world-systems theory is as follows:

> It is the articulation of the *processes* of the world-scale division and integration of labor and the *processes* of state-formation and deformation (the latter in the twin context of interstate relations and relations of imperium) that constitute the system's formation and provide an account, at the most general level, for the patterns and features of its development (hence, of the patterns and features of modern social

change). The articulation of the two sets of processes necessarily results, in the theory, in the network of relations among political formations (states, colonies, etc.) being patterned like the network of relations among production-accumulation zones (core-periphery), *and vice versa* (Hopkins, 1982, p. 12).

In addition to its capitalist economic organization, the other basic aspect of the modern world-system is that it is comprised of competing sovereign nation-states, n one of which has b een able t o eliminate i ts counterparts. Indeed, writes Wallerstein:

> It is the peculiarity of the modern world-system that a world-economy has survived for 500 years and yet has not come to be transformed into a world empire—a peculiarity that is the secret of its strength (Wallerstein, 1974, p. 348).

Precisely because of the multiplicity of states in the system, Wallerstein argues, has capitalism flourished. This large "arena" allowed economic factors to operate beyond the control of any single political entity. "This gives capitalists a freedom of maneuver that is structurally based. It has made possible the constant e conomic expansion of the w orld-system, albeit a very skewed distribution of its rewards" (Wallerstein, 1974, p. 348).

Besides nation-states, o ther components o f W orld-Systems theory include economic zones, social classes, and status groups. Borrowing from Dependency theory, World-Systems theorists utilize the terms "core", "semi-periphery", and "periphery" to categorize the world social division of labor. These terms, states Hopkins, "designate complementary portions of the world-economy and only derivatively pertain to its political division" (Hopkins, 1982, p. 11). Core states are understood to be economically and politically dominant states in the world-system which have access to the most advanced technological processes and thus specialize in manufacturing the most sophisticated goods. As well, core states' military power is superior to the other economic zones of the system. Although initially confined to Europe, the U.S. and Japan are understood to have attained core status in the twentieth century.

At the other end of the world-systems spectrum are those states and colonies in what is referred to as the periphery. Relatively weak in terms of military power, states in the periphery are technologically deficient and engage in more labor-intensive production. Consisting of most states in South and Central America, Africa, and Asia, "production for export was concentrated on raw materials and agricultural commodities" in these states for "most of the modern era" (Shannon, 1989, p. 25).

Existing as a mid-point between core and periphery states, and which also act to mediate between these two extremes, are what are known as semi-peripheral states. Exhibiting a mixture of more-or-less technological sophistication in production mechanisms relative to their core/periphery counterparts, the organization—both political and military—of these semi-peripheral states (e.g. Brazil and Argentina) grants them a degree of autonomy envied by states in the periphery, though their subordinate status in the world-system maintains their dependent status on the core states.

With regard to social classes, world-systems theorists follow Marx's classification of differentiating social groupings according to their relationship to the means of production. In contrast to world-empires which preexisted the modern world-system where the basic distinction was between those who controlled the state machinery and those who did not, under the modern capitalist world-system, the basic distinction "is between those who own the means of production and those who are denied ownership" (Shannon, 1989, p. 27).

A final social cleavage which world-systems theorists recognize is that of status-groupings "whose solidarity derives from cultural identification" based on factors such as "religion, language, race, or ethnicity" which, in the modern era, have "become organized into nations or peoples governed by a single state." The significance of these groupings for world-systems theory is that these identifications have often "prevented global class solidarity of both the capitalist class and the proletariat" (Shannon, 1989, pp. 27-8).

While world-systems theory constitutes a relatively new perspective by which to analyze international relations, one of its most promising studies (Boswell & Chase-Dunn, 2000) relates directly—if only as postulating an alternative conception of democracy from that being promoted by the NED—to the thesis of the present dissertation. In theorizing the prospects for what they call "global democracy," these theorists analyze antisystemic social and labor movements from 1848 to the present which have overcome the worst forms of domination including slavery and colonialism, and they postulate "a spiral of economic expansion and social progress by which the modern world-system has expanded and intensified to become the global political economy of today" (Boswell & Chase-Dunn, 2000, pp. xi-xii).

Rejecting teleological claims which postulate the inevitability of progress, Boswell and Chase-Dunn utilize structuralist and materialist theories in light of the impact of cultural factors and individual decisionmaking to formulate a response to what they see as "the current ideological hegemony of neoliberalism" (p. xii). With the world economy as their level of analysis, they recognize certain systemic trends and cycles which have molded the world-system over the long-term. As well, they acknowledge "the impermeability of the global capitalist system," asserting that the various attempts of communist or socialist states to break out of the system were "never feasible in practice" (pp. 3-4). Nonetheless, they argue that the parameters of the world-system are not impervious to social action from below as witnessed by the change in rules governing global capitalist relations over the past 500 years including the abolishment of slavery, the liberation of colonies, and the winning of democracy in various areas of the world. However, they warn, individual action at the state level is not sufficient to generate permanent change in the world-system; on the contrary, they write, "institutions and relations at the global level must be changed in order to foster equality and end exploitation in every state" (p. 5).

Boswell's and Chase-Dunn's conception of global democracy has a dual characteristic in that it advocates for "democratic institutions governing the ever more integrated world economy" while, at the local level, they call for "economic management and social administration as well as politics and the state open to democratic participation." In this regard, they assert, "[d]emocracy includes civil and individual human rights, without which democratic institutions are meaningless." Moreover, they argue, "rights in the economy, and links between the economy and the polity, are also fundamental to any conception of democracy that can actually produce social justice and equality" (pp. 5-6). Consequently, they reject the simple notion which equates the mere presence of popular elections with democracy. Without economic democracy, they argue, what results are "highly unequal, class-divided societies" g overned by "an elected polyarchy." This is the form of democracy, they assert, which currently "exists in the United States and is promulgated world-wide by the U.S. [National] Endowment for Democracy as the political basis for the neoliberal globalization project" (p. 6).

Rejecting the necessity for state ownership of the means of production to achieve their goals of meeting basic social needs, sustainable development, social justice, and peace, they nonetheless believe that the actions of workers worldwide can, through the twin processes of market competition and c lass conflict, contest the standards and r ules of the current capitalist world order. The accumulation of capital alongside its cycles of expansion and stagnation "produces a spiraling growth in production forces that, however unevenly, always offers periods with the possibility of improving people's lives" (p. 10). Admitting that an alternative response to capitalist globalization could well be led by forces of national chauvinism which "can easily devolve into racism and xenophobia," they argue that it is f or this reason that t he "contemporary transnational drive toward heightened exploitation can only be checked by," what they refer to as "transnational p olitics." In particular, they argue:

Global labor standards, environmental regulations, and women's rights form a single starting point.[68] Through institutions of global democracy, labor and allied movements can direct market competition away from cheaper wages and toward increasing human productivity. In world historical terms, this is the essence of the term "progressive" (Boswell & Chase-Dunn, 2000, p. 13).

The present study with its focus on the NED and the export of a U.S. brand of democracy abroad in an attempt to secure U.S. hegemony in the post-Cold War world and into the 21st century, draws selectively from each of these globalist theoretical paradigms. Historical materialism provides an understanding of the animating aspects of both societal and material development and the underlying dialectical tensions in the historical epoch of capitalism. In addition, Gramsci's further elaboration of historical materialism as presented in Chapter 1 provides insight into the necessity for a would-be ruling class to provide leadership without simply relying on the use of force so as to engender a socio-political moral ethic to win legitimacy for its programs and rule, thus exerting sufficient hegemony necessary for its reproduction and continuity. And while Dependency theory's distinctions between core and periphery are useful in categorizing asymmetries of power and wealth internationally, its understanding of exploitation as occurring between states fails to account for the new processes associated with globalization which are beginning to bring pockets of wealth to these traditionally neglected areas in the Third World while exacerbating disparities of wealth within core societies themselves, albeit the major economic divide still rests between the so-called developed and developing nations.[69] On the other hand, the broad international systemic context presented by World Systems theory, positing a truly global system, currently capitalist in orientation, provides the fundamental framework for analyzing the evolution and integration of the world capitalist economy and the interdependencies of social classes, states, status groups, their effect upon struggles both within and between states, the effect the overall system has recursively on these struggles, while highlighting the antisystemic movements which act to alter current constraints of the global capitalist system. Because the capitalist mode of production is dominant throughout the system, the level of analysis it posits for international relations theory rests at the level of the global economy. However, this writer agrees with Halliday (1999) that World Systems theory's implicit assumption that all antisystemic movements opposed to capitalism are "necessarily part of a broader emancipatory process" conveys too much of a unity on them "and commonality of direction" (pp. 306-7). Moreover, as Halliday points out, many of the social movements since the mid-1960s were "anything but emancipatory" including:

> right-wing populist mobilisations in the USA that heralded the advent of Reagan in 1981, mass racist movements in Western Europe in the 1980s and 1990s, [and] fundamentalist mobilisations of Muslims, Jews and Hindus (Halliday, 1999, p. 307).

Indeed, Halliday's central criticism of World Systems theory is its assertion that the whole world is inextricably capitalist in orientation. The theory posits, for example, that the Soviet Union and its Eastern European satellites were part of the capitalist world system. If there has only been one system, then oppositional forces to communism "were part of the same world-wide movement as those opposed to capitalist states"; however, if there were indeed two world systems during the existence of the Soviet Union in conflict with one another, "then those opposed to the system on one side were, by dint of this opposition, supportive of the system in the other." In this case, he writes:

> The 'antisystemic' movements within the established 'antisystemic' were therefore 'prosystemic': this, indeed, was what the historical function of the opposition movements in the East turned out to be. In a systemically divided world, two negatives make a positive (Halliday, 1999, p. 307).

The state-capitalist nature of the Soviet Union has been argued by many including Resnick and Wolff (Summer 1993), with the central aspect of this latter critique pointing out that the social surplus failed to be appropriated and allocated by the direct producers. On this basis, the accumulation of surplus by the state and its managers often mimicked processes of accumulation in the developed capitalist states. And while this writer agrees with this analysis, it is nevertheless arguable that the Soviet Union and those countries which followed its lead represented nascent, though ultimately unsuccessful, attempts to move beyond the capitalist world system, thus providing historical experience from which to draw upon. With their collapse, however, even the remaining nominally communist regimes have, more or less, opened up their societies to market-based economics, operating under the principles of profit maximization and privately-appropriated extraction of surplus.

Writing on the nature of revolutions—i.e. the ultimate antisystemic movement—and their impact on the world system, Halliday proposes a seismologic analogy which underscores the systemic level of analyis for IR. "[R]evolutions," he states:

occur in particular places, as do volcanoes and earthquakes, but we can only understand these specific explosions by looking at broader contexts and structures within which the revolutions, their causes and their contexts, are located. An earthquake or a volcano tells us to look at underlying structures and faults in the earth's surface as a whole, not just at the site of the explosion itself (1999, p. 310).

And though not all antisystemic movements are revolutionary in nature, the key aspect of Halliday's analogy is that analyses which focus only on individual countries to explain change or potential changes "will miss the ideological, or economic, or power political context" in which such crises occur. Neither, he warns, can the international or systemic level be the sole focus, for "this will not explain why states pursue the policies they do, nor why such policies have the outcomes they have." With a broader "internationalised perspective" that encompasses socioeconomic and ideological structures, then not only will we be able to understand the particular forces that generate revolutions, but, as well, and contrarily, such a wider perspective will also help to explain "why, given the vast range of potential causes, domestic and international, there is not more upheaval in societies than there is" (pp. 310-11). What is proposed by Halliday with his seismologic analogy arising out of his study of revolutions "is not the displacement of the state, but rather its redefinition: states are to be seen not as undifferentiated legal-territorial entities, nor as units that operate in an abstract international system, but as the coercive and administrative entities that political and social forces both challenge and appropriate" (p. 311). In this respect, states are sites of contention, and changes within them affect the constitution and stability of the international system. And just as coercive and administrative practices of reward and punishment occur within states as dominant classes seek to perpetuate the economic and social bases of their rule, so too at the level of the global capitalist system are there constraints along with benefits and rewards in addition to punishments meted out in order to maintain and extend the system.

In addition to his reconceptualization of the state, Halliday argues for linkage between the socio-economic context and that of ideology or culture. Thus in examining the socio-economic aspects of a regime, we should "also look at the ideology that underpins it, and at the preconditions, internal and external, for that stability" (p. 314). Yet, he notes, approaches which stress the importance of ideas and culture must be distinguished from that which "bases its account of change on the role of human will." The latter does not follow from the former, he argues. To the contrary, he writes:

Ideas, culture, and language may be part not of the domain of human volition and of meaningful collective action, but rather of that which contextualizes and constrains: individuals are born into a world of realities they cannot change, and these include the culture, religion, language, the texture of social meaning that envelops them. These are constraints as important as social and economic structure. When they change, they can, equally, be part of that convulsion of the system that takes individuals and social groups along with it (Halliday, 1999, p. 313).

Lastly, in his reassessment of international relations theory and approaches, Halliday argues for the incorporation of social movements and classes. Social movements, he writes, challenge states both internally and externally, and the successful ones that make revolutions "are formed in an international context." The broader, transnational forces which actually make revolutions prompt Marxists to posit "classes as both internationally constituted and internationally active" while likewise prompting behaviouralists to view such events as "affected by, and in turn affect, the conduct of others, through demonstration effects and a range of transnational linkages." Both approaches, argues Halliday, pose a conception of IR "that displaces the primacy of states and seeks to locate individual revolutions, or political processes in general, within a broader context of transnational action" (1999, p. 315). Revolutionary situations always break down the barriers between states and societies. In this regard, Halliday writes: "1789 challenged 1648, 1848 challenged 1815, [and] the twentieth-century revolutions repeatedly defied schemes for the maintenance of international order." The permanence of transnational influences engendered by revolutions persist for some time, though "the stability of societies presupposes, *inter alia*, a favourable international economic climate, and the reinforcement, by shared practice, of the political and social practices of the country in question." Here the factor of a dominant ideology must not only be instilled within particular societies but as well "reinforced from outside by an appearance of naturalness" (Halliday, 1999, p. 316). Values and ideology thus reflect the constitution of transnational social groups and classes who exhibit a convergence of interest, shared values and ideology due to the simularity of conditions produced by transnational forces. The same transnational forces constitute similarities in values and ideology for the dominated as well, including workers, peasants, and intellectuals. Halliday notes, however, that while social groups and classes may be said to have a convergence of interests "in the sense that their security, prosperity and wealth is to a considerable extent dependent on international conditions... [this] does not, however, entail that classes have a transnational identity or consciousness" (1999, p. 317). Pointing out that the possessing classes, the bourgeoisie, have been globalizing their interests since the Second World War, he notes, to the c ontrary, that the dominated classes—including both service and part-time workers which are a product of transnational forces in the late twentieth century—have been less able to put forward their interests internationally, "for the dominated," he argues, "do not have the investments, the material incentive, to articulate an international interest that the dominant do." In this respect, the "dominant have more resources—money, air tickets, conference centres, [computers,] adminis-trative support, time itself—than the dominated." In the ensuing conflict between transnational and national forces, Halliday is cautious to remind the reader that "[s]ocial movements act in a context of states and, in the longer run, serve to reinforce states, internally and externally" (1999, p. 318). But in acknowledging the ground on which such movements are played out, he nonetheless asserts that such changes which are produced in revolutionary periods cannot be explained "by a logic of states, bal-ances of power and *idées reçues*" nor by such logic can their impact on the international system itself be explained. To the contrary, he argues: "Only a dual perspective, incorporating both state and society, can en-compass the international dimensions of revolutions" (Halliday, 1999, p. 319).

The "inescapable context" in which societal conflicts are played out in the modern world—including revolutions, conflicts between states, social classes and ideologies, is, he writes, a combined and uneven pro-cess. Drawing on Trotsky's formulation of the laws of uneven and com-bined development (cf. Trotsky, 1932; 1931/1969) which respectively pointed out how backward countries are compelled to make leaps to catch up ideologically, technologically, etc. with their relatively developed coun-terparts while simultaneously combining different stages of development in this leap forward, Halliday notes that it is this broad contradictory context which explains "how ideas, and forms of conflict, like forms of technology or economic activity, could be transposed to contexts very different from that in which they originated" (1999, p. 320). In concluding that "the combination would prevail over the unevenness," Halliday states that this Marxist approach to the laws which anticipated a "world revolu-tionary cataclysm" (i.e. the combination) failed due to "the fragmentary character of states, the spatial and political distributor of that uneven-ness" (1999, pp. 320-1). This unevenness is particularly exacerbated in the current period of capitalist globalization, as evident with the ever-widen-ing gaps between rich and poor on a global scale. Globalization impacts on the level of states as well as the socioeconomic and ideological levels. Writes Halliday:

States and communities exist in a world increasingly unified by economic and social processes, by both transnational formation and by the pressure on societies to conform with each other with an increasingly unified, and unequal, world. Part of this transformation involves the reproduction of separate political and economic forms, the 'nation-states', but part involves the reproduction within each society of the tensions and conflicts characteristic of the modern world as a whole (Halliday, 1999, p. 321).

In recognizing the accompanying globalization of social conflicts as a consequence of the production of the global system itself, Halliday is quick to note that such conflicts are first located and fought out within particular states, although he remarks this "does not contradict the fact that it is a global phenomenon"; after all, he writes, "nationalism…by definition the most self-regarding of ideologies, is universal—literally no country can be without it" (1999, p. 321). Indeed, nationalist forces present one of the most potent threats to the present global capitalist system that may eventually thwart the present campaign by the U.S. to introduce its brand of democracy within the borders of other countries.

While the strength of Marxian analyses "located politics and social behaviour within a global context, that of the spread of an uneven but increasingly globalised capitalism," Halliday nonetheless faults Marxism on two counts: 1) "in the depreciation of the endurance of states, and the ideologies associated with it"; and 2) "in ascribing to this globalisation a direction, a teleology, that would lead necessarily to its destruction and supersession by another political and social formation" (1999, pp. 321-22).

The present analysis rejects any teleological understanding either of the democracy-promotion activities of the U.S. or of the antisystemic movements which such interference in the affairs of other states engender. General tendencies and exposition and analysis of the particular practices undertaken within their historical context, however, do provide explanation and insight into the varying forces at work in this regard. Moreover, one of the basic underlying assumptions of this study is that the socioeconomic, political, and ideological contexts in which the NED has arisen and continues to operate is as the creation and tool of a particular national social formation, *viz.* the USA. In this respect, while certain tendencies explored below point in the direction of the supersession of these efforts away from national states and the possible solidification of a truly transnational elite directing such efforts, it is argued herein that it is the particular circumstances which the U.S. currently enjoys with its dominance in the world system which necessitates not only its involvement in democracy-promotion activities to secure its hegemony but as well to set the agenda and direction, including the ideological form democracy promotion takes in its implementation.

It is with this exposition and understanding of present international relations that we now look at previous U.S. efforts to promote democracy abroad by focusing on its long involvement in the regions of Latin America and the Caribbean, areas in which the U.S. has most successfully implemented its hegemony under the banner of promoting freedom and democracy.

III. Past U.S. Attempts to Export Democracy in Latin America

> It may seem odd for me, a military man, to adopt such a comparison. Truthfulness compels me to. I spent 33 years and 4 months in active service as a member of our country's most agile military force—the Marine Corps. I served in all commissioned ranks from second lieutenant to Major-General. And during that period I spent most of my time being a high-class muscle man for Big Business, for Wall Street and for the bankers. In short, I was a racketeer for capitalism (Butler, 1935-36, p. 8).

> —Marine Corps Major General Smedley D. Butler. Under fire 121 times, twice wounded in action and twenty times decorated, Smedley Butler saw military action in Mexico, Nicaragua, the Philippines, Honduras and China and was also one of the few Americans to be twice awarded the Congressional Medal of Honor.

Throughout the Cold War, and indeed going back to the 1823 Monroe Doctrine, U.S. foreign policy pronouncements have been presumptuous in claiming to speak for all of the countries which make up the Americas, for this is in truth an aggressive hegemonistic position which denies any particularity or relative autonomy to the multiplicity of countries which comprise South, Central and North America. Historically, however, U.S. domination of the Americas has oftentimes proved this singularity of voice by the U.S. to be true in fact, at least as a matter of practice. And though these countries still remain largely under the influence of U.S. control, they nonetheless have asserted their relative independence from U.S. dictates within the last thirty years or so either by challenging U.S. leadership in the United Nations or by cutting their own deals with the former Soviet Union, China, Cuba, and other countries. Hence, it is more accurate and less presumptuous to replace the concept of "American," with that of "U.S." foreign policy as I have done here. However, such a descriptive change is unlikely to occur in practice, because one of the essential aspects of U.S. foreign policy has always been its expansionist tendencies. And when a country has expansionist tendencies, it requires a corresponding language to point toward the expansionist goals sought while simultaneously incorporating those elements of the new territories and peoples which can be assimilated and vigorously countering, suppressing and writing out of existence those aspects which tend to undermine the ideological unity needed to carry out such expansionist goals.[70] Such was the case with the Monroe Doctrine which declared the Americas off-limits to further European colonization (cf. Perkins, 1941/ 1946). At the turn of the 20th century, expansionist terminology became, in President Woodrow Wilson's words, a fight "for democracy, for the right of those who submit to authority to have a voice in their own Governments" (Wilson, *President Wilson's War Message*, in Barlett, 1947, p. 457) which, following the election of FDR in 1932, got translated again into the "Good Neighbor Policy" of nonintervention (cf. Roosevelt, *The Good Neighbor Policy*, in Barlett, 1947, pp. 551-2; see also Pike, 1995).[71] One should note that in this interwar period of presumed U.S. isolationism/ noninterventionism, FDR did pledge to be a "good neighbor" in his inaugural address of 1933 and did commit the U.S. to a policy of nonintervention at the December 1933 inter-American conference in Montevideo, Uruguay. But, as Pike notes: "From the very beginning, however, the new U.S. president demonstrated that when it came to nonintervention he would pursue a Talleyrand-like course of tricksterism; he would show that nonintervention was a policy meaning fundamentally very much the same thing as intervention" (Pike, 1995, p. 173). Such was the case in Cuba when the U.S. refused to recognize the nationalist government of Ramón Grau San Martín and acquiesced when Fulgencio Batista overthrew Grau in January of 1934 and replaced him with Carlos Mendieta as President, whose government Washington recognized within five days of the coup d'état. Pike also notes that FDR's nonintervention policy acted similarly to the previous U.S. interventionist policy in other ways as well, as, for example, FDR's stationing of warships in Cuban waters as a show of strength and U.S. resolve or the U.S.'s retention of military forces in Guantánamo Bay, Cuba and in the Panama Canal Zone. Concludes Pike, "Yankee intervention had ended but it still persisted; and Latin Americans understood they might very well derive advantages from two diametrically opposed policies if they played their cards right" (Pike, 1995, pp. 173-4). Changed conditions after WWII, however, at the onset of the Cold War with the Soviet Union, called for a policy of "containment" of the communist menace which in turn further necessitated a policy of global interventionism to protect those countries fighting communism through the establishment of a U.S.-dominated international governing body, otherwise known as the United Nations. And, for a short while with regards to Latin America, U.S. President John F. Kennedy proclaimed the "Alliance for Progress" which ostensibly sought to "assist democratization in Latin America through socioeconomic aid and thus inhibit the spread of communism" (Wiarda, 1990a, p. 104).

The theoretical bedrock of the Alliance for Progress was rooted in an amalgam of perspectives which came to be known as *modernization theory* (see Chapter 2 above). Associated with individual scholars such as Walt W. *Rostow (The Stages of Economic Growth: A Non-Communist Manifesto*, 1960), B. Hoselitz (*Sociological Aspects of Economic Growth*, 1965), D. McClelland (*The Achieving Society*, 1961), et al., modernization theory characterized Western Europe and North America—the so-called "First World"—as "the centres of modernity, innovation, industrialization, dynamic entrepreneurship, achievement, rationality, democracy and freedom."[72] With modernization theory blaming Latin American underdevelopment on powerful, entrenched oligarchs, "inherited, long-standing inertia, corruption, and careless inattention to economic and social problems," and a culture noted by "a pattern of flawed character traits, medieval cultural traditions, and defective institutions," Park writes that the Alliance for Progress became widely upheld and accepted as policy because its optimistic outlook "captured the mood of the time and expressed the traditional American sense of mission." The mission, presumably, was to go into Latin America and root out these long-standing problems. "Fundamentally," though, Park notes, "that mission remained what it had been throughout the postwar period: defense of the noncommunist world" (Park, 1995, pp. 217-20). Hence, U.S. intervention in the Dominican Republic in 1965, called into question modernization theory and, as Park notes, "together with military coups in Brazil in 1964 and Argentina in 1966 darkened the assessments of the Alliance for Progress during the remainder of the decade and infused them with a sense of disillusionment" (Park, 1995, p. 224). In an article in *Saturday Review* in 1970, Senator Edward M. Kennedy added, perhaps, the final stake to the Alliance for Progress as he wrote that: "For the vast majority of Latin Americans, the alliance has failed...." The Senator went on to characterize the failure as "a major economic disappointment," "a social failure," and "a political failure" (Kennedy, October 17, 1970, pp. 18-19). Park summarizes:

> Its putative failure was less a result of Latin American events than of momentous cultural and political changes within the U.S., which sharply curtailed the liberal agenda and also reduced the public's already notoriously short attention span for things Latin American.

The consensus that had upheld the Alliance for Progress early in the Kennedy administration failed primarily because of those changes, but the decade also witnessed a growing challenge to modernization theory by a new paradigm, which brought into doubt the theoretical underpinnings of the Kennedy program and undermined confidence in its ultimate success (Park, 1995, p. 204).

This new paradigm was called Dependency Theory. Based on the writings of Andre Gunder Frank (*Latin America: Underdevelopment or Revolution*, 1969), Samir Amin (*Accumulation on a World Scale: A critique of the Theory of Underdevelopment*, 1974), Fernando Henrique Cardoso and E. Faletto (*Dependency and Development in Latin America*, 1979), and, perhaps most especially, to Raúl Prebisch (*Change and Development—Latin America's Great Task: Report Submitted to the Inter-American Development Bank*, 1971), dependency theory saw development and underdevelopment as two aspects of the same historical process which gave rise to European colonization and led to an international division of labor, *viz.* the process of capitalist development.

As Dependency theory displaced Modernization theory, the policies promoted by the Alliance for Progress were soon forgotten, and in the 1970s during the so-called "decade of the generals" (which had actually begun with the CIA-backed Brazilian *coup d'etat* of 1964), bureaucratic-authoritarian regimes headed by military governments ruled in most every Latin American country.

Thus whether it was the Monroe Doctrine, Wilson's "fight for democracy", FDR's Good Neighbor Policy, "containment", or JFK's Alliance for Progress, all of these policies had a corresponding language which attempted to maintain U.S. hegemony. And while the U.S. made inroads into Africa, Asia, the Middle East and Western Europe after WWII, nowhere has its hegemonistic desires had a more prolonged, enduring, and brutal history than with the countries of Latin America.[73] And nowhere other than in Latin America has the U.S. acted with so singular a public purpose of acting under the guise of promoting "freedom and democracy."

Following the independence movements of most South American countries in the first quarter of the nineteenth century, the U.S. responded with the Monroe Doctrine in 1823 which publicly declared Latin America off-limits to further European colonization while implying that, in effect, as political scientist Michael Parenti notes,

the United States would be the sole political and colonizing power in the New World, and that the western hemisphere was to be an American sphere of influence.... A year after the Doctrine's promulgation, [Secretary of State] Adams informed South American liberator Simon

Bolivar that the Doctrine 'must not be interpreted as authorization for the weak to be insolent with the strong.' Bolivar, as early as 1829, mournfully and prophetically forecast the next hundred years: 'The United States appears to be destined by Providence to plague America with misery in the name of liberty' (quoted in Parenti, 1971, p. 16).

And, indeed, misery for Latin America came in the form of U.S. interventionism to maintain U.S. hegemony in the region which allowed easy access for U.S. investors and extraction of the region's vast quantities of raw materials. Thus before the Open Door Policy was proclaimed regarding China in 1899, the U.S. had intervened over 20 times in Latin American countries as far north as Mexico in 1847 and as far south as Chile in 1891. One classic example of U.S. intervention in Latin America is that of "the strange career of William Walker" (Houston, in Walker, 1860/1985, p. 1), the American filibuster who, acting in a private capacity, in the seven year period from 1853 till his death by a Honduran firing squad in 1860, first proclaimed himself "President of Lower California", then proclaimed the Mexican department of Sonora "free" while designating himself as "President of the Republic of Sonora" as well and, when those ventures failed, attempted four times—killing 12,000 people in the process—to take control of Nicaragua (even managing between 1855 to 1857 to have himself elected Chief Executive of the Republic of Nicaragua) in an attempt to further U.S. boundaries down through Central America.[74] The rage of U.S. citizens to become "filibusters" or "freebooters" following the successful filibustering action of Sam Houston in prying away Texas from Mexico in 1836, and after the U.S. succeeded in taking half of Mexico following the subsequent war with that country over the annexation of Texas ending in the 1848 Treaty of Guadalupe-Hidalgo, "was acceptable to a large part of the thirty million Americans," Houston argues, "as long as it could be somehow justified by our messianic duty to spread democracy." And he continues, "[i]f now we address our rhetoric to fighting communism, then [i.e. in the 19th century] we addressed it to fighting ignorance, colonialism, the shameful inability of 'effete and decadent' races to govern themselves properly—anything that stood in the way of Progress" (Houston, in Walker, 1860/1985, p. 1). So supportive of filibustering was the American public in the mid-nineteenth century, that even the failed attempts by General Narciso López to "liberate" Cuba and offer it to the Americans virtually assured him the status of a hero when the Spanish executed him and his band on his third attempt in 1851. Indeed, when López's second attempt in 1850 failed to inspire the Cuban population to rise up and welcome him and instead forced him to flee back to the U.S. where he was charged with violating the Neutrality Law of 1818, "public opinion was so sympathetic toward the filibusters that three successive juries disagreed.

Prosecutions in New York and Ohio," writes Bailey, "met with similar failures" to convict López (Bailey, 1940/1946, p. 308). As regards the widespread belief in the fundamental legitimacy of American expansionism, Representative Anderson of Missouri spoke for many when he stated:

> "Let no technical impediment be thrown in the way of our Americanizing Central America. Humanity, philanthropy, and Christianity, demand that it shall be done at no distant day. Such is our Manifest destiny; and why should we be afraid to proclaim it to the world?[75] Wave upon wave of immigration will roll in upon that country, until, ere long, its internal wars, ignorance, superstition, and anarchy, will be supplanted by peace, knowledge, Christianity, and our own Heavenborn institutions" [Cong. Globe, 35 Cong., 2 sess., p. 299, January 10, 1859] (quoted in Bailey, 1940/1946, pp. 294-5).

Pro-slavery interests in the Southern U.S. states, "satisfied of their inability to carry slavery into Kansas [by the 1850s], were then prepared to concentrate their labors on Central America..." (Walker, 1860/1985, pp. 364-65).[76] The repeated attempts at colonizing Nicaragua presented advantage for the U.S. government as well which could deny any backing for Walker's adventures should they fail while readily accepting any newly "liberated" state into the Union should the subject population prove to be relatively pacified and passive to Yankee rule.[77]

In his account of his 1854-57 war in Nicaragua, Walker several times makes it a point to indicate that the U.S. government failed to back him in his adventures and even acted to thwart his activities; but that such pronouncements of U.S. disinterest in expanding into Central America were not widely believed is indicated by Walker's own explanation below:

> Often, it has been semi-officially announced that the United States government was determined to force open the road across Nicaragua; but as no justification for so violent an act on the part of the United States has been presented, it must be presumed that such declarations are intended merely for popular effect. In fact the American authorities, by an arbitrary act of force, interrupted the only effort which, since December, 1856, has promised successfully to restore the passage across Nicaragua to citizens of the United States (Walker, 1860/1985, pp. 365-66).

The American diplomatic historian, Dexter Perkins, however, is much more forthcoming about the U.S. government's attitude towards Walker's filibustering as indicated below:

> The filibustering expedition of William Walker, his seizure of the

government of Nicaragua, the tolerance and finally the recognition accorded him by President Pierce and his advisers, all seemed to show that unscrupulousness and covetousness had more to do with American policy than anything else. There had been the Mexican War less than a decade before; there had been a bullying policy toward Mexico almost ever since, except for a few brief years of Whig rule (and these not impeccable); and now there was the toleration of this ruthless, if unofficial, imperialism (Perkins, 1941/1946, p. 104).

The legacy of William Walker, writes Houston, is that he is remembered all over Central America "as the pattern and paradigm for American intentions." Houston continues:

There's not a schoolchild who doesn't know his name and his story. Parents for generations have been frightening children to sleep with his name. He has become the core around which their national myths have been created (and all countries define themselves by their national myths): the heroic and successful struggle of the people of Central America against the arrogance and power of the North Americans—as they see it—has sustained them through all the years of other American interventions since Walker's first and "unofficial" one. Whoever their internal enemies are, they know for certain from which direction their external enemy has traditionally come (Houston, in Walker, 1860/1985, p. 9).

And though the U.S. government did not always openly back such private colonial ventures in the 19th century, the opposition to direct U.S. intervention in the 20th century has forced it to reexamine the path of private initiative and the security cloak of plausible deniability it provides. But all of this rethinking on the part of U.S. government policymakers had to wait, for in the nineteenth century the public clamor and support for outright imperialism was then in its heyday.

In the aftermath of the 1898 Spanish American War, Teddy Roosevelt's "Big Stick" policy led to multiple military interventions mostly in Central America and the Caribbean in Cuba, Honduras, Dominican Republic, Nicaragua, Haiti, Mexico and in the newly-created state of Panama—which gained its independence from Colombia with U.S. contrivance and gunboat diplomacy so that a canal could be built linking both oceans and reducing the travel time for transoceanic shipping.[78]

With the election to the presidency of Woodrow Wilson in 1912, U.S. intervention in Latin America continued, though it now occurred under the auspices of protecting constitutional government in the hemisphere and "making the world safe for democracy." But lest anyone believe that support for democracy was the basis of U.S. intervention in

Latin America in the past, one need only be reminded of the words of the much-decorated Major General Smedley Butler of the U.S. Marine Corps who had a completely different perspective of just in fact whose interests he was protecting when he recapitulated his past military exploits thusly:

> I helped make Mexico and especially Tampico safe for American oil interests in 1914. I helped make Haiti and Cuba a decent place for the National City Bank boys to collect revenue in. I helped in the raping of half a dozen Central American republics for the benefit of Wall Street. The record of racketeering is long. I helped purify Nicaragua for the international banking house of Brown Brothers in 1909-12. I brought light to the Dominican Republic for American sugar interests in 1916. I helped make Honduras "right" for American fruit companies in 1903. In China in 1927 I helped see to it that Standard Oil went its way unmolested.
>
> During those years, I had, as the boys in the back room would say, a swell racket. I was rewarded with honors, medals, promotion. Looking back on it, I feel I might have given Al Capone a few hints. The best *he* could do was to operate his racket in three city districts. We Marines operated on three *continents* (Butler, 1935-36, p. 8).

As Parenti notes, "[s]ome saw no contradiction between Wilson's professions and General Smedley's statement—including Woodrow Wilson himself. In their view," Parenti argues, "to bring the energetic blessings of capitalism to Latin America was as much a part of the nation's sacred mission as was disseminating Christianity and constitutionalism" (Parenti, 1971, p. 18).

Twenty-six years of constant interventionism from 1914-34, which included, amongst others, the 19-year occupation of Haiti, the 18-year occupation of the Dominican Republic, multiple interventions in Panama including those of 1918 and 1925, and the eight-year occupation of Nicaragua (this latter being the third such military occupation into that country by the U.S.), were ended with the ascendancy to the U.S. presidency by Franklin Delano Roosevelt in 1933. FDR, however, only replaced military diplomacy with dollar diplomacy as his "Good Neighbor" policy towards Latin America continued to install, arm, and foot the bills for despots like Somozo in Nicaragua and Trujillo in the Dominican Republic. Yet it should be noted that FDR's Administration sought to rely more on liberal trade policies than the constant use of force and intervention which had characterized previous U.S. policy on the Latin American continent. The Caribbean also experienced U.S. interventionism as WWII saw the U.S. Navy occupy Jamaica, Antigua, Trinidad, Bermuda, St. Lucia, and the Bahamas. As well, in order—at least officially—to curb Nazi activities and German influence in the region, the U.S. shortly before its entry into the war in

December 1941, had begun establishing military missions throughout Latin America to serve as "liaison agencies between the military establishment of the United States and those of Latin American countries, and mission personnel became advisers to the Latin American military" (Meditz and Hanratty, 1989, p. 249). This U.S. military assistance program to the region laid the basis for subsequent programs designed to ensure U.S. hegemony in the region.[79]

This fifteen year period of relative non-interventionism from 1933 to 1947 (i.e. aside from those necessitated by WWII) was transformed once again, however, as President Truman took over after FDR's death in 1945 and institutionalized what would be the cornerstone of subsequent U.S. foreign policy for the ensuing 40 years. And whether one refers to the Truman Doctrine which vowed U.S. aid "to support free peoples who are resisting attempted subjugation by armed minorities or by outside pressures" (Truman, quoted in Ambrose, 1971/1979, p. 150) or National Security Council Resolution Number 68 which delineated the view that the conflict with the Soviet Union involved "the fulfillment or destruction not only of this Republic but of civilization itself" (NSC-68, 1950/1975, p. 51) or whether one merely uses the original term of "containment" as formulated by George Kennan (cf. Kennan, 1947, p. 575), all of these policies pointed to basically the same goal: containing communism and rolling it back wherever possible.[80] In short, the U.S. launched itself on a holy crusade against communism whether against Stalin and the Soviet Union and the threat posed to Western Europe or against presumably Soviet allies in Latin American or other parts of the globe or even internally within the U.S. itself against those charged with aiding and abetting the "communist menace" as charged by the then junior senator from Wisconsin, Joseph R. McCarthy.[81] In consequence, this unfortunate trajectory in many ways not only forestalled much democratic development, particularly in Latin America, but oftentimes worked diametrically against it.

In the case of Cuba, American diplomacy, rooted in anticommunism, contained what William Appleman Williams referred to as "the fundamental elements of tragedy" (Williams, 1959/1972, p. 2). Specifically, he noted four tragic elements of American diplomacy in Cuba which could be generalized to most of the United States' subsequent relations with the countries of Latin America in that they entailed—*viz.* 1) vastly asymmetrical power between the U.S. and the governments it dealt with, 2) the failure or inability to use that power to create a reality in these other cultures which correlated with professed American ideals of democracy and freedom and respect for self-determination and the modernization of the economy, 3) the abandonment of those reformist elements in other countries who did support the goals of American democracy, and 4) a reactionary behaviour exhibited towards any reform movement which consistently played into the hands of the most extreme radicals in other countries (Williams, 1959/1972, pp. 3-4). Thus the underlying roots of this U.S. behavior rooted in anticommunism meant that any efforts for reform in these countries were met with a virulent American response in that the U.S. countered most genuine efforts at reform by claiming it was "communistic" and then acted to oust the reformers. As such, the original expansionist motivations of the U.S. were very much present, i.e. the drive to extend U.S. power and hegemonic influence. However, during the Cold War, this drive took on a different clothing, so to speak, which, on the one hand, did have some basis in fact (in the sense that there were active, though very small, relative to the dominant political parties operating in each country, Communist Parties operating in most Latin American countries as in the U.S. as well), but which, on the other hand, was only another chapter to be added to the continuing saga of further expansion and extension of U.S. domination. Taken individually, accounts of U.S. intervention sometimes fail to reveal a coordinated and encompassing plan to suppress movements aimed at reform; juxataposed together, however, U.S. efforts to establish and extend its hegemony illuminate an all-around general functional mission which characterizes U.S. foreign policy.

As in other regions of the world, so too in Latin America, the U.S. needed particular instruments to aid in its policy of continued hemispheric dominance. One of the most effective, at least initially, of these instruments was the Organization of American States (O.A.S.) created in Bogota, Colombia in 1948 which was set up so as to coordinate and develop unified pan-American policies. Latin American nations had already committed themselves a year earlier in 1947 to the Inter-American Treaty of Reciprocal Assistance (i.e. the Rio Treaty) which was a mutual defense pact committing its members to provide mutual assistance in the event of aggression; specifically, in the post-WWII context of the Cold War, this meant communist aggression. The O.A.S., with its provisos which allowed for the U.S. to intervene in Latin American states to "protect the peace" sanctioned U.S. imperialist policies under an ostensibly Latin American controlled organization thus allowing the U.S. to avoid the appearance of taking unilateral measures or abandoning its Good Neighbor policy of nonintervention. The Rio Treaty was followed by the Mutual Security Act of 1951 which solidified Latin American security in U.S. hands. Subsequent U.S. meddling—like the 1954 overthrow of Jacobo Arbenz Guzman in Guatemala and the sending of U.S. and Latin American troops to the Dominican Republic in 1965—were both given legal sanction by the O.A.S. as its member states were cajoled into issuing a resolution which declared that international communism constituted outside intervention in the hemisphere which required strong countermeasures—specifically, in these cases, permission for the U.S. to intervene to protect Guatemala and the Dominican Republic from falling under the treacherous sway of communism.

But "communism," in particular in the case of Guatemala in 1954, amounted only to a land redistribution program instituted by the reform-minded Arbenz in 1951, building on an earlier reform program initiated shortly after WWII.[82] Specifically, uncultivated land from farms of over 300 hectares was distributed to peasants, with compensation to those suffering expropriation to be calculated on the basis of their land's declared taxable value. And as was the case with most of the big farms and especially with the land owned by the U.S. corporation United Fruit Company—which owned the largest amount of cultivable land in Guatemala—the owners would receive the least compensation percentage-wise since they had reported their land's declared taxable value at far lower rates than its real worth. Incensed, at what would be considered in later years a mild reform program in the region, United Fruit reacted quickly and, with the help of the new Eisenhower Administration, launched a sustained public-relations campaign to convince the U.S. public and the world that Guatemala had been taken over by communists. "But," as Gabriel Kolko observed,

> neither [Secretary of State John Foster] Dulles nor Eisenhower wanted a mere coup...; rather, they sought to exploit the occasion to inhibit nationalists in the other nations of the hemisphere, many of whom had supporters and programs comparable to those in Guatemala, and to deepen U.S. political control of the Organization of American States in order better to be able to utilize it in the future (Kolko, 1988, p. 103).

The resulting CIA-controlled invasion thus followed and within two weeks was able to persuade the Guatemalan army (many of whom had close ties to the oligarchy) to transfer power to Castillo Armas, the leader of the invasion force whom United Fruit had personally selected.[83] Neither the alleged communist Arbenz nor the small Guatemalan communist party (which never numbered more than four thousand persons) chose to fight.[84] The subsequent terror of the new Armas regime, however, was, as Kolko notes, "merciless":

> unions were banned, parties suspended, a majority of voters disenfranchised, and at least nine thousand persons arrested and an unknown number killed. The new regime abolished the post-1945 reform legislation, and United Fruit had its huge estates returned. As the pre-1944 order was fully restored and the government sank into corruption, Guatemala became the leading example of the kind of hemisphere the United States sought to create (Kolko, 1988, p. 105).[85]

Aside from its opposition to land redistribution schemes, the U.S. also sought to maintain a tight control over labor movements in Latin America. Labor relations are important to any state, and especially in a capitalist economy where there is a stark division between the classes, between those with capital who own and control the means of production and those who must necessarily sell their labor-power to the business owners in exchange for a wage in order to eat, pay rent, maintain and reproduce themselves, etc.[86] Thus the U.S. government monitors very closely labor relations and seeks to influence and oftentimes control the labor relations in other countries. As Wiarda notes,

> the chief purpose of course is to prevent Communist unions from gaining the upper hand and using their positions of strength within the labor movement to launch a Marxist-Leninist revolution or seize control of the organs of the state, which would be detrimental to American foreign policy interests. The task of preventing such Communist takeovers of union movements abroad has been in large part entrusted to the American labor movement (Wiarda, 1990b, p. 119).

This U.S. anti-communist labor program was set up at the beginning of the Cold War when Stalin's armies were completing their takeovers of Eastern Europe and western Europe was devastated from the war, its infrastructure in shambles. At the time, large communist parties existed in France, Italy, Greece and other European countries, and their unions were well organized. The U.S. feared that these parties would come to power if they did not circumvent this development.[87] Hence, the U.S. government enlisted the American labor movement, funded by "CIA money and sometimes CIA personnel," to bolster and provide financial and material support to non-Communist trade unions.[88] In large part, the move was successful, for the U.S. government built up "the Christian-Democratic trade unions in Italy and the Socialist (but non-Communist) union movement in France to the point where their strength was equal to or exceeded Communist union strength" (Wiarda, 1990b, p. 119).[89] Along with Marshall Plan aid, the economies of Western Europe recovered and remained decidedly capitalist in structure and the non-communist trade unions "were able to serve as a check on the Communist unions and to prevent the possibility of Marxist-Leninist revolution in Western Europe." Consequently, Wiarda concludes, "American foreign policy goals were thus served" (Wiarda, 1990b, pp. 119-20).

Because of this success, the CIA expanded their efforts to the Third World in the late 1950s when many new nations emerged by throwing off their colonial oppressors, and when prospects for additional Cuban revolutions threatened the Western Hemisphere with the prospect of Marxist regimes in what was considered the U.S.'s own "backyard." Utilizing the AFL-CIO, a program called the American Institute for Free Labor Development (AIFLD) was established in 1961 inside the AFL-CIO union structure with the purpose of supplanting communist union strength in other countries with generally nonpolitical unions which would operate according to the American model of collective bargaining.[90] Passing initially as an educational institute with its main office in Washington D.C., field offices were quickly set up in virtually every capital city in Latin America. Not only did the funding come from the CIA, but "often the personnel—the labor attachés sent to the American embassies abroad to work on creating anti-Communist labor movements—were still CIA" (Wiarda, 1990b, p. 120).

This close association between the AFL-CIO and the CIA prompted Victor Reuther, then international affairs director of the United Auto Workers, to charge in 1966 that the AFL-CIO's department on international affairs was involved with the Central Intelligence Agency and that "the AFL-CIO and some of its affiliates 'have permitted themselves to be used by the Central Intelligence Agency as a cover for clandestine operations abroad'" (Reuther, quoted in Morris, 1967, p. 7). The split in the labor movement as represented by Victor Reuther's remarks were directed primarily at then AFL-CIO President George Meany and his "global affairs operational man" Jay Lovestone. By the end of 1966, the split over organized labor's foreign policy practices turned into a rupture as Walter Reuther, Victor's brother and then president of the UAW, "announced his union would henceforth follow a course independent of AFL-CIO policies." This was followed a year later, in 1967, with Walter Reuther's resignation from the vice-presidency and the Executive Council of the AFL-CIO (Morris, 1967, p. 9).

Organized as a training institute, the AIFLD operated to sever ties local unions had with fraternal unions and international confederations. Indeed, during the 1960s the AFL-CIO itself severed its ties with the International Confederation of Free Trade Unions (ICFTU) and the International Labor Organization (ILO). As Hirsch and Fletcher document, the AIFLD, in conjunction with its regional offices of six International Trade Secretariats (ITSs), "established a network of subagents in the ranks and leadership of unions throughout the continent" [of South America]....
"The strategic value of this network," they point out, was to operate "as a fifth column, waiting with cobra fangs to strike out, to poison, and where possible, to destroy popular attempts to terminate transnational corporate domination..." (Hirsch and Fletcher, 1977, pp. 7-8). Also, because of the pro-capitalist ideology of many AIFLD union officials which prevented them from being able to identify with the stark material and social condi-

tions which their counterparts in the Third World faced, many of their attempts to supplant communist dominated unions there proved unsuccessful. Moreover, once it was found out that CIA funding was behind the activities of certain unions in the Third World, this "was often the kiss of death to the local labor movement that accepted AIFLD assistance," and "the labor group that received it was discredited and often destroyed as a result" (Wiarda, 1990b, pp. 120-1). Often, the AIFLD did help to mobilize reactionary forces and did succeed in overthrowing left-wing governments in many areas of the Third World. But more often, "the AFL-CIO all but ruined the local labor movements, thereby stimulating more pro-Communist and anti-American sentiment, which was what the program was designed to prevent in the first place" (Wiarda, 1990b, p. 121).

As indicated by this anti-communist orientation of the AIFLD, one can understand why the AFL-CIO, then and afterwards, for years, sided with the U.S. government whenever it invaded another country, or engaged in subversive activities in the Third World, or supported aid to the Somoza dictatorship or the dictatorship in El Salvador, or backed repressive regimes in numerous other countries. It also becomes apparent why the labor movement here in the U.S. has so little power and influence, for they have indeed been compromised by both their anti-communist activities abroad and by the corresponding need not to appear too radical on the home front. And, as regards the average union member's knowledge of such clandestine activities, Hirsch and Fletcher note: "The AFL-CIO process of penetration, with labour apparati in most parts of the world, is highly fragile because it operates almost totally without the knowledge, understanding, or consent of the members of the unions comprising the AFL-CIO" (Hirsch and Fletcher, 1977, p. 12). In return for the AFL-CIO's assistance in helping to secure capitalism internationally, unions initially were able to organize many branches of U.S. industry, although by the late 1960s and 1970s, as organized capital—i.e. the major corporations acting through their political fronts (e.g. the Business Roundtable, U.S. Chamber of Commerce, the National Association of Manufacturers, the Business Council, and hundreds of other industry and trade associations)—fought back with the misnamed "Right-to-work" laws, union strength greatly deteriorated and union membership greatly diminished. Consequently, this relationship between organized labor and the capitalist state, i.e. the representatives of organized capital who dictate U.S. governmental policies, began to split as many rank and file members began to castigate their union officials as mere pawns of corporate America; indeed, the growing recognition by workers of the real power of corporations behind governmental policies led to an ousting of class collaborationist union leadership in the '90s and their replacement by more militant, anti-corporate activists.

The election of new leadership in the AFL-CIO in October 1995 led by John Sweeney, Richard Trumka, and Linda Chavez-Thompson thus may presage a new period of militancy in the ranks of organized labor in the U.S., though it is still too soon to determine whether the new leadership will alter the AFL-CIO's activities abroad. One should note, however, a report that one of the first actions taken by the new leadership was to reject the heretofore annual payment by the CIA to the AFL-CIO of $9 million for such activities (stated in a speech by CPUSA Vice-Chair Jarvis Tyner at the University of Massachusetts on October 30, 1996). Nonetheless, as one of the four core partners of the National Endowment for Democracy (NED) and the NED's major grant recipient (averaging approximately $6 million dollars in grants annually from 1990 to 1999), the AFL-CIO is still compromised by the dependency developed from such payments. Still, an indication of the fightback against class collaborationist policies in the 13 million member union was graphically illustrated just three months before the union's convention in August of 1995 when, for the first time in its history, the sitting AFL-CIO president, Lane Kirkland (praised by the *Wall Street Journal* for his "yeoman service against communism" in August of 1995), was driven from office. It is also noteworthy that in April 1999, the NED presented "Democracy Service Medals" to former AFL-CIO President Lane Kirkland and to former Polish President and Solidarity Union leader Lech Walesa "for their roles in the demise of communist rule in Poland" (*NED Annual Report 1999*, 2000, p. 7).

Another recent indication of the renewed surge in labor organizing in the U.S. as well as the response of corporate America to what they see as a dangerous new militancy can be seen in the successful victory in August 1997 by the International Brotherhood of Teamsters against the United Parcel Service. As *The Boston Globe* described it: "Atlanta-based United Parcel Service settled a contentious 15-day strike by 185,000 Teamsters late Monday, ending a dispute that hampered thousands of businesses and cost the company $650 million or more" (Diane Lewis. Wednesday, August 20, 1997. "UPS accord seen lifting Teamsters, other unions," *The Boston Globe*, p. A1). Since the successful strike, however, Teamster President Ron Carey was expelled from the union by a three-judge federal panel which found Carey responsible for a scheme to funnel $850,000 in union money to his union election campaign, even though the government supervised the balloting and taxpayers paid $17 million for the election. Some see this as a Republican and rightwing vendetta against the new Teamster militancy, especially given the unequal focus on campaign irregularities of James P. Hoffa, Jr., the loser in the 1996 Teamster election and subseqently the winner in the 1998 court-mandated election, who is seen by many as a trojan horse for business unionism (Gaboury, October 25, 1997, *People's Weekly World*).

82   *Exporting 'Made-in-America' Democracy*

The labor upsurge of the Teamsters, however, only encouraged delegates to the 21st Constitutional Convention of the AFL-CIO in September of 1997 to unanimously remove the anti-communist clause in the AFL-CIO constitution which barred members of the Communist Party from full participation in the AFL-CIO or its subordinate bodies. Such action sends a bold message to corporate America that the gloves are coming off in labor's fight for the basic interests of all working people. This new militancy represents a milestone development in the AFL-CIO's effort to renew and reenergize the U.S. labor movement, though it is still too soon to determine how long it will endure.

It is impossible within the confines of this thesis to go over all the other instruments and instances of U.S. intervention in Latin America.[91] For example, we would have to look at the U.S. Southern Command (SOUTHCOM) at Fort Gulick in Panama and the U.S. Army School of the Americas (SOA) at Fort Benning in Columbus, Georgia (provisions of the 1977 Panama Canal Treaty forced the SOA's move to Georgia from Panama in 1984) which provide military and police training to the countries of Latin America and examine how this training (particularly its counterinsurgency and "interrogation" [i.e. torture] methods aimed at fighting the "communist" menace) served to shore up many of the subsequent dictatorships which arose in that region.[92] We would also need to look at several new forms of intervention in Latin America including the use of the air-waves as seen by the propaganda tools of Radio and TV Marti which are beamed into Cuba, this latter a violation of the International Telecommunications Union rules and hence in violation of International Law. In addition, we would need also examine recent U.S. intervention programs operated under the auspices of "drug interdiction" in Bolivia, Brazil, Peru, Colombia, etc. which often are disguised attempts to route out leftist insurgents in these countries. As Stan Goff, a retired 20-year veteran of the U.S. military who trained Colombian Special Forces in 1992 and who served in seven Latin American countries, stated: "In Colombia, it is well known that those who profit the most by the drug trade are members of the armed forces, the police, government officials and the big businessmen of the urban centers."[93] But drugs are only the pretense for intervention, Goff notes, for the more significant factor is the "billions of dollars in markets for U.S. products in Colombia and Latin American nations" which will require "the continued bleeding of those nations' economies through external debts owed to American-dominated financial institutions." Referring to a June 1999 OAS meeting where Clinton administration representatives proposed an American-led multinational military force "'to intervene in threatened environments'" to "'protect democracy'" in Latin America, Goff writes:

Colombia will be the foothold for this force, because it is under the most immediate threat. The guerrillas are the foes of democracy, of course. And the government of Colombia is the nominal democracy. They have elections. Only a tiny fraction of the population has the means to recruit and promote candidates, and terror is part of the political machinery. But they have elections (Goff, July 29, 1999).

The "most egregious and systematic human rights violations currently taking place in this hemisphere," argues Goff, are hidden by what he calls "the democratic facade" by which U.S. interventionary activity is justified. But many of these interventions—either directly or by proxy or by other indirect means—are already familiar to most.

And, of course, there are the more notable examples of U.S. interventions such as the 1973 overthrow of the democratically elected Marxist government of Salvador Allende Gossens which came to power in Chile in 1970. While the case of Chile also reveals the U.S. government's past preference for dictators and repressive regimes in the hemisphere (as exemplified by the Pinochet regime which succeeded Allende and which institutionalized widespread torture and government-sponsored murder)—a preference which was paramount in the 1970s—the example of Chile also demonstrates that the U.S. could never accept "the verdict of democratic politics in any nation where anti-Yankee sentiment was overwhelming," because, as Kolko notes, there is a "fear of seeing not only its local investments lost but also encouraging anti-United States economic legislation elsewhere in the hemisphere" (Kolko, 1988, p. 221). In this regard, Kolko especially notes that in Chile, the coalition fighting against the U.S.

> was centrist as well as leftist, revealing that the historically dominant hemispheric trend toward nationalist economic strategies certain to constrict, if not exclude, U.S. investment was more vital and dangerous than ever. Indeed, the very nature of this nationalist vision created a hemispheric consensus that was politically still far more widespread and effective, and therefore threatening, than conventional Left ideologies. Had it survived, the Chilean example would have posed an unprecedented, grave challenge to Yankee hegemony. Allende's failure to neutralize the military immediately was his decisive error, however, and that, too, was a moral all those of similar persuasion were certain to understand" (Kolko, 1988, pp. 221-2).

Other more recent examples of U.S. intervention to protect its hegemony in the region include the Contra War against Nicaragua in the early '80s as well as the invasion of Grenada in 1983, Panama in 1989, and Haiti in 1994. Of particular interest of late has been the indictment, extradiction, conviction, and imprisonment of governmental leaders, including General Manuel Noriega of Panama and Chief Minister Norman B. Saunders and Minister of Commerce and Development Stafford Missick of the Turks and Caicos Islands, actions which violate the principle of sovereignty embedded in the foundation of international law and the modern states system (Meditz and Hanratty, 1989, pp. 579-80).[94] These examples of intervention only scratch the surface of the constant, extensive, and oftentimes brutal policy of interference and intervention by the U.S. in Latin America.

What is suggested here is that this U.S. policy in Latin America is not new and is one which seeks continued hegemonic dominance over the region, its resources, and its peoples, and acts as a testing ground for hegemonic schemes launched elsewhere in the world. Furthermore, this is a policy which at first asserted a U.S. right to be the sole exploiter of the region, was followed by a period of private "filibustering" imperialism, which then led to a period of blatant military interventions and outright imperialism, and which since 1934 and especially since the onset of the Cold War in 1945 has witnessed the U.S. attempt to mask its interventions through hemispheric instruments like the O.A.S., the AIFLD, and, presently, the National Endowment for Democracy (NED) while ultimately relying on the military structures in each country to secure continued U.S. hegemony and Latin American subordination. And, finally, the U.S. has consistently claimed it was intervening in Latin America to promote the cause of "freedom and democracy."

Since the 1980s, U.S. policy has sought to move away from support of dictatorships in Latin America, especially following the revolution in Nicaragua in 1979. Such dictatorships were seen as easy targets for leftist revolutionary agitation. The policy has thus been to support regimes which have democratic elections, understood as elections between two or more market-oriented (i.e. capitalistic) parties and to fund, not government-to-government aid, but rather directly private initiatives in Latin America, as was originally proposed by David Rockefeller in 1963 (Colby and Dennett, 1995, p. 665). But does this mean that the U.S. has lost some control over these Latin American governments? Not necessarily, for while democratic politics (albeit capitalist in form) are once again allowed to be practiced, the U.S. has sought to retain ultimate control over these regimes through extensive ties with the region's militaries. Thus, the training and supplying of Latin American military personnel through the U.S. Southern Command and the School of the Americas is still pursued in order to develop close ties with the ultimate arbiters and guarantors of political power in these countries.

And as recent events have attested to in Haiti, where the democratically elected, eight-month-long, government of Jean-Bertrand Aristide was charged with moving too far to the left (French, 1991, p. A10), he was removed hastily through a U.S.-backed *coup d'etat* on September 30, 1991 (Norton, 1991, pp. 1, 8). And even though he was the first freely elected president of Haiti in over 186 years and had won over 67% of the vote, he apparently had pushed the parameters of what the U.S. considered acceptable politics beyond reasonable give and take. His subsequent installation back into power in October of 1994 (after Clinton replaced Bush as U.S. president) by U.S. military intervention (referred to as "Operation Uphold Democracy") was implemented only after Aristide agreed to a prominent U.S. role in Haiti and also after securing Aristide's promise not to run for reelection in 1995 (which he was kept to) (Fineman, May 1, 1998, *The Los Angeles Times*).

Moreover, U.S. congressional action in the 1990s with both the Torricelli Law (the Cuban Democracy Act of 1992) and the Helms-Burton Act (the Cuban Liberty and Solidarity Act of 1996) has attempted not only to tighten the U.S. embargo on Cuba by prohibiting foreign subsidiaries of U.S. companies from trading with Cuba but also by denying U.S. visas to executives of foreign companies that engage in trade or have investments in Cuba.[95] In addition, the Helms-Burton Act seeks to negate any popular gains of the Cuban Revolution of 1959 by allowing U.S. citizens—including Cuban who became U.S. citizens after the 1959 revolution—to sue for property abandoned or nationalized by the Cuban government and to sue foreigners who use property seized by Castro's government from U.S. companies or citizens.

Given this prior and present history of U.S. intervention, current U.S. efforts to promote democracy abroad become uncomfortably suspect. Still, questions must be posed as to whether this policy of supporting restrained democracies will work to ensure continued U.S. dominance of the region or will lead only to further disillusionment and hence to further challenges to U.S. hegemony as the more familiar cases of Guatemala, Cuba, Chile and Nicaragua have demonstrated. Lessons from this U.S. history of promoting democracy in Latin America have no doubt influenced present efforts by the NED to promote democracy abroad in the post-Cold War world. We will now turn to an examination of the nature and form of this brand of U.S. democracy being exported abroad along with an analysis of its grant-funding activity from its first decade and a half of existence.

IV. Origin, Structure, & Grantfunding Practices of the NED

> Some people think that there is only one democracy and only one oligarchy. This is not true, and therefore one should not forget how many differences there are between constitutions and how many different ways there are of combining them (Aristotle, *The Politics*, 335-322 B.C.E./1984, Book IV, Ch. I, para. 1288b39, p. 237).

Though the current effort by the U.S. to promote democracy abroad was initiated at the federal level in 1983 by National Security Decision Document 77, it took Public Laws 98-164 and 98-166 to 1) authorize "Project Democracy," a program which would fund projects supporting democratic institutions abroad through the United States Information Agency (USIA), the United States Agency for International Development (USAID), and the U.S. State Department and 2) grant a two year authorization for the National Endowment for Democracy (NED) in November 1983 and appropriate 18 million dollars for the NED's fiscal year 1984 operations (GAO/NSIAD-84-121, 1984, pp. 3-4).[96] NSDD 77, signed on January 14, 1983, and entitled "Management of Public Diplomacy Relative to National Security," created the International Political Committee (IPC), one of four interagency standing committees reporting to the Special Planning Group (SPG) of the National Security Council. The IPC was given the responsibility for planning, coordinating and implementing international political activities in support of U.S. policies and national security interests including providing "aid, training and organizational support for foreign governments and private groups to encourage the growth of democratic political institutions and practices." Instructed to work with labor, business, universities, philanthropy, political parties and the press, the IPC was given the task to "build up the U.S. Government capability to promote democracy" and to "initiate plans, programs and strategies designed to counter totalitarian ideologies and aggressive political action moves undertaken by the Soviet Union or Soviet surrogates" (NSDD 77, 1984, pp. 131-2). As then-Secretary of State George P. Shultz testified before Congress, the third goal of the U.S. foreign policy agenda was the U.S. "commitment to expanding the forces of democracy and freedom."[97] Echoing President Reagan's words spoken before the British Parliament in June 1982, Shultz pointed out to Congress the perceived need "to move decisively to strengthen the infrastructure of democracy—free press, free trade unions, free political parties—institutions," the Secretary stated, "which allow people to determine their own future" (Shultz, 1983, p. 2).

Supporting the institutions and proponents of democracy abroad, Shultz proclaimed, was worthwhile because "only in democracies is there inherent respect for individual liberties and rights," "freedom of expression and real participation in choosing leaders," and "economic vitality." Moreover, Shultz claimed, democracies "do not invade or subvert their neighbors" (Shultz, 1983, p. 8).

That the U.S. should engage in the export of democracy abroad was necessary, or so it was claimed, due to both the distortion of what U.S. democracy stood for and because "practical assistance" was required by those who would emulate it.[98] Those who called for merely keeping the "beacon" of democracy "bright" at home by "meeting the economic, social and political needs" of the American people were less than far-sighted, Shultz implied, for it was "naive to believe," he claimed, that democracy's mere "existence somewhere in the world is sufficient incentive for its growth elsewhere" (Shultz, 1983, p. 9). Heralding past U.S. successes in "providing assistance" to post-war Western Europe and Japan and noting how this assistance "in some instances...became a function of covert activity," Shultz stated that U.S. support for democracy abroad "should be done openly." Finally, Secretary Shultz claimed, destabilization was not the goal sought with Project Democracy—as the entire effort was referred to—for "[c]hange must come from within, not be imposed from outside" (Shultz, 1983, p. 10). The CIA, he testified, would not be a recipient of any funds from the project and all funds were to be publically accounted for.

Building on previous and on-going programs—"with a proven track record"—which sought to influence political developments abroad, such as the Asia Foundation and the American Institute for Free Labor Development (AIFLD), Project Democracy sought to channel funding into five key areas: "leadership training, strengthening the institutions of democracy, education, conveying ideas and information, and developing closer ties between American organizations and individuals and their foreign counterparts" (Shultz, 1983, p. 4). Privileging links between Western Europe and the U.S., Shultz's statement reiterated the desire to strengthen the perception "of shared values and a common destiny" between the citizens of Europe and the U.S., for, he felt, "our young people...are drawing further apart" (Shultz, 1983, p. 12).

Thus, as initially set out by Secretary Shultz, the promotion of democracy abroad by the U.S. assumed that indigenous democratic forces were active in other countries, that there was a shared understanding between these forces abroad and the U.S. government as to what is meant by "democracy" and "democracy promotion" or "democracy-building", that the U.S.—acting through the instruments of Project Democracy like the NED—would only be providing assistance for these forces to act on their own, that such assistance was not aimed at destabilizing existing governments, that the U.S. had successfully provided such assistance in the past as indicated by the stable democracies of Western Europe and Japan, that this practice would be good for establishing links with American organizations and individuals and their foreign counterparts, that it would correct the supposedly distorted view of what U.S. democracy stood for, and would be a worthy goal in itself for democracies respect individual rights and freedoms and are nonaggressive, and would serve to strengthen bonds of a common destiny between Western European and American youth.[99]

Caught in a quagmire in Central America in the early 1980s and still reeling from the effects of the Iranian and Nicaraguan revolutions, the second OPEC oil shock in addition to the Soviet move into Afghanistan, the growing strength of marxist regimes in Africa, as well as the electoral wave which brought social democrats to power in Europe at the beginning of the decade, most notably in France, Italy, Spain, Portugal and Greece, and also confronted in the early '80s by an anti-nuclear movement in Europe which, at the time, produced the largest mass demonstrations in history, the Reagan administration realized that its massive arms build-up, by itself, was insufficient to counter the revolutionary rumblings then emanating from many areas of the globe. Reagan himself acknowledged this when he stated in his 1982 London speech that "the ultimate determinant in the struggle now going on for the world will not be bombs and rockets, but a test of wills and ideas, a trial of spiritual resolve..." (Reagan, 1982, p. 549). More importantly, as Wiarda notes, one prime motivation behind the Reagan Administration's enthusiasm for Project Democracy was that it came to realize that "Congress, the media, public opinion, church and labor groups, to say nothing of our allies, are much more cooperative and supportive when the goals of our policy are presented as 'democracy'" (Wiarda, 1990a, p. 147). Indeed, one NED critic writes that it was the exposure of CIA criminal activities as revealed by the Church Senate committee, the Pike House committee, and the President's Rockefeller Commission in the 1970s which prompted the shift of these interventionary activities "to a new organization, with a nice sounding name—The National Endowment for Democracy." As Blum writes: "The idea was that the NED would do somewhat overtly what the CIA had been doing covertly for decades, and thus, hopefully, eliminate the stigma associated with CIA covert activities" (Blum, 2000, p. 179). But, as Barbara Conry of the libertarian CATO Institute remarks:

> The debate over NED is not a debate about democracy; no one is disputing that democracy and liberty are worthwhile goals. Rather, the controversy surrounding NED questions the wisdom of giving a quasi-private organization the fiat to pursue what is effectively an independent foreign policy under the guise of "promoting democracy."

Noting that NED proponents argue that a private structure is necessary "to overcome t he restraints t hat limit t he activities o f a g overnment agency," she likewise points out

> the inherent contradiction of a publicly funded organization that is charged with executing foreign policy (a power expressly given to the federal government in the Constitution) yet exempt from nearly all political and administrative controls (Conry, November 8, 1993).

Moreover, Conry adds, the Cold War argument that was previously used to justify the NED, as a counter to Soviet ideology, is no longer relevant since the demise of the Soviet Union. But on what basis can the U.S. claim a right to intervene in the domestic affairs of other countries? And what form of democracy does the U.S. wish to promote abroad and for what ends?

In an attempt to justify its intervention in other countries' affairs, the U.S. promotion of democracy abroad, so claims the NED's Statement of Principles and Objectives, is rooted

> in universally recognized principles of international law. The Universal Declaration of Human Rights and other United Nations agreements (including the Conventions of the International Labor Organization), as well as the Helsinki Final Act, commit governments around the world to honoring the fundamental human rights that are guaranteed to citizens of the United States and other free societies.

In what one scholar favorable to the NED notes as "a considerable leap of logic and interpretation" (Wiarda, 1990, p. 150), the NED statement concludes that it is

> therefore in keeping with established international law for the American people, through an institution such as the National Endowment

for Democracy, t o help o thers build d emocratic institutions a nd strengthen democratic processes that will promote individual rights and freedoms (NED SPO, 1992, p. 1).

To the extent that such an interpretation of these conventions has any validity at all, one still must acknowledge that any intervention in another state's affairs also contradicts internationally r ecognized principles o f sovereignty; c onsequently, whatever intervention does o ccur must be understood either as the prerogative of the dominant power due to the absence of any reliable enforcement mechanism by international bodies to check such interventionary activities, or to the tacit acceptance of a host country owing to their relative weakness *vis-à-vis* the hegemon.[100] Also, while intervention in another state's affairs in any form is generally suspect, such a transgression of state sovereignty becomes particularly egregious when it takes a political form which seeks to influence domestic power relationships and national political development. The NED's justification for intervention, therefore, is not likely to win the admiration and respect of the governments it deals with.

In the U.S., however, in a climate where the foreign policy establishment has, since late 1991, lost its main organizing principle of the previous 45 years, *viz.* anticommunism, the NED's *raison d 'être* was welcome news to a defense establishment whose 300 billion dollar annual Cold War budgets are harder to defend in a post-Cold War world. Such was the sentiment uttered by the Chairman of the Coalition for a Democratic Majority, Ben Wattenberg, who argued that "embarking on a crusade for democracy can help persuade the American people to keep defense budgets high 'to prevent Soviet imperial recidivism'" (Wattenberg, quoted in Maynes, 1990, p. 14). Moreover, as political scientist Charles Maynes surmised: "Most Americans probably would be willing to defy international law," not only "to support the use of military force to spread the cause of democracy if the cost were low" but, moreover, they "probably will also accept covert efforts to promote democracy, that is to say, other forms of interference, including violence, that are barred by international law." Arguing that most Americans "do not have the time or background to become terribly troubled over long-term costs," Maynes concluded, therefore, that "[i]f the end is democracy, officials can persuade them that the end justifies the means. The average American will rely on his government to exercise good judgment in carrying out this policy" (Maynes, 1990, p. 15). Still, there are limits to which the American populace will support such a policy; thus Maynes warned that if the U .S. supports only "facade democracies" (e.g. all the governments in Central America except Costa Rica before the 1990s), then "significant groups within the United States will object vehemently" (Maynes, 1990, p. 16).

The question of "facade democracies" versus, say, "real democracies" raises the question of the particular form U.S. exported democracy takes. Hence, we must turn to the National Endowment for Democracy Act itself, where the avowed six purposes of the NED are stated as follows:

> 1) to encourage free and democratic institutions throughout the world through private sector initiatives, including activities which promote the individual rights and freedoms (including internationally recognized human rights) which are essential to the functioning of democratic institutions;
>
> 2) to facilitate exchanges between United States private sector groups (especially the two major American political parties, labor, and business) and democratic groups abroad;
>
> 3) to promote United States nongovernmental participation (especially through the two major American political parties, labor, business, and other private sector groups) in democratic training programs and democratic institution-building abroad;
>
> 4) to strengthen democratic electoral processes abroad through timely measures in cooperation with indigenous democratic forces;
>
> 5) to support the participation of the two major American political parties, labor, business, and other United States private sector groups in fostering cooperation with those abroad dedicated to the cultural values, institutions, and organizations of democratic pluralism; and
>
> 6) to encourage the establishment and growth of democratic development in a manner consistent both with the broad concerns of United States national interests and with the specific requirements of the democratic groups in other countries which are aided by programs funded by the Endowment (National Endowment for Democracy Act, pp. 1039-40).

These NED purposes, in turn, are to be guided by the following seven principles as reiterated in the NED's 1992 Statement of Principles and Objectives:

> 1) that democracy involves the right of the people freely to determine their own destiny;
>
> 2) that the exercise of this right requires a system that guarantees freedom of expression, belief and association, free and competitive elections, respect for the inalienable rights of individuals and minorities, free communications media, and the rule of law;
>
> 3) that a democratic system may take a variety of forms suited to local needs and traditions, and therefore need not follow the U.S. or any other particular model;
>
> 4) that the existence of autonomous economic, political, social and cultural institutions is the foundation of the democratic process and

the best guarantor of individual rights and freedoms;

5) that private institutions in free societies can contribute to the development of democracy through assistance to counterparts abroad;

6) that such assistance must be responsive to local needs and seek to encourage—but not to control—indigenous efforts to build free and independent institutions; and

7) that the partnership between those who enjoy the benefits of democracy and those who aspire to a democratic future must be based upon mutual respect, shared values, and a common commitment to work together to extend the frontiers of democracy for present and future generations (NED Statement of Principles and Objectives, 1992, pp. 3-4).

As these six purposes and seven principles indicate, the conception of democracy proposed by the NED is, in many instances, vague and leaves room for discretion as to what constitutes a democratic institution, group, electoral process, etc.[101] What is emphasized, however, are procedural rights of freedom of expression, belief and association and the rule of law while making no mention of substantive rights such as the right to work, education, health care, social security, housing, etc. Furthermore, private-sector political, social and cultural institutions are privileged as the best guarantors of individual rights and freedoms. In so offering these procedural rights over substantive rights, the NED's conception of democracy does not stray far, if at all, from that which dominates within the U.S. internally.

The particular brand of democracy being exported is further revealed when examining NED's funding priorities, which emphasize three major functional areas: pluralism; democratic governance; and education, culture and communications. The goals of these programs include "the strengthening of civil society, democratic political institutions, and democratic culture, respectively." These three areas are deemed by the NED as "essential to the achievement and maintenance of stable democratic orders" (NED SD, 1992, p. 4). Two other areas involving research on democratic development and regional and international cooperation receive more modest funding from the Endowment. All NED programs, however, are devoted to encouraging democratic *political* development without mentioning economic or social development (NED SPO, 1992, p. 4). And democratic political development is primarily oriented around independent private-sector organizations—especially trade and business associations. So again, we see that the emphasis is not on changing the economic underpinnings of undemocratic governments, but rather on effecting legal and political alterations, i.e. superstructural changes.[102]

Funding by the NED is primarily directed at fostering a cooperative and bipartisan effort to promote democracy by enlisting the support

of the Republican and Democratic parties, the labor movement and organized business interests. Four core institutes of the NED—the Center for
International Private Enterprise (CIPE), associated with the U.S. Chamber
of Commerce; the American Center for International Labor Solidarity
(ACILS), an arm of the AFL-CIO; the Democratic Party's National Democratic Institute for International Affairs (NDIIA); and the Republican Party's
International Republican Institute (IRI)—receive the majority of NED grant
monies.[103] And of the these four institutes, the AFL-CIO's international
institute, through 1995, received the overwhelming largess of NED funds,
receiving between 40-50% or nearly half of all NED funds annually. However, since 1996, following the ouster of Lane Kirkland the year before
from the presidency of the AFL-CIO, labor's share of NED grants has been
nearly proportional to the NED's other three core institutes. These core
institutes also receive funding from the U.S. Agency for International
Development (USAID). The NED itself receives the bulk of its monies for
grantmaking from annual appropriations from the U.S. Information Agency
(USIA), the U.S. Agency for International Development (USAID), and the
Department of State (DOS). But with USIA's integration into the DOS as
of October 1999, funding decisions for the NED will likely reside with the
State Department's Undersecretary for Public Affairs and Public Diplomacy. Also, the "Endowment collects U.S. Government funds by filing
requests for direct funding and by presenting payment vouchers against
letters of credit when it disburses cash for program grants and administrative costs" (NED Annual Report 1999, 2000, p. 81). Recipients of NED
funding must apply for grants on an annual basis—which are doled out
quarterly by the NED's Board of Directors.

In its first few years in the 1980s, the NED allocated nearly half of
its funding to programs in Latin America. By the late 1980s, however,
programs targetting first Eastern Europe and then the Soviet Union were
in full swing. These areas—Central and Eastern Europe, Latin America,
and, by 1992, the former Soviet Union or the so-called "Newly Independent States (NIS)"—were declared by the Endowment to be "post-breakthrough" countries. These were broken down further into two categories
including, firstly, "emerging democracies, i.e. countries that have achieved
democratic breakthroughs but not yet consolidated democratic institutions," and, secondly, "transitional countries where repressive political
authority is collapsing and democratic groups committed to peaceful transitions and the establishment of alternative structures exist and need support" (NED SD, 1992, p. 8). NED sponsored programs in these countries
thus "seek to defend recent democratic gains, consolidate the democratic
process, and a void reversals." As such, programs in these countries
focus on "party-building efforts, economic reform initiatives, electoral
monitoring and training, human rights monitoring, and the establishment

of a free and independent press" (NED *1991 Annual Report*, 1992, p. 13). And while many of the programs in these regions are still ongoing, the focus of NED grantmaking in the 1990s shifted more towards East Asia (particularly China), Africa, and the Islamic countries of the Middle East. These latter regions of the globe are termed "pre-breakthrough" societies and these are further subcategorized into "closed societies that repress all institutions independent of the state, and authoritarian systems that tolerate the elements of civil society but where democratic development can only be viewed as a long-term prospect" (NED SD, 1992, p. 8). NED programs in these areas "are more likely to focus on facilitating the free flow of information, enhancing democratic civic consciousness, promoting human rights, and creating political space in which democratic activists can operate" (*NED 1991 Annual Report*, 1992, p. 14). These latter pre-breakthrough societies continued to receive increasing priority in the late '90s and into the new century while post-breakthrough regions' funding has diminished from approximately 80% of all obligated program funds in fiscal year 1991 to approximately 59% by 1999 (NED SD, 1992, p. 8; *NED Annual Report 1999*, 2000). This 80% in 1991 was further broken down into 49% of funds devoted to "emerging democracies" and 31% to "transitional countries." As for the remaining 20% of obligated funds in 1991 geared toward pre-breakthrough societies, 6% went toward "closed societies" while 14% was earmarked for "authoritarian systems" (NED *1991 Annual Report*, 1992, p. 25).

A more dynamic view of the history of the NED grant funding can be gleaned by examining the funding breakdown by region for the years 1990 to 1999. In Table 1 below, we can see that Central and Eastern Europe funding topped the list for the decade with nearly $53 ½ million, followed by a slightly lesser amount of over $48 ½ million for Latin America and the Caribbean, nearly $46 million for Asia, over $40 million for the Newly Independent States of the former Soviet Union, over $34 ¾ million for Africa, nearly $20 ½ million for the Middle East and North Africa, with $11 ¾ million designated as Multi-Regional funding. In addition, since 1996, the "Miscellaneous" funding category which funds had previously comingled under the "Multi-Regional" heading became a separate category and has since received nearly $5 ½ million for various non-region-specific purposes (See Table 2). Likewise in Table 3, a breakdown by year of funding for the NED's four core institutes (which are annually the largest grant recipients) reveals that the AFL-CIO's American Center for International Labor Solidarity (ACILS) was by far the largest grant recipient garnering over $60 ½ million, followed in a distant second by the nearly $34 million for the Chamber of Commerce's Center for International Private Enterprise (CIPE), over $30 ½ million for the Democratic Party's National Democratic Institute for International Affairs (NDIIA), and nearly

$31 million for the Republican Party's International Republican Institute
(IRI). The "post-breakthrough" societies of Central and Eastern Europe,
the Newly Independent States of the former Soviet Union, and the countries of Latin American and the Caribbean received 58% of all NED funding
allocated to its six regions from 1990-99, comparing similarly to the per-
centage of funding these regions received in the year 1991 taken alone,
although the amount of funding for the "pre-breakthrough" regions of
Asia and the Middle East/North Africa since 1991 nearly doubled and
tripled for these two regions by 1999. Funding for Africa appears to have
remained stagnant during the decade, though the constancy of funding
for this region must take into account the recategorization of the Middle
East which now incorporates as well the area of North Africa as of 1998,
which likewise reduces the scope of the Africa region category.

Table 1
National Endowment for Democracy
Grant Funding by Region, 1990-1999
(In U.S. Dollars)

YEAR	AFRICA	ASIA	C. & E. EUROPE	L. AM. & CARIB.	M. EAST & N. AFRICA	NIS (FORMER U.S.S.R.)	MULTI-REGIONAL
1990	1,811,750	1,706,922	12,751,675	6,476,140	—	1,399,207	586,865
1991	3,378,682	2,613,627	4,089,096	4,046,492	516,453	1,104,132	803,202
1992	4,271,308	3,189,056	3,947,726	4,984,440	454,150	4,022,787	1,517,251
1993	3,650,311	3,575,635	3,117,553	5,623,034	1,297,712	5,090,253	1,210,059
1994	3,933,214	5,177,825	4,559,206	5,932,451	2,489,740	6,236,156	1,307,675
1995	3,500,015	6,107,370	4,959,872	5,391,708	2,638,509	5,010,488	1,604,426
1996	3,518,551	7,600,660	4,145,354	4,205,964	3,518,014	4,121,226	481,061
1997	3,567,176	5,870,670	4,849,171	3,712,534	3,003,875	3,940,306	747,920
1998	3,715,603	5,793,414	4,542,898	3,433,392	3,378,323	4,686,326	1,531,675
1999	3,405,770	4,351,111	6,476,899	4,837,172	3,153,904	4,769,835	2,006,138
TOTAL	$34,752,380	$45,986,290	$53,439,450	$48,643,327	$20,450,680	$40,380,716	$11,796,272

NOTE: "Miscellaneous" spending which had previously been comingled
under the "Multi-Regional" heading was made into a separate category in
1996 with various non-region-specific grant funding as depicted in Table
2 below:

Table 2
National Endowment for Democracy
Miscellaneous Grant Funding, 1998-1999
(In U.S. Dollars)

YEAR	MISCELLANEOUS
1996	1,060,025
1997	1,301,858
1998	1,483,994
1999	1,633,615
TOTAL	$5,479,492

Table 3
National Endowment for Democracy
Grant Funding To Its Four Core Institutes, 1990-1999
(In U.S. Dollars)

YEAR	CIPE	ACILS	IRI	NDIIA
1990	1,996,159	7,117,411	2,645,022	2,106,843
1991	2,472,340	4,875,909	1,201,317	1,191,834
1992	3,034,427	5,766,102	1,673,000	2,172,723
1993	2,672,194	7,735,119	2,234,342	2,455,333
1994	3,323,315	9,095,722	2,941,675	3,305,418
1995	3,516,821	8,441,082	3,163,841	3,241,360
1996	3,577,463	4,320,721	3,826,277	4,095,361
1997	4,603,606	4,124,999	4,333,001	3,811,098
1998	4,104,988	3,885,790	3,989,645	3,888,815
1999	4,545,189	5,171,624	4,828,512	4,248,113
TOTAL	$33,846,502	$60,534,479	$30,836,632	$30,516,898

[NOTE: CIPE=Center for International Private Enterprise; ACILS=American Center for International Labor Solidarity (formerly the Free Trade Union Institute FTUI); IRI=International Republican Institute; NDIIA=National Democratic Institute for International Affairs.]

In 1990, the NED began to issue its own *Journal of Democracy* published quarterly by the Johns Hopkins University Press which is said to have both a scholarly orientation and be accessible to general readers interested in worldwide democratic developments, in particular analyses of international democratic movements and the cultural, political and social factors that affect the institutionalization of democracy. Some of the contributors to the journal include political scientists Samuel P. Huntington, Philippe C. Schmitter, Arend Lijphart, Enrique Baloyra, Guillermo O'Donnell, Seymour Martin Lipset, former State Department analyst and now RAND Corporation analyst Francis Fukuyama, and 1998 Nobel Prize winner and economist Amartya Sen, in addition to "leading democratic activists" such as Chinese dissident Fang Lizhi, Russian parliamentarian Oleg Rumyantsev, Kenyan human rights lawyer Gibson Kamau Kuria, playwright-cum-president of the Czech Republic Václav Havel, Peruvian novelist Mario Vargas Llosa, and "His Holiness" the Dalai Lama. Since 1994, the *Journal of Democracy* has come under a new arm of the NED called the International Forum for Democratic Studies which bills itself as "a leading center for analysis of the theory and practice of democratic development worldwide. It also serves as a clearinghouse for information on the varied activities and experiences of groups and institutions working to achieve and maintain democracy around the world." Marc F. Plattner and Larry Diamond not only direct the Forum but they also coedit the *Journal of Democracy*. Three additional programs have been initiated by the Forum including a Democracy Resource Center, a Research and Conferences Program, and a Visiting Fellows Program that "enables distinguished scholars and democratic activists from around the world to spend from three to ten months in residence at the Forum." The Democracy Resource Center itself has set up its own moderated listserv on the Internet called *DemocracyNews*, which it claims "facilitates an exchange of news and information among NED grantees and other democracy activists, scholars, and practitioners" ("Forum: International Forum for Democratic Studies, National Endowment for Democracy," March, 1999). In addition, a number of anthologies of articles from the *Journal of Democracy* have been published separately by the Johns Hopkins University Press.

Also, in 1996, an NED website was initiated on the World Wide Web delineating many of the NED's policies and programs.[104] A highlight of the *"DemocracyNet"* website is an online "Democracy Projects Database" of NED grants from 1990 to the present, in addition to grants made by newly affiliated Canadian and European democracy-promotion organizations including the Westminster Foundation for Democracy (Great Britain), the International Centre for Human Rights and Democratic Development (Canada), the Foundation Jean Jaurès (France), and the Alfred Mozer

Foundation (The Netherlands). However, there are several drawbacks to this online grant database, including the fact that only grants for one region and for only one grantee can be searched at any one time, thus preventing the online researcher from perusing all grants for all regions by year, though in 1999 the NED began placing its annual reports online.[105] Links have been established as well to the NED's four core institutes who are also now online at the following web addresses or Uniform Resource Locators (URLs): CIPE <http://www.cipe.org/>, ACILS (formerly the FTUI) <http://www.ned.org/grantees/center.html>, IRI <http://www.iri.org/>, and NDIIA <http://www.ndi.org/>.[106]

In addition to these efforts, the NED in 1998 launched what it terms "The World Movement for Democracy," holding its first meeting in February 1999 in New Delhi, India with 400 participants representing over 80 countries. Described as "a dynamic network of democrats, both individuals and organizations, who aspire to work in a coordinated way to address proactively the toughest challenges to the advancement of democracy and human rights in the world today," the NED's 1999 Annual Report states that this first assembly

> established the World Movement as a unique global forum for mutual support, exchange, and cooperation, and highlighted the potential for using new information technologies, especially the Internet, to meet the challenges posed by authoritarian regimes and to support democratic development (pp. 5, 9).

With plans for a follow-up conference in São Paulo, Brazil, from November 12-15, 2000, a Steering Committee has been established to guide the World Movement's development, with the NED designated as the Movement's current secretariat (*NED Annual Report 1999*, 2000, p. 9). It is also noteworthy that the World Movement for Democracy's first assembly in New Delhi was funded by both private and public resources including: The Starr Foundation, The Ford Foundation, CIVITAS, Freedom House, Godrej & Boyce Mfg. Co. Ltd., the Holdeen India Fund, the Industrial Development Bank of India, RPG Enterprises, Tata Steel, and the U.S. Department of State's Bureau of Democracy, Human Rights and Labor (*NED Annual Report 1999*, 2000, p. 9).

To see how NED practice conforms (or not) to its own rhetoric, we need to examine some of the programs NED funds more directly. Looking at NED's *1991 Annual Report* and its rather sketchy description of grant allocations, we can see that there were 50 grant recipients for all of Africa in fiscal year 1991 (See Table 4). The largest single grant recipient was a $330,000 grant to the Joint Center for Political and Economic Studies to enable the Institute for a Democratic Alternative for South Africa

(IDASA) to support a regional office in Natal Province. The second largest recipient was a $230,000 grant to the Free Trade Union Institute (FTIU) to allow the African-American Labor Center (AALC) to hold three leadership seminars in the U.S. for African trade union leaders and to develop worker education course materials. In Asia, 30 grants were made with the largest, a $363,000 grant, going to the FTUI to allow the Asian-American Free Labor Institute (AAFLI) to support the strengthening of free trade union institutions in the Philippines. A lesser grant of $318,337 was also given to the FTUI to enable the AAFLI to support trade unions in Taiwan, Pakistan, India, Malaysia, Hong Kong, Nepal a nd several "sub-Asian regional union organizations." In Central and Eastern Europe, NED funded 51 grantees in 1991 with the four largest grants goint to the FTUI to fund labor organizations i n Bulgaria, Hungary, and Poland and to assist in regional independent trade union development. As for the republics of the former Soviet Union, 22 grants were made, with, by far, the largest grant of $1,000,000 going to the FTUI to provide support for independent trade unions in the region. A much lesser grant of $250,000 was given to the International Republican Institute (IRI) to conduct conferences i n Moscow on institution-building and political training. NED programs for Latin America and the Caribbean had 56 recipients in fiscal year 1991, by far the largest number of active programs of all the regions. Again, the FTUI received the largest grant of $294,650 to enable the AIFLD to monitor human and trade union rights in Latin America. This was followed by a $215,000 grant to the Ethics and Public Policy Center to sponsor a *Libro Libre* publication program of books which promote democracy. The last region to receive funding was the Middle East where just 11 grants were made in 1991 with the largest grant for $272,955 given to the Center for International Private Enterprise (CIPE) in order to publish a new *Journal of Economic Reform* for the region.

By 1999, the number of grants for all regions except for the Latin America/Caribbean region had increased, going from 50 to 76 in Africa, from 30 to 74 in Asia, from 51 to 90 in Central and Eastern Europe, from 11 to 41 in the Middle East/North Africa region, and from 22 to 93 in the Newly Independent States, with only the Latin America/Caribbean region declining in the number of grants going down from 56 in 1991 to 52 in 1999. Two of the three largest grants for the Africa region in 1999 were given to ACILS, with $142,000 allocated so as to "increase participation of the Union Nationale des Syndicats des Traveilleurs du Benin and the Centrale des Syndicats Autonomes du Benin in the 1999 parliamentary electoral process" and $162,385 allocated to ACILS so that it could "work with the Union des Syndicats des Travailleurs du Niger to r everse the current deterioration of worker and trade union rights." The second largest grant for the Africa region in 1999 went to the NDI for a total of $150,120 to "help prepare key political party figures for the competitive multiparty elections in March 2000" in Zimbabwe (NED Annual Report 1999, 2000, pp. 12, 15, 18). In Asia in 1999, four of the five largest grants went to ACILS with the largest, for an amount of $551,232, going to "support the protection of workers' rights and the institutional development of trade unions in Thailand and Malaysia" while the second largest grant for $489,716 went to the IRI for its work in China to "support further progress and consolidation of electoral reform at the village level, and to conduct programs on legislative reform at the national and provincial levels" (NED Annual Report 1999, 2000, pp. 26, 29). The one grant that stands out in Central and Eastern Europe in 1999, and by far the largest of all regional grants that year, was for $735,177 allocated to the IRI in order to "establish a regional field office in Bratislava, Slovakia, from which IRI will organize and implement a variety of programs involving participants from one or more of 12 countries" (NED Annual Report 1999, 2000, p. 39). A grant for $284,284 allocated to the IRI so that they can "conduct an international election observation mission during the October and November 1999 presidential elections in Ukraine" tops the list of funding in the Newly Independent States (NED Annual Report 1999, 2000, p. 48). Likewise, the IRI received the largest grant in the Latin America/Caribbean region for 1999 with an amount of $310,507 allocated so they can "work with the Cuban Democratic Revolutionary Directorate to promote a peaceful, democratic transition in Cuba" (NED Annual Report 1999, 2000, p. 53). And, lastly, ACILS received the biggest grant for the Middle East/North Africa region in 1999 with an allocation of $353,897 in order to "work with the Working Women's League in Lebanon and the International Institute for Peace and Democracy to build democratic trade union institutions, empower working women, raise consciousness about child labor and migrant labor issues, and develop intra-Arab union networks to promote democracy thoughout the Middle East/Northern Africa region" (NED Annual Report 1999, 2000, p. 63).

Table 4
National Endowment for Democracy
Number of Grants By Region And Year,
1990-1999

YEAR	AFRICA	ASIA	C. & E. EUROPE	L.A. & CARIB.	M. E. & N. AFRICA	NIS (FORM. U.S.S.R.)	MULTI-REGION
1990	21	23	94	71	0	23	6
1991	50	30	51	56	11	22	6
1992	58	43	54	63	7	43	10
1993	49	42	39	67	19	55	9
1994	63	49	53	65	34	61	8
1995	58	62	60	63	39	54	10
1996	58	58	53	50	48	67	3
1997	62	47	60	42	42	74	5
1998	74	58	70	50	41	84	11
1999	76	74	90	52	41	93	17
TOTAL	569	486	624	579	282	576	85

NOTE: The number of grants in the newly autonomous "Miscellaneous" category are depicted in Table 5 below:

Table 5
National Endowment for Democracy Miscellaneous Number of Grants,
1998-1999

YEAR	NUMBER OF GRANTS
1997	9
1998	9
1999	11
TOTAL	**29**

That the NED annual reports are vague as to the specific breakdown of its individual grants has been noticed also by the U.S. government's General Accounting Office which in 1991 investigated 36 NED projects—accounting for a total of 20 million dollars—and concluded that only one had been evaluated adequately. In addition, there were several instances of petty graft including $10,000 spent on unauthorized office renovations, inappropriate loans made with NED funds, funds spent on a rental car for an individual later arrested for dealing drugs and then further unapproved expenditures to cover the cost of rental fees on the impounded vehicle. More to the point, however, the GAO also found itself unable to get the General Workers Union of Portugal to assist in accounting for how it spent its $2.6 million grant it had received from the FTUI. And though the NED brushes off such problems by claiming that it works with mostly small activist organizations working under trying conditions, *Nation* columnist David Corn states that given this atmosphere of lax oversight, it is apparent that NED recipients are "clearly learning one vital lesson of U.S.-style democracy: Taxpayer dollars...are funds just waiting to be burned" (Corn, 1991, p. 548). In its March 1991 report, the GAO stated that since the

> GAO's last report in 1986, the Endowment has not significantly improved its capability to evaluate and report on the effectiveness of its total program. The Endowment has not given adequate attention to systematically planning program objectives and assessing program results. In addition, the Endowment has not developed an adequate evaluation capability to independently evaluate and report on the effectiveness of its total programs (GAO/NSIAD-91-162, 1991, p. 3).

And while instances of petty graft and vague financial reporting point to certain administrative problems at NED which perhaps, if the political will exists, may easily be addressed, other funding programs raise questions as to NED's priorities in its efforts to promote democracy and indicate the narrowness of its ideological orientation. For example, in May 1989, the NED held its first "world conference of democratic activists" whose invitees were strictly disciples of free market capitalism including Hernando de Soto, the free market Peruvian economist and author of *The Other Path*; the anti-Soviet activist Vladimir Bukovsky; the Polish free-market advocate Leszek Kolakowski; and the Mexican neoconservative Octavio Paz. Award winners at this event included the "renowned" Chinese dissident Fang Lizhi, Nicaraguan President Violeta Chamorro and Václav Havel, current president of the newly-renamed Czech Republic [which separated from Slovakia in 1993]. Offering the invocation for the 1991 Democracy Awards ceremony at the convention was Tibet's Dalai Lama. And to conclude the program, Vice President Dan Quayle praised Havel and Chamorro as representing "democratic statesmanship at its very finest" (Quayle, quoted in NED 1991 Annual Report, 1992, p. 9). Since 1989, the NED has hosted approximately 17 other conferences including one in March, 1997 entitled "Consolidating Democracy in Taiwan" which promised to examine "the Taiwanese political landscape in the wake of its historic March 1996 presidential elections to identify obstacles to the strengthening of Taiwan's democracy, and to explore the impact of international factors on Taiwan's future prospects" (NED: International Forum Conference Reports <http://www.ned.org/pubs/intercom.html>).[107]

That the 1989 convention featured, as did the others which followed, many of the heroes of the conservative right is not surprising. Still, other funding programs spell out this orientation more clearly. A 1984 FTUI grant to Panamanian union activists was used to promote the presidential candidacy of one Nicolas Barletta who the U.S.-backed Panamanian military endorsed. Such support for particular candidates not only violates NED principles but is against U.S. neutrality laws. Also in 1984, the FTUI gave secret grants to two French groups opposed to French President Francois Mitterand. One grant for $500,000 went to a rightwing activist group which proceeded to stage protests against Mitterand. The other secret grant for $800,000 went to a CIA-connected trade union called *Force Ouvriere* which acted to counter socialist and communist controlled unions. In these latter two grants, not only did NED funding raise questions about engaging in destabilization campaigns, especially against a democratic ally of the U.S. but, moreover, the fact that these activities were funded secretly again violated both NED principles and U.S. law.[108]

In another effort at destabilizing an elected government, the NED in 1990 allocated more than $615,095 to the Bulgarian Union of Democratic Forces with another $232,695 going to its newspaper in an attempt to defeat the Bulgarian Socialist Party in the June 1990 elections. When even this financial aid failed to prevent a BSP (which formerly had been the Bulgarian Communist Party) victory, the NED, Blum writes:

> stepped in with generous funding and advice to the specific opposition groups which carried out a campaign of chaos lasting almost five months: very militant and disruptive street demonstrations, paralyzing labor strikes, sit-ins, hunger strikes, arson...parliament was surrounded, the government was under seige...until finally the president was forced to resign, followed by some of his ministers; lastly, the prime minister gave up his office (Blum, 2000, p. 157).

In the subsequent 1991 Bulgarian elections, NED-backed political allies prevailed, or as Blum writes, "what NED calls the 'democratic forces' won" (Blum, 2000, p. 157).

Still other NED practices not only suggest impropriety, if not illegality, but also certain individuals and groups NED has working for it tarnishes its stated commitment to democratic goals; moreover, what goals NED does have only further indicates that in truth it merely pursues U.S. foreign policy aims—which have more to do with selfish state interests, e.g. accumulation of wealth and expansion of power, than in promoting democracy. For example, in one 1990 grant given to the University of South Carolina, the university took a ten percent administrative charge for handling the funds and passed the rest on into several vaguely described Chilean projects with money being deposited directly into the personal account of the director of one of the Chilean projects with no further documentation on how it was spent. As investigative reporter Holly Sklar and political analyst Chip Berlet note, "the university was used essentially as a money laundry" (Sklar and Berlet, 1991-92, p. 13). Also in 1990, it was found out that former pro-Nazi Arrow Cross official Laszlo Pasztor, a convicted Nazi collaborator, was helping to channel NED funds to his friends in Hungary by translating a nd evaluating grant requests from Hungarian and Czechoslovak groups to the National Republican and National Democratic Institutions for International Affairs. Just two years before, Pasztor had been forced to resign from President Bush's 1988 presidential campaign when it was found out that the campaign's Coalition for American Nationalities, headed by Pasztor, had numerous ties to anti-Semitic and openly fascist organizations (Berlet and Sklar, 1990, pp. 450-51). In September 1991, a scandal erupted in the Philippines after the U.S. attempted to buy the support of Philippine Senator Ernesto Herrera for the treaty to keep U.S. bases in the country. Herrera is also the general secretary of the Trade Union Congress of the Philippines (TUCP) which received NED grants via the FTUI and the Asian-American Free Labor Institute (AAFLI). After criticizing the treaty as being against Filipino workers' interest, "Herrera reportedly switched his vote in favor of the losing treaty after AAFLI promised $3.7 million in additional TUCP support" (Sklar and Berlet, 1991-92, p. 59). NED funding activities, or rather the lack thereof in one noticeable 1991 case, came under fire when Congressman William P. Gray III (D.-Pa.), the House Majority Whip at that time, was able to temporarily strike NED funding in retaliation for the apparent unwillingness of NED to distribute $10 million in aid to political groups helping victims of apartheid in South Africa. The money had been approved as part of a 1990 supplemental appropriations bill and yet 14 months later, the funding still had not occurred. But before Gray could move to eliminate NED's $26 million in funding for 1991, the House quickly dropped NED funding from HR 2608 in order to avoid a full debate (Biskupic, 1991, pp. 1594-5). NED funding was reintroduced and passed later in the year in the 1992 appropriations process, but the racist implications of NED action, or rather inaction, opened the NED up to further scrutiny.

The degree to which the NED will go to subvert a country's sovereignty can perhaps best be gleaned from its funding of anti-Sandinista groups in Nicaragua. Prior to 1986, for example, part of $3.5 million in NED grants to Nicaragua went to an organization called PRODEMCA which

funded the Sandinista opposition newspaper *La Prensa* while simultaneously taking out advertisements supporting Reagan's contra war. To
obviate criticism which resulted from this practice, funding for *La Prensa*
was taken up by the Washington-based Delphi International Group which
later became a key NED grant operator in Nicaragua. More blatant interference was witnessed in 1989 when NED pumped in nearly $9 million to
help fund Nicaragua's anti-Sandinista United Nicaraguan Opposition (UNO)
in the February 1990 elections. That the NED had gone overboard is
indicated by the fact that the Endowment never, prior to 1989, spent more
than $2.8 million for opposition movements in Chile, Poland, Panama and
the Philippines, and all but Panama had larger populations than Nicaragua's
1.6 million voters (Overt Meddling, 1989, p. 408). And though by Nicaraguan law half the aid had to go to Nicaragua's Sandinista-dominated Supreme Electoral Council, the NED partisan funding raised questions as to
whether NED had violated its own principles and charter as well as U.S.
law by working to elect individual candidates, in the present case UNO's
presidential candidate Violeta Chamorro, and by paying the salaries of
municipal candidates (GAO/NSIAD-90-245, 1990, pp. 24-25). The money
was supposed to be used as per Public Law 101-119 to promote democracy and national reconciliation in Nicaragua, including assistance for free
and fair elections held in February 1990 for activities such as voter regis-
tration, get out the vote activities, and monitoring the results (GAO/NSIAD-
90-245, 1990, pp. 1-2). But as *The Economist* magazine noted, the funding
would help build up the opposition's infrastructure but "would not, in
theory, directly finance the opposition's campaign (but that is the greyest
of all grey electoral areas)" (Cash for Violeta, 1989, p. 28). Gray indeed was
this supposedly neutral aid to "build party infrastructure" as indicated by
NED grants of upwards of $200,000 to fund a video center (a program
endorsed by former President Bush's son, Jeb Bush, and approved by
retired U.S. Army General [and former NATO head, White House Chief of
Staff, and U.S. Secretary of State] Al Haig's daughter, Barbara, a program
director at NED), part of the $9 million congressional appropriation for the
1990 Nicaraguan elections, which churned out slick campaign commer-
cials for Chamorro's UNO Party.

     Of particular interest as regards the allocation of NED funds
spent building the UNO party infrastructure was the payment of $743,000
for an initial purchase of 88 vehicles for UNO operatives plus $800,000 in
sales taxes and customs duties to cover the vehicles, followed by an
unreported amount spent on the additional purchase of eight boats, 190
bicycles, 60 motorcycles, 19 generators, and an undetermined amount of
radios and office equipment (GAO/NSIAD-90-245, 1990, p. 19). That the
Nicaraguan Supreme Electoral Council was more than lenient in allowing
this sort of blatant interference in the country's internal domestic affairs is

quite apparent. The Electoral Council, however, did have to put its foot down when an NED-funded group called the Center for Training and Electoral Promotion (CAPEL) proposed to airdrop nearly two million "civic education leaflets" at the final political rallies of both the UNO and the Sandinista Frente on February 18 and 21, 1990, respectively. The Council also decided not to allow a CAPEL produced videotape to air on Nicaraguan television (GAO/NSIAD-90-245, 1990, p. 22). As a report by the Institute for Media Analysis (IMA), a New York-based nonprofit which monitored the 1990 Nicaraguan television campaign, stated: "'The U.S. defines the Nic[araguan] electoral campaign in terms of a battle between the [Sandinista] Frente and the UNO despite the fact that there are eight other contenders. However, the money that the U.S. is giving to UNO will turn this definition into a reality. It is totally distorting the electoral process and this is only the beginning'" (IMA quoted in Branan, 1990, p. 14).

Why the Sandinistas allowed NED funding to begin with is a telling case of the coordinated pressure tactics used by the U.S. to—in Ronald Reagan's words—get the Sandinistas "to cry uncle." Economically strangled by U.S. control or dominate influence over international markets and international lending agencies and under pressure by Washington to make concessions to the opposition in order to end U.S. backing for the counterrevolutionary guerrilla bands known as "the Contras", the Nicaraguan government figured it had little choice but to allow the funding. However, in order to thwart the impact of NED funding, the Sandinistas passed in 1989 a new electoral law—mentioned above—which required that half of all funds donated to political parties from non-Nicaraguan groups must be turned over to the government's electoral council as a tax to help pay administrative costs of the election (Nichols, 1990, pp. 266-67). With regard to the NED, about half of its $2.1 million granted to the UNO by Public Law 101-119 went to the Electoral Council for taxes (GAO/NSIAD-90-245, 1990, p. 18). The Nicaraguan law, however, did not envision nor could defend against millions of other dollars in U.S. aid which also flowed to the Sandinista opponents including $47.9 million authorized under U.S. Public Law 100-276 and $49.75 million authorized under U.S. Public Law 101-14 for the "Nicaraguan Resistance" (GAO/NSIAD-90-245, 1990, p. 8).

As the victory of Violeta Chamorro in the 1990 elections proved, overt, perhaps even more than covert, U.S. funding can have a powerful influence in manipulating the internal politics of other countries. Indeed, current efforts to undermine the Cuban government are running along full-speed ahead. With help from the anti-Cuba Torricelli bill signed into law by President Bush on October 23, 1992 and the Helms-Burton Act signed into law by President Clinton on March 12, 1996, external pressure to tighten the then 34-year-old U.S. blockade of Cuba by attempting to cut off international trade by penalizing companies doing business in Cuba on properties owned by U.S. companies and citizens prior to the 1959 revolution, denying U.S. visas to executives of companies doing business in Cuba, allowing lawsuits by U.S. citizens—including Cubans who have since the revolution become U.S. citizens—for reclamation of land nationalized by the Castro government, will be complementing NED funded anti-Castro groups which in turn could produce what years of CIA covert activities have been unable to do, *viz.* the overturning of the Cuban revolution.[109] And though on June 27, 2000 (following the Elian Gonzalez saga) the U.S. House of Representatives voted to ease sanctions on delivering food and medicine to Cuba for the first time in 40 years, it remains to be seen whether other aspects of the trade embargo against Cuba will be relaxed or not by the new administration following the November 2000 elections.[110]

One of the key NED grantees in the anti-Castro operation is known as the Cuban American National Foundation (CANF) founded and originally chaired by a wealthy Miami businessman and virulent anti-Castro activist Jorge Mas Canosa.[111] Mas and CANF came under scrutiny as Mas continued to receive large NED grants through 1992 and, in turn, funded campaigns of scores of candidates for federal office, including that of former chair of the House Foreign Affairs Committee, who was also a founder of NED and its first acting chairman, Representative Dante Fascell (D.-Fl.) (Nichols, 1988, pp. 389-90).[112] Indeed, Representative Robert Torricelli, sponsor of the Cuban Democracy Act of 1992, received thousands of dollars in funding from CANF. And as *U.S. News & World Report* correspondent Linda Robinson wrote: "It is less clear whether their (CANF) goal is promoting democracy in Cuba or restoring 1950s style rule by a wealthy elite. In fact, Mas was said to have already chosen positions for his cohorts in Miami to serve under him as president in a post-Castro Cuba" (McAfee, March 23, 1994, *Movimiento Cubano por la Paz*). These NED-funded activities in Cuba intended to overturn the Castro government "leads to the probability," states former CIA agent Ralph McGehee, "that [the] CIA uses [the] NED for cover and that NED's hundreds of so-called non-governmental organizations (NGOs)—many of them human rights groups, are little more than fronts for the operations of the CIA." Furthermore, he argues: "Since NED sponsors human rights groups and other NGOs in about 80 countries, this creates a massive worldwide mechanism for subversion" (McGehee, September 6, 1996).

Since 1990, and especially since the collapse of the Soviet Union in 1991, the NED has funneled millions of dollars for political organizing and independent trade union development into Russia primarily through its four core institutes. These efforts have been supplemented by millions of dollars more from other U.S. foreign policy agencies including the USIA, USAID, DOD, and the State Department. As the GAO noted, the "democracy assistance program in Russia seeks to capitalize on the historic opportunity to build democracy in place of a centralized Communist system" (GAO/NSIAD-96-40, 1996, p. 2).[113] For the years 1990 till June of 1999, NED funding has exceeded $38 million for Russia and the former states of the Soviet Union. Although the GAO reported that democracy related projects under their review were seen as "generally valuable" by Russian reformers and others, they stated there were mixed results as far as the projects contributing to significant changes in Russia's political, legal, or social system and concluded that "the most important factors determining project impact were Russian economic and political conditions" (GAO/NSIAD-96-40, 1996, p. 2). While citing a "new openness" of the newly independent media as indicated by their "frequently aired views highly critical of the Communist government," the report also noted insufficient advertising revenues were forcing many media organizations "into bankruptcy or joining larger affiliates, thereby curtailing their independence and capacity to produce their own programs." Also noted was the pressure faced by many print and broadcast outlets "from local political authorities or from organized crime, in large part due to their dire financial situations" (GAO/NSIAD-96-40, 1996, p. 3).

Regarding the NED funded activities to promote free trade union development, the GAO recognized the FTUI for providing "important equipment and training for the first independent, non-Communist unions that arose in the late 1980s, that backed Boris Yeltsin and other reformers, and that played a key role in the breakup of the Soviet Union." However, the report notes, the "influence of the successors to the official Communist trade unions, the inexperience and isolation of democratic unions, the apathy of Russian citizens, and the weakness of the economy" continues to hamper the new democratic unions (GAO/NSIAD-96-40, 1996, p. 5). As of late 1994, there were between three to five million workers in the "independent" or "democratic" labor movement (encompassing such unions as Sotsprof with 300,000 members; the Confederation of Maritime Workers with 86,000 workers; and a regional affiliate of the Independent Miners' Union of Russia with about 95,000 members), while the overwhelming majority of workers, more than 50 million, were still affiliated with the Communist dominated unions. Leaders associated with the "independent" labor organizations cited their biggest obstacle to establishing independent unions as laying in the continued control of the social insurance fund by the official trade unions, through which they could disperse benefits such as workers' vacations and sick pay (GAO/NSIAD-96-40, 1996, pp. 31-33). Citing the need to give workers a means of participating in the new political and economic environment, NED program documents and U.S. and Russian officials warned that "if workers are not given a voice during this transitional period and believe that free markets and democracy only work to their disadvantage, then they could pose a threat to social peace and political and economic development" (GAO/NSIAD-96-40, 1996, p. 30).

With reference to political party development in Russia, the GAO noted that U.S. funded activities "had not significantly strengthened reformist national political parties, either organizationally or in terms of increased membership or performance in elections." Despite NED funding of $956,000 to the NDIIA and the IRI between 1990 and 1992 to support the anti-Communist Democratic Russia Movement, as well as funding to conduct civic education and grassroots organizing programs for Russians at the national and local levels in addition to over $200,000 to monitor the April 1993 elections and to send Russian party leaders to the U.S. for "training," on top of over $17 million spent by USAID on similar efforts during this same period, "reformist political parties," the GAO reported, "performed poorly in the December 1993 elections." As the report pointed out, "reformist parties have been either unwilling or unable to form broad-based coalitions or build national organizations and large segments of the Russian public have not been receptive to their political message" (GAO/NSIAD-96-40, 1996, p. 37). Since the 1993 elections, the situation for reformist parties has "only marginally improved," such by the December 1995 parliamentary elections, "the two large pro-reform election blocs of 1993, Yabloko and Russia's Choice, had split into 11 different parties and movements." Russian political reform activists lamented that viable reformist political parties "may only emerge after more than a decade" and that "they will only win elections when the Russian people are receptive to a reformist, democratic political message." As for now, the report notes that reformist parties are bogged down by "the unpopularity of their free market message" and the "historical negative view of 'party' (a harsh memory from the days of Communist party control)" (GAO/NSIAD-96-40, 1996, pp. 40-41). Moreover, local elections held countrywide in 1994, notes the GAO, "raised concerns about future national elections, as these elections were marked by many irregularities and low voter participation" (GAO/NSIAD-96-40, 1996, p. 27).

Civic education programs funded by the NDIIA and the IRI were cited as a way to better promote democracy in Russia. In particular, political party participants "spoke favorably of U.S. support for sending Russians to the United States for training." Such efforts, it was stated, may convince Russians to support the reformist parties' message. Because of a lack of success with political party development, USAID has been encouraging the NDIIA and the IRI "to place less emphasis on their party training programs and more on their work with civic organizations" (GAO/NSIAD-96-40, 1996, p. 43).

Given the foregoing NED funding activities, it is fair to say that

U.S. democracy promotion is tainted and contradicted when advanced through secrecy, money laundering, vote buying, kickbacks, paid junkets to the U.S. for "training", and blatant acts which violate national sovereignty. That the U.S. has been successful in achieving its aims in several areas of the world is undeniable—the election of Violeta Chamorro being a classic case in point. But short-term gains can have long-term negative consequences as witnessed by CIA coup d'états and other covert activities in Iran, Guatemala, Nicaragua and elsewhere before and during the Cold War which continue to lend fuel to fire virulent anti-American sentiment in these countries. It is true that the presumably overt nature of much NED funding may help to dispel some of this resentment, but NED proponents should not be surprised if the new beneficiaries of this made-in-America brand of democracy begin to reject this export seeing it as just another attempt to mask U.S. desires for world hegemonic dominance.[114] And such a rejection is most likely to occur when the supposedly liberatory institutions of this capitalist, market-based brand of democracy fail to deliver material goods adequate to the promises given. For, indeed, are not compliant and/or submissive publics for the better part satiated, while those whose needs have long gone unmet stirred to revolt? Nevertheless, the U.S. continued to pursue this course of "promoting democracy" abroad in the Clinton administration. In fact, before he was sworn into office, the then president-elect Clinton was quoted in *The New York Times* as stating that he wanted a Secretary of State who possesses "a commitment to global growth and economic regeneration here and the fulfilling of our responsibility as the world's sole superpower to try to promote democracy and freedom..." (Clinton, quoted in Friedman, 1992, p. A19).[115] For the most part, Clinton, in his two terms in office, has not had to confront the multiplicity of anti-U.S. rebellions and revolutions around the world which marked most U.S. administrations throughout the years of the Cold War. Certainly the demise of the Soviet Union has contributed to the lessening of international tensions. But one could argue that U.S. interventionary behavior like those carried out by the NED may likewise be impacting on the present absence of major international conflicts. NED advocate Cohen argues the case that "[t]o the extent that U.S. foreign policy and diplomacy fosters the spread of democracy, the world will become more hospitable to freedom." Moreover, long-term support for democracy promotion, he predicts, will yield "a less contentious community of nations, regional stability, freer societies with few refugees, and freer economies that spread prosperity to their citizens while opening markets to all" (Cohen, 2000, p. 846). That this view is shared by the present administration can be witnessed by the adoration of Secretary of State Albright who, on May 16, 2000, praised the NED stating that it "is one of my favorite institutions." The NED, she remarked:

has pioneered the use of our own civil society to work with supporters of democracy from other countries and cultures. It's had extraordinary success in helping democracy-builders learn from each other by sharing experiences across national lines. And by so doing has helped to give global impetus to the movement to democracy (Albright, May 16, 2000).

Secretary Albright's claims of success may be more than just cheerleading as the U.S. has perhaps found an answer to what years of Cold War arms and advisors often failed to achieve, namely, pacification of hostile foreign populations. And though the NED's actions constitute only a small part of overall U.S. government activity abroad and much less of the overall activity associated with globalization and the tying together of the world's various regions into a single global market, the NED is nonetheless actively coopting political elements in the developing nations which, to the consternation of both anti-U.S. and/or anti-capitalist activists, otherwise might be susceptible to following indigenous oppositional rule.[116]

Whether this commitment to promoting democracy abroad continues with the new U.S. administration elected in November 2000 remains to be seen, though at present, the bipartisan consensus supporting the NED appears to remain constant, thus solidifying this component of U.S. foreign policy for the foreseeable future. As NED President, Carl Gershman, stated in 1999: "Today, the Cold War is almost a distant memory, and democracy-promotion has become an established field of international activity, and a pillar of American foreign policy" (NED Annual Report, 2000, p. 4). Shared assumptions about the nature of the liberal capitalist state and its foundation in the presumed virtues of civil society will assure that the U.S. is committed to this foreign policy path whether the party in power is Republican or Democratic and with the active support of both the AFL-CIO and the Chamber of Commerce. The successful export of a political philosophy, however, especially one closely intertwined with an economic program, requires the ability to influence, coordinate, and sometimes direct economic decisions, policies, and trends in countries targeted for democracy promotion. In the next and final chapter, U.S. transnational economic extension and leadership will be analyzed as to the likelihood that the world capitalist system under the tutelage of the U.S. hegemon might act to mediate and facilitate transitions to the U.S. model of democracy or generate sufficient resentment and antipathy to this U.S.-led export so as to negate its goals.

V. Capitalism, Hegemony, and Democracy

During the last years, the power of money has presented a new mask over its criminal face. Above borders, no matter race or color, the Power of money humiliates dignities, insults honesties and assassinates hopes. Re-named as "Neoliberalism", the historic crime in the concentration of privileges, wealth and impunities, democratizes misery and hopelessness.

— (Subcomandante Insurgente Marcos, January 30, 1996, *La Jornada*, "The EZLN calls for an intercontinental anti-liberalism gathering." Mexico: Chiapas Mountains.)

Can the U.S. successfully export its own brand of democracy abroad? Can this "revolution" towards democratic capitalist structures be effected in a passive manner or will it create the type of convulsions historically awakened by external intervention of one state into the affairs of another? Indeed, does not this U.S. brand of democracy contain contradictions of political obligation which could forestall such transitions? Intended to foster U.S. hegemony and, hence, the functioning of the world capitalist system under its leadership, will not such transitions to liberal democracy in fact impede or obstruct the necessity to accumulate capital as national resentment against the U.S. hegemon and its foreign export grows? And, in this event, which interests will likely dominate? In this concluding chapter, I examine certain aspects of global capitalist development since WWII and the affect this development is having on the relations between the so-called "developing nations" *vis-à-vis* the so-called "developed nations." As well, the accelerated globalization of the world market in the 1990s demands a look at the established international economic bodies including the newly formed World Trade Organization (WTO). Utilizing a Marxian class analysis, I then construct a basic theoretical model of capitalist production as it operates within the current global market and attempt to analyze the concomitant effect on the U.S. export of democracy in general. In this regard, an assessment is made of the degree to which the U.S. attempt to promote democracy abroad falls within the prescription for hegemonic rule as outlined by Gramsci (in the sense of domination combined with political leadership). Indeed, the possibility arises of a division between the interests of international capital from that of U.S. national interests proper and, hence, the necessity by internationally organized capital to create its own instruments for the implementation of its policies, e.g. the Multilateral Agreement on Investments (MAI), and/or expand existing instruments, e.g. the World Trade Organization (WTO), the International Bank for Reconstruction and Development (IBRD; otherwise known as the World Bank), the International Monetary Fund (IMF), and the United Nations (UN).[117] As such, can this U.S. policy be pursued successfully solely within the framework of a national state acting as the hegemonic leader or will a supranational or international framework need be constructed and/or expanded in order to legitimate and enforce the capitalistic democratic values being exported? In short, is the western liberal (i.e. capitalist) democratic state under U.S. hegemony the best form for the realization of continued capitalist accumulation or does this form of state and hegemonic relationships produce its own irreconcilable contradictions which undermine this very hegemony?

A Short History of the Post-WWII LIEO

Arthur Jensen (played by actor Ned Beatty), CEO of CCA (a fictional corporation) in the 1976 film "Network" to TV network anchorman turned on-air prophet and madman Howard Beale (played by actor Peter Finch) after Beale went on air criticizing a proposed buyout of CCA by the Western World Funding Company, a corporation bankrolled by Arab money.

Arthur Jensen: You have meddled with the primal forces of nature Mr. Beale, and I won't have it! Is that clear?!
  You are an old man who thinks in terms of nations and peoples. There are no nations. There are no peoples. There are no Russians. There are no Arabs. There are no Third Worlds. There is no West. There is only one holistic system of systems, one vast and immense interwoven, interacting, multivariate, multinational dominion of dollars—petro-dollars, electro-dollars, multi-dollars, reichmarks, rheims, rubles, pounds, and shekels. It is the international system of currency which determines the totality of life on this planet. That is the natural order of things today. That is the atomic and subatomic and galactic structure of things today! And you have meddled with the primal

forces of nature! And you will atone!
Am I getting through to you Mr. Beale?
You get on your little 21-inch screen and howl about America and
democracy. There is no America. There is no democracy. There is
only IBM and ITT and AT&T and Dupont, Dow, Union Carbide, and
Exxon. Those are the nations of the world today.
What do you think the Russians talk about in their councils of
state? Karl Marx? They get out their linear programming charts,
statistical decision theories, minimax solutions, and compute the price/
cost probabilities of their transactions and investments just like we
do. We no longer live in a world of nations and ideologies Mr. Beale.
The world is a college of corporations inexorably determined by
the immutable bylaws of business. The world is a business Mr. Beale.
It has been since man crawled out of the slime. And our children will
live, Mr. Beale, to see that perfect world in which there is no war or
famine, oppression, or brutality—one vast and ecumenical holding
company for whom all men will work to serve a common company
for whom all men will work to serve a common profit in which all men
will hold a share of stock, all necessities provided, all anxieties tran-
quilized, all boredom amused. And I have chosen you Mr. Beale to
preach this evangel.
Howard Beale: Why me?
Arthur Jensen: Because you're on television dummy. Sixty million
people watch you every night of the week, Monday through Friday.
Howard Beale: I have seen the face of God!
Arthur Jensen: You just might be right Mr. Beale.

— "The corporate cosmology of Arthur Jensen"

Following World War II, a Liberal International Economic Order
(LIEO) was established under U.S. tutelage at the historic Bretton Woods
Conference in New Hampshire. Building on the Articles of Agreement of
the 1944 Bretton Woods conference, the LIEO which was constructed
included several institutional instruments to help facilitate the expansion
and security of market forces. The conferees to the 1944 conference
wishing to avoid the ubiquitous imposition of trade barriers and the widespread practice of competitive devaluation, which in the late 1920s and
1930s exacerbated the Great Depression, thus knew that to alleviate the
fear and distrust of governments a means would have to be devised to
determine the fair value of each country's currency relative to others (i.e.
the necessity for convertible currencies) so that trade could proceed in an
orderly and uninterrupted fashion.[118] With specialized agencies like the
International Monetary Fund (IMF), the International Bank for Reconstruction and Development (IBRD; a.k.a. the World Bank), and the International Trade Organization (ITO), the Bretton Woods agreements laid

the basis for a postwar economic structure which was to rest on three political conditions: "the concentration of power in a small number of states, the existence of a cluster of important interests shared by those states, and the presence of a dominant power [the U.S.] willing and able to assume a leadership role" (Spero, 1981, p. 23). A system of fixed exchange rates was adopted which forced all participatory countries to balance their finances while keeping their exchange rates within narrow set limits with their currencies earmarked to the U.S. dollar so that they could be sold or redeemed in the different exchange markets around the world.[119] U.S. dominance in the post-WWII international economy kept the parity of the dollar's value relatively high *vis-à-vis* most other of the world's currencies, hence its agreed upon status at Bretton Woods as the standard bearer was psychologically reinforced by its seeming invulnerability up to the 1970s. And because the U.S. dollar acted as the standard by which all other currencies' exchange rates were set while retaining a relatively high parity in relation to most other currencies, the U.S. was able to act relatively unhindered as the capitalist world's banker as the dollar became the currency of preference for international transactions and investment.

An agreement on a new international trade order proved more elusive than on a monetary order, however. Whereas the U.S. had dominated decision making at Bretton Woods, it was unable to dictate the structure of trade rules formalized in the Havana Charter. Immediately from the start, exemptions from generalized rules by member countries participating in the trade negotiations weakened the dominant role of the U.S. and made the ITO a watered down institution. And though the U.S. did not formally abandon the ITO until 1950 (by not submitting the Havana Charter to Congress where it faced certain defeat), an interim treaty drawn up by the U.S. in 1947 (which came into force in 1948) known as the General Agreement on Tariffs and Trade (GATT)—which was to serve until the Havana Charter was ratified—by default became "the expression of the international consensus on trade" (Spero, 1981, p. 78).

While acknowledging as "useful and necessary" the contention that the configuration of state power in the world political economy is the most basic factor required for the existence of an international economic regime—the so-called "hegemonic stability thesis" (Kindleberger, 1973; Gilpin, 1981; Keohane, 1980 & 1984), Ruggie argues that the existence of a LIEO "has more to do with the international projection of a particular configuration of domestic state-society relations than it does with the projection simply of state power" for, in a liberal order pride of place is given to market rationality, and "political authority is designed to give maximum scope to market forces rather than constrain them."[120] Hence, Ruggie notes: "An (sic) LIEO will exist, then, when this form of state-society relations enjoys a hegemonic status among the major economic powers" (Ruggie, 1984, p. 35). Once the major economic powers achieve this congruence in the balance of their state-society relations, the collective purposes of these regimes must still be operationalized and justified as policies. And this, Ruggie argues, "largely depends upon the prevailing bodies of economic theory and ideology to which the regime-making states hold." When the gold standard prevailed prior to WWI, for example, state abstinence was advocated and understood within the framework of classical economics and justified by the *laissez-faire* ideology. The interwar period saw no reigning theory or ideology states Ruggie. In the post-WWII period, however,

> among the capitalist countries social democratic doctrines and methods have coexisted with more traditional economic forms, but there has been a substantial area of theoretical and ideological overlap in the Keynesian middle (Ruggie, 1984, p. 36).

The neoclassical-Keynesian synthesis, he argues, provided "the means both to legitimate the prevailing social objectives of the major economic powers as well as to operationalize those objectives into specific policies that the economic regimes were programmed to coordinate" (Ruggie, 1984, p. 37).[121]

Though U.S. predominance in the post-war period could guarantee the establishment of a LIEO, a much more complicated task was to secure legitimacy for the system in order to make it work. This was to be achieved, first, through the principle of *comparative advantage* which was to reflect the formal equality of those states party to the agreements. This "mutual-gain" approach, as Bhagwati (1984) refers to it, stipulated that "any two nations will benefit if each specializes in those goods that it can produce relatively cheaply and exchange for goods that it can produce only at a higher cost" (Kegley and Wittkopf, 1981/1985, p. 172). Specialization was thus to ensure effective low-cost production while the benefits of unfettered trade were to accrue to all participating nations, more so than would otherwise be possible in a system of protective trade barriers. And, secondly, the principle of *non-discrimination* was incorporated in the designation of Most Favored Nation (MFN) status which meant that each member country had to treat all of its fellow GATT members equally, extending favorable trade conditions it had made to one country to all fellow countries, as well as prohibiting quantitative restrictions on imports (although these restrictions were deemed to be suitable measures for safeguarding balance of payments) (Ruggie, 1984, p. 37).[122] In addition, this high level of mutual economic interaction among states involved in what were deemed to be relatively symmetrical relationships on an even playing field was to lead to an interdependence between states thus legitimating the system.

In practice, however, the principle of mutual-gain gave way to self-gain as competition rather than cooperation became the n orm.[123] Concomitantly, nations repeatedly interfered with free trade practices, continuously trying to get an edge in market shares and exchange rates while playing favorites in deciding who was to be granted MFN status. Indeed, as per section 5 of the Trade Agreements Extension Act of 1951 (P.L. 82-50), President Truman suspended MFN status to the Soviet Union and all countries of the then Sino-Soviet bloc.[124] The presumed equality of states was thus hit with the reality of their inequality as states with greater resource reserves and productive capacities, as well as with more advanced technologies and a skilled work force, could use this leverage to ensure unequal t rade patterns. This had the political consequence o f perpetually subordinating those nations less well-endowed. Interdependence thus gave way to dependence. Indeed, as Danaher argues: "The unwritten goal of the World Bank and the IMF—one that has been enforced with a vengeance—has been to integrate countries into the capitalist world economy." Rhetoric about development and the alleviation of poverty, asserts Danaher, merely cover the fact that the central function of these multilateral lending agencies [i.e. the World Bank and the IMF] is to draw weaker states "more tightly into a world economy dominated by large, transnational corporations." "[T]he Bretton Woods institutions," he adds, "enforce economic policies written in Washington, where both the Bank and the Fund are based. For many in the Third World, this harkens back to colonial times" (Danaher, 1994, p. 2).

And since post-war decolonialization saw the rise of independent states mostly in the southern hemisphere (hence the terminology: "the South"), the objective condition of these emergent countries' economies *vis-à-vis* the capital intensive and technologically advanced "North" led to the formation of political alliances in the South and the creation, first, of the Non-Aligned Movement (NAM) in 1955 at Bangdung, Indonesia where 29 Asian and African nations met to devise plans to combat neocolonialism which grew into an institutionalized organization by 1961.[125] Choosing, or rather desiring, to remain outside of the superpower confrontation of the Cold War, the nonaligned countries attempted to maintain bilateral and cooperative relations with both the Western capitalist and Eastern communist blocs, establishing mixed economies which incorporated frequent state interventions while not totally nationalizing all capital.

The disenchantment of developing nations was again vocalized at the June 15, 1964 United Nations Conference on Trade and Development (UNCTAD) in Geneva, where a joint declaration by 75 (two other countries later joined in the declaration to make it known as the "G-77" declaration) developing countries called for "a new international division of labour oriented towards the accelerated industrialization of developing countries…supplemented and strengthened by constructive international action" (*Joint Declaration of the Seventy-Seven Developing Countries Made at the Conclusion of the United Nations Conference on Trade in Development*, June 15, 1964, Geneva, Switzerland). While UNCTAD became a forum for the expression of the South's woes and subsequent demands, the G-77 countries established a permanent organization to push for multilateral cooperation within the UN framework to alter the marginalization of the world's developing nations.[126]

The 1960s and early 1970s witnessed attempts by these developing countries to "extend the international normative consensus in favor of independence to international support for development" with official development assistance targets, preferential trade arrangements, etc. in order to "close the gap" (Ruggie, 1984, p. 33). The key issues in this North-South conflict (or "dialogue" as Ruggie et al. refer to it; cf. Jones, 1983) have subsequently revolved around the economic and political claims of the world's "have-nots" versus those of the world's "haves," with political independence and sovereignty as well as economic assistance and development monies constituting the primary thrust of these negotiations.[127]

It was the triumph of the Organization of Petroleum Exporting Countries (OPEC) in the 1970s, however, which suggested to the developing countries of the South "that other commodities could be cartelized to extract resources unilaterally from the North" (Bhagwati, 1984, p. 23).[128] With the credibility of commodity power strengthened by OPEC's lead, the South sought not only to expand cartelization to other commodities but, moreover, to overturn the LIEO established at Bretton Woods insisting that "the entire range of international economic issues—trade, money, aid, energy, raw materials, etc.—be negotiated together." What was called for was nothing less than a New International Economic Order (NIEO) which was "proclaimed at the 1973 Algiers Non-Aligned Conference and embraced at the UN General Assembly's 1974 Sixth Special Session" (Bhagwati, 1984, p. 25). At this stage, developing countries pursued a strategy of "Global Negotiations" seeking resource transfers to the South arguing that such transfers would stimulate Southern growth which, in turn, would lead to increased demand for Northern exports, thus "pulling the North out of recession without rekindling inflation" (Ruggie, 1984, p. 34). Before the South's newfound commodity weapons could be deployed, however, world oil prices stabilized and the cartelization of oil proved unable to be successfully duplicated with other commodities. As Northern vulnerability declined, demands by the South for Global Negotiations went unheeded. Bhagwati contends that the lack of Northern response was also due to a weakened macroeconomic situation in the advanced capitalist countries which hampered "their political and financial capability to respond constructively, especially in regard to redistribution measures such as foreign aid flows" (Bhagwati, 1984, p. 26). And though a temporary resurgence in demands for Global Negotiations followed the 80 percent rise in oil prices stemming from the 1979 revolution in Iran, a circumvention of OPEC by the North by obtaining other sources of oil and by increased production by Saudi Arabia and Kuwait followed by a subsequent reduction in oil prices diffused the crisis thus stalling the Global Negotiations further. While energy conservation played a role in easing the vulnerability of the North, Bhagwati noted that "ultimately the world recession, following on the tight-money policies of the Federal Reserve combined with the expansionary budget deficits and the resulting phenomenal rise in US interest rates, delivered the coup de grace" (Bhagwati, 1984, p. 27). Thus with Southern inability to demonstrate any comparable commodity power to get the attention of the North as oil had, and with the North feeling less vulnerable and, hence, less willing to listen to Southern demands for resource transfers, once the cartelization of OPEC was rendered harmless (for the time being, at least), interest in Global Negotiations waned a s the South found itself without a ny bargaining p ower. Thus, the lack of state power on the part of the South led to the stalled Global Negotiations, for in trying to establish a "regime" under the rubric of the NIEO to counter the LIEO of Bretton Woods, the South's relative power *vis-à-vis* the North was greatly inferior.[129]

The disunity of the South also hindered its ability to establish a counter-regime to Bretton Woods. Specifically, this related to the newly industrialized countries (NICs)—what are often referred to as the semiperiphery countries—such as Brazil, Taiwan, and Singapore who, once entering the world's financial markets, were no longer interested in solutions l ike "generalized d ebt relief" to North-South d isparity issues (Bhagwati, 1984, p. 7). Thus with developmental gradations in its ranks, the South was unable to agree on the collective purpose their NIEO regime was to pursue.

While the South was vulnerable due to its lack of congruence in the balance of its state-society relations, such was not the case with the emerging international society of the North, whose collective purposes—though altered over time—had nonetheless held the major capitalist oriented nations together for over 50 years at this writing.[130] And though Ruggie concludes that "[t]he North-South dialogue has had little to do with transforming international economic regimes," he counters that, nevertheless, the dialogue "has not been entirely irrelevant to this process" as indicated in three areas which these negotiations have impacted: first, in putting such issues on the international agenda; second, in creating a normative impact as "the ritual of negotiations provides a useful instrument in the global legitimation struggle because it is carried on in universalistic terms and in the language of common interests"; and third, the North-South dialogue has impacted the institutional level by embedding development policy constituencies in the bureaucracies of all the industrialized countries, "in large measure," he admits, "because of the need to prepare for a nd respond t o the never-ending rounds o f the dialogue" (Ruggie, 1984, pp. 40-41).

Without a formal mechanism governing international economic relations following the collapse of the Bretton Woods system in 1971, the idea of regional trading blocks emerged in the late 1970s and '80s building on the success of the European Economic Community (EEC) which began in the early 1950s. The European Community (EC) itself is a byproduct of the Cold War, as a working relationship between post-WWII France and Germany was seen as necessary to anchor the non-communist countries of Europe into a unified and workable system (Fontaine, 1997; Pryce in Duff, et al., 1994, p. 10). This integration was endorsed and overseen by the United States which, as Pryce notes, "began by strongly encouraging the formation of the EC, and shielded it in its early years from British hostility..." (Pryce in Duff, et al., 1994, pp. 8-9). The European Coal and Steel Community (ECSC) was the first joint treaty which paved the way to further cooperation.[131] This was followed with the Treaty of Rome on March 25, 1957 establishing the European Economic Community (EEC) which abolished customs duties on trade between signatory states as well as quantitative limits on trade. "Between 1958 and 1970, the abolition of customs duties had spectacular effects: trade within the community increased sixfold while EEC trade with the rest of the world went up by a factor of three. Average gross national product in the EEC over the same period went up by 70%" (Fontaine, 1997). With its initial success, the EC began to enlarge, beginning in the 1970s, and in 1979 the first direct elections to the European Parliament in Strasbourg were held, though the non-elected European Council still controls most of the important decisions.[132]

By the mid-1980s, EC countries were ready to abolish many additional obstacles to free trade within its member states' borders and thus signed on February 17, 1986 the Single European Act (SEA) which set January 1, 1993 as the date "by which a full internal market was to be established" (Fontaine, 1997). As Cafruny and Rosenthal note, the SEA "was ultimately passed because it corresponded to the perceived national interests of Europe's most powerful nations. Governments recognized that international capital mobility had rendered 'Keynesianism in one country' obsolete; they saw the SEA as an extension of new domestic strategies of economic and financial liberalization" (Cafruny & Rosenthal, 1993, p. 4). The SEA was followed by the more decisive political as well as economic union resulting from the signing of the Maastricht Treaty on February 7, 1992 which came into force on November 1, 1993 and created "a vast internal market of over 340 million people providing free movement within it, with only limited exceptions, for goods, capital and services and the citizens of the member states" (Pryce in Duff, et al., 1994, pp.6-7). Although an initial Danish rejection of the Maastricht Treaty in June of 1992 was overcome a year later with a majority "yes" vote in a second referendum in May of 1993, the fact that only Denmark and France (amongst EC members) held public referendums on the treaty, with the Danish referendum requiring to be run twice while the French majority was less than three percent of the vote (51.05% to 48.95%), indicates a possible division of interests between European financial and political elites and the populations of these countries (Duff in Duff, et al., 1994, pp. 54-65).[133] Nonetheless, Maastricht ushered in the transformation of the European Community into the European Union (E.U.) and, in the process, transferred "a great deal of power from states to EC institutions" (Cafruny & Rosenthal, 1993, p. 4). Perhaps the most important consequence of the Maastricht Treaty, however, is the decision to enact an economic and monetary union (EMU) buttressed by the establishment of a single European currency—the *Euro*—which came into existence on January 1, 1999. While the introduction of the single currency is, for Fontaine, the "final, logical stage in the completion of the internal market" (Fontaine, 1997), Cafruny and Rosenthal note that "monetary union would certainly represent an unprecedented and fundamental assault on the nation-state." Pointing out that the power to issue currency is "a fundamental aspect of national sovereignty and the most important means by which governments regulate national economies," they denote the decision to adopt "one currency and one central bank by the year 2000" as clearly constituting "the major achievement of Maastricht" (Cafruny & Rosenthal, 1993, p. 6).[134] Maastricht was followed on January 1, 1994 with the establishment of the European Economic Area (EEA) joining together in one single market the 15 members of the E.U. with five members of the European Free Trade Association (EFTA): Austria, Finland, Norway, Sweden, and Iceland.[135] The EEA, at that time, became "the world's largest free trade zone, comprising 372 million people," thus making the E.U. "one of the three most important players on the world economic scene alongside the USA and Japan" (Pryce in Duff, et al, 1994, p. 7). The latest addition to these documents constituting the unification of Europe is the signing on October 2, 1997 of the Treaty of Amsterdam which more fully expands on social and political consolidation of the Union while revising aspects of the Maastricht Treaty; in effect, it represents the new treaty on European

Union.[136] The Amsterdam treaty is intended to consolidate "the three great 'pillars' which have been the foundation for the Union's work since the Maastricht Treaty of 1 November 1993: the European Communities (first pillar); the common foreign and security policy (second pillar); and cooperation in the fields of justice and home affairs (third pillar)" ("The four major objectives...", July 31, 1997). European plans for the immediate future center around the "Agenda 2000" political agreement reached by EU leaders on March 26, 1999 at the end of a special European Council held in Berlin. The agreement opens the way for the enlargement of the European Union to a first wave of countries from Central and Eastern Europe beginning in 2002, including the first six applicants—Cyprus, the Czech Republic, Estonia, Hungary, Poland and Slovenia. Bulgaria, Latvia, Lithuania, Romania and Slovakia have also applied for membership ("Presidency Conclusions," March 24-5, 1999; "Agenda 2000...," March 26, 1999).

One further grouping to emerge out of the economic turmoil of the 1970s to attempt to direct and control the international capitalist economy by coordinating state economic policies was the so-called Group of Seven (G7) launched in 1975 and consisting of the seven major industrialized democracies (the United States, the United Kingdom, France, Germany, Japan, Italy and Canada). Since the mid-1990s, Russia has become a junior partner in this grouping, hence the nomenclature change to G8 or Group of Eight; though, because of Russia's precarious economic condition, some still refer to the grouping as the G7/G8. Increasingly, the EU, as a separate composite entity, is also being included in G8 discussions and summit meetings. It is the annual summit meetings which form the basis of this organization, which is "relatively informal and relatively unencumbered by bureaucracy." The G8 also has a secondary structure of regular policy coordination meetings between these states' foreign and finance ministers and a third structure of regular meetings of lower-level officials which, in the mind of one analyst, "has achieved respectable results on many economic, political and other global issues" (Hajnal, June 11, 1998).

The New World Order of Global Capitalism

Entering the decade of the 1990s, and especially following the collapse of the Soviet Union and its eastern European allies, with the return of capitalist market economies to the countries in these regions, the North-South terminology has in large part been supplanted in the literature by more common references to the dichotomy between developed market economies and developing countries. With the loss of the Soviet Union, many of their former client states in the so-called Third World were set adrift and left to negotiate their own deals with the U.S., Japan, or the

European Union. And particularly, these countries quickly learned that in this New World Order proclaimed by President Bush in 1990, state-to-state economic relationships often give way either to state-to-corporation deals or, as is the preference with the transnational corporations, private corporation-to-corporation arrangements and agreements, which further threatens and undermines many of these developing nations' ability to democratically and, hence, publicly control their own development, much less enact conscious long-term public development plans and projects. In this regard, though it might be objected that nationalism and the states system is outdated and that many developing countries exhibit little democracy in practice, it is nonetheless clear that the developed market economies, particularly the U.S., are exceptions to this general pattern of the depreciation of state control. Thus, contrary to the Francis Fukuyama's 1989 declaration of "the end of history" and the ultimate victory of liberal democracy as the most effective and just organization of human society (Fukuyama, Summer 1989, December 1991, & 1992), what many developing countries now feared was "the history of the end" of their sovereign integrity.[137]

As regards oil resources necessary to fuel this New World Order constituted around the American hegemon, the U.S. achieved with its victory in the 1991 Gulf War (however temporary or long-lasting) a decisive advantage in forcing the Persian Gulf allies into greater dependence upon its military and security capabilities thus ensuring a continuous flow of relatively cheap oil to developed market economies for the near-term future. Acting on the precarious situation of Iraq—just two years out of the economically and socially devastating Iran-Iraq War which left Iraq over $100 billion in debt and with at least 150,000-200,000 casualties, the U.S. successfully goaded Iraq's Saddam Hussein to invade oil-rich Kuwait in 1990 (Horwitz, December 1988, p. 75; Ogden, April 1, 1991, p. 36; Agee, October, 1990; see also Baker, 1995, p. 274), thus providing the pretext for the subsequent 1991 Gulf War which, though comprised of international forces, was heavily dominated by U.S. personnel, including, and especially, the top general staff which directed the two-month war. And though the Gulf War did not secure the overthrow of Hussein's government, it nonetheless did strategically position U.S. forces around the key global oil reserves in the Middle East, ensuring a long-term presence of the 5th Fleet in the Persian Gulf—a virtual floating base—which operates out of Bahrain, as well as securing agreements for a constant presence of over 20,000 U.S. troops at bases in Saudi Arabia, Kuwait, and Bahrain, the ability to pre-position stocks of armaments and material in the region, all of which decidedly has shifted control over the Middle Eastern oil reserves in favor of the U.S.[138] And, indeed, the continued existence of unfriendly governments (i.e. *vis-à-vis* the U.S. and its allies) in Iraq and

Iran serves to both perpetuate and legitimate a U.S. military presence in the region, at least amongst U.S. allies. This U.S. presence is supplemented by a regime of United Nations sanctions (Goshko, May 21, 1996, pp. A1 & A14; Hoagland, January 15, 1998, p. A14) which dictate whether and how much oil Iraq can produce and sell on international markets, in addition to allowing for numerous other violations of Iraqi state sovereignty, including controls over production and storage of military stocks, circumvention of Iraqi air space, other trade sanctions, etc. The subsequent Pax Americana (anchored by the U.S. client states of Israel, the Gulf Cooperation Council (GCC) states, Turkey, and Egypt), however, is not a secure one, for the political reality of U.S. dominance in the region has and will likely continue to threaten to undermine the very regimes the U.S. depends upon to operate in this region of the world.[139]   Indeed, U.S. ability to secure its presence in the Persian Gulf region is a consequence of the other major event of the early 1990s: the collapse of the Soviet Union and its eastern European allies.

The United States's biggest nemesis throughout the Cold War, the Soviet Union—beset with internal feuding spurred on by the electoral victory claimed by Boris Yeltsin to the Presidency of the Russian Soviet Federated Socialist Republic in June of 1990 by the Russian parliament, followed in 1991 by Yeltsin's popular election as President of the Russian republic, compounded with the resignation of Mikhail Gorbachev as head of the Communist Party of the Soviet Union (CPSU) in December 1991—collapsed and was replaced by the Confederation of Independent States (CIS) on Christmas Day 1991.[140]   Gorbachev himself had supported the drive towards privatization of the Soviet economy when he initially backed the 500-day plan to move the Soviet Union from a centrally-planned economy to a market economy within a year and a half, as drafted by the economists Stanislav Shatalin and Grigory Yavlinsky. As former *Washington Post* correspondent David Remnick stated in his book *Lenin's Tomb*, Shatalin and Yavlsinsky had done nothing less during the summer of 1990 than "plotted, in civil tones and bureaucratic language, the dismantling of the System." Upon returning to Moscow from his summer holiday on the Black Sea, Gorbachev "told the legislature he was 'inclined' to support the plan." As Remnick writes: "That was all the hard-liners had to hear. The fight for their political life, a war that would rage for the next eleven months, had begun" (Remnick, 1993, p. 359). And because Gorbachev was forced to scrap the 500-day plan, this sent signals to other free marketeers that reform could not come from within the system (Zaks, 1997). Consequently, internal pro-capitalist forces and free market advocates then lent all of their available resources to back Boris Yeltsin to accomplish the job. As one analyst concluded at the time: "Whereas Gorbachev seemed unable to part with the dream of a Soviet empire, Yeltsin built both his economic and political programs on the assumption of full sovereignty for all republics" (Shlapentokh, 1993, p. 165). External efforts also contributed to the downfall of the Soviet Union as both overt and covert assistance came in the form of funds—over $40 million between 1984 and 1990—from the National Endowment for Democracy. Indeed, describing the U.S. intelligence community's role as constituting a "full court press", one writer notes that the U.S. cooperated with at least 50 other organizations, including British, German, French, and Israeli intelligence agencies to take advantage of the internal turmoil in the Soviet Union estimating that alone the "CIA was probably spending $160 million per year on intervention operations in the Socialist Bloc."[141] Noting that this U.S.-led intervention "was probably one of the largest coordinated covert operations ever set in motion," Gervasi concludes that:

> An "anti-communist putsch" or "coup" is not a "democratic revolution." Conservatives in this country [i.e. the U.S.] cannot have it both ways: If the U.S. and others intervened in the Soviet Union in the ways and to the extent that the evidence suggests, then we have not witnessed a "democratic revolution" but a victory in a new kind of warfare. The debate about the "collapse of communism" needs to be seen for what it is: the propaganda which accompanies this new kind of warfare—a kind of warfare which, given its (at least) short-term success, is bound to be reproduced and exported around the world (Gervasi, Winter, 1991-92, p. 9).

With the shift in political power to the developed market economies (particularly the U.S.) and the path now open to virtually unrestrained global exploitation and marketing of commodities and services, international economic integration became the order of the day.[142] In this respect, the U.S. moved in quickly, first, setting up a regional trade pact encompassing Canada, Mexico, and itself—otherwise known as the North American Free Trade Agreement (NAFTA) in 1993—which became effective on January 1, 1994. The basic provisions of NAFTA included an agreement to eliminate tariffs on all products by 2009. Tariffs on certain goods were dropped immediately, while others are schedule to be phased out within 15 years.

Secondly, in that same year of 1993, President Clinton called for a summit on Blake Island in Seattle, Washington of the Asia Pacific Economic Cooperation community (APEC) to establish the framework for a free trade area spanning 18 Pacific Rim countries, including the existing then six member Association of South East Asian Nations (ASEAN), as well as China. APEC's combined 1994 GNP of more than 13 trillion dollars represented "about half the world's total annual output" and "about 46 percent of the world's total trade in merchandise" ("Overview of APEC,"

May 12, 1997).[143] In November of 1994, the APEC leaders, meeting in Bogor, Indonesia, issued a call "to usher in an era of free trade and investment in the region by not later than the year 2020" (APEC Finance Ministers' Meeting, April 24, 1995, p. 368). In Osaka, Japan on November 19, 1995, APEC ministers adopted an Action Agenda dealing with trade and investment liberalization and facilitation along with furthering economic and technical cooperation. This was followed the next year by the Manila Action Plan for APEC (MAPA) adopted on November 25, 1996 which called for progress reports on opening member economies to trade and investment and noted the establishment of several joint activities including the APEC Educational Network (EduNet), the Asia-Pacific Energy Research Center (APERC), the APEC Labor Market Information Network (LMI), and the Trade and Investment Data Database. The first annual review of member countries' progress towards market liberalization took place in 1997 at the APEC Ministerial Meeting in Vancouver, Canada. Also at the 1997 meeting, Peru, Russia, and Vietnam were admitted as new members to APEC, following which a 10-year moratorium on new membership was announced (APEC News Announcements, January 8, 1998). And, at the November 18, 1998 meeting in Kuala Lumpur, Malaysia, the APEC leaders met amidst a staggering financial crisis which threatened to undermine the political foundations of many Asian countries, as indeed it had already done in Indonesia with the removal from office of President Suharto on May 21, 1998 who had ruled that archipelago nation of 17,000 islands since his overthrow of President Sukarno in a 1965 *coup d'état*, killing hundreds of thousands in the process. Despite the impending financial cataclysm gripping Asia, the APEC leaders renewed their commitment to pursue "a cooperative growth strategy" with the "goals of achieving free and open trade and investment within APEC" ("APEC Economic Leaders Declaration," November 18, 1998). And at the 7th APEC economic leaders' meeting in Auckland, New Zealand, which met from September 12-13, 1999, "economic reform" (i.e. privatization) and "liberalization" were the primary items being discussed even though many of the region's countries were still recovering from the financial crisis the year before. Moreover, the leaders reaffirmed their commitment to "promoting open, transparent and well-governed markets (particularly domestic financial markets) and to achieving the goals of free and open trade and investment in APEC by 2010/2020, as they had agreed at the 2nd APEC Economic Leaders' Meeting in Bogor, Indonesia" ("APEC 1999 Summit - Aukland, New Zealand," 2000).

Third, the eighth round of GATT negotiations, launched at Punta del Este, Uruguay in September 1986 (and which had dragged on for over seven years by 1993) quickly accelerated its proposals for a permanent regulation of trade by establishing on December 15, 1993 an institutionalized World Trade Organization (WTO), centered in Geneva, which would from now on regulate the developing globalized economy. Signed by 123 countries which at the time accounted for 90% of world trade, the Uruguay Round of GATT mandates "a more than one-third across-the-board reduction in tariffs" as well as the elimination or reduction of many non-tariff barriers to free trade, including "quotas, discretionary licensing, import bans, or voluntary export restraints." Even in the highly contested area of agricultural trade, new market access provisions require countries "to provide a minimum level of import access opportunities for certain products, usually set at 3% of domestic consumption" (Fact Sheet: Uruguay Round, July 1995, p. 20). The 550 page Final Act of the WTO was signed on April 15, 1994 in Marrakesh, Morocco, and was approved by the U.S. Congress in December 1994, and officially came into force on January 1, 1995. Encompassing the most detailed body of rules ever constructed to govern international trade relations, the WTO is also unique in that it establishes a semi-judicial structure referred to as the Dispute Settlement Body (DSB) which has binding authority to settle trade disputes among states as well as adjudicate over rights and obligations arising out of the WTO agreements and its dispute settlement process. Some analysts see this as the beginning of the end of the hallowed principle of state sovereignty in international relations (Jones, December 1996/January 1997; Weissman, January/February, 1996, p. 5). Indeed, weakening of U.S. state sovereignty as a consequence of joining the WTO has political conservatives and progressives in the U.S. up in arms as indicated by condemnations from independent socialist Rep. Bernie Sanders (I-VT) (cf. "Left-Right Coalition…") to conservative commentator and Presidential aspirant Patrick Buchanan (Buchanan, "The Rise of Sovereignty Fears"; Raum, January 19, 1996). Speaking before Congress on May 14, 1996, Representative Cliff Stearns (R-FL) stated:

> I believed then, and still maintain, that our sovereignty is endangered by our membership in the WTO. Simply put, we are not equal to other nations. We have the world's most powerful economy, the world's most desirable markets, and the world's most advanced and forward-looking environmental, health, and safety laws. In other words, we have the most to lose. Entry into the WTO made no sense to us; we saw it as a means toward the demise of our sovereignty, the weakening of our standards and laws, and as a means toward the subversion of our already precarious trading position (Rep. Cliff Stearns, May 14, 1996, p. H4904).

"To be sure," argues one pro-WTO analyst, "WTO members have an obligation under *international law* to comply with the WTO rules, but the

WTO itself has no means to force countries to honor those obligations" (Schott, September, 1996, p. 4). Like its non-institutionalized predecessor—GATT (which remained in force until the end of 1995 and whose agreements have all become incorporated into the WTO), which operated on the principle of comparative advantage and Most Favored Nation status—the only remedy for noncompliance and unequal treatment is retaliation (once authorization is permitted by the WTO) by the injured state. Thus, again, the more powerful states, particularly the U.S. and the European Union (E.U.), will continue to maintain their asymmetrical domination over the world's markets and, hence, over weaker states.[144]

Fourth, at the Summit of the Americas in December 1994 in Miami, Florida, attended by 34 heads of state from the western hemisphere, with only Cuba not represented, President Clinton laid the framework for the Free Trade Area of the Americas (FTAA) which would establish a free trade area encompassing the entire western hemisphere, except for Cuba, from Canada to Chile by the year 2005 (Fact Sheet: Summit of the Americas, May 1995, pp. 31-2). With 850 million people or 13% of the world's population, the FTAA would represent a "buying power of $13 trillion in goods and services" (Pomeroy, January 28, 1995, p. 7). The ministers of the 34 states of the proposed FTAA met in Denver, Colorado on June 30, 1995; a second time on March 18-21, 1996 in Cartagena, Colombia and vowed to strengthen their commitment to conclude the pact by 2005 by establishing working groups to facilitate the economic integration of the hemisphere ("Joint Declaration," March 21, 1996); a third time on May 16, 1997 at Belo Horizonte, Brazil where a Working Group on Dispute Settlement was established; a fourth time on March 19, 1998 in San Jose, Costa Rica where they made final preparations for the Second Summit of the Americas held in Santiago, Chile on April 18-19, 1998 by approving the San Jose Declaration; and a fifth time on November 4, 1999 in Toronto, Canada where the ministers reaffirmed their commitment to liberalization and vowed to "strongly support the widening and deepening process of economic integration in our Hemisphere, including sub-regionally, bilaterally and through the adoption of unilateral liberalization measures in some of our economies" ("FTAA Declaration of Ministers Fifth Trade Ministerial Meeting, Toronto, Canada," November 4, 1999).[145] At a preparatory meeting for the Second Summit of the Americas, Sven Sandström, Managing Director of the World Bank, acknowledged that "at least one-fourth of the total population in the Region—or somewhere on the order of 110 million people—continue to live in poverty" while "another quarter live just above the poverty line" and, yet, he stated:

> Throughout the Region, there has been tremendous economic progress—through the liberalization of trade, the privatization of state-

owned enterprises, the freeing of markets, and the reform and redirection of state activities. Accompanying this process of fundamental economic reform has been an equally historic process of democratization and an opening up of political systems to enhanced popular participation, new forms of representation, and the flourishing of grassroots organizations and civil society (Sandström, October 1, 1997).

With one-half the population of the region just above or below the poverty line, even the most uncritical proponents of the FTAA should question what type of democracy is being established and to what extent is it accompanied by popular participation. Moreover, as foreign debt of a combined group of 23 Latin American and Caribbean countries reached $644 billion in 1997—a growth of 50% between 1991 and 1997—it becomes increasingly questionable whether free trade liberalization is the panacea or problem to removing the region's debt obligations ("Poor Countries Debt Rises," January 27, 1998, p. B5).

An effort similar to the free trade pact for the Americas has been devised with regard to the countries of Africa. After five years in the making, the African Growth and Opportunity Act, sardonically nicknamed the "NAFTA for Africa" bill, was finally passed by the U.S. Senate with a vote of 77-19 and signed into law by President Clinton on May 18, 2000. It was the first major trade legislation approved by the U.S. Senate since the 1994 legislation which led to the creation of the World Trade Organization. Seeking to establish a new trade and investment policy for sub-Saharan Africa, the Act would provide sub-Saharan African countries—as well as Caribbean nations—with increased foreign aid and U.S. trade concessions, while helping to establish a free-trade area amongst countries in the region.[146] Though Africa possesses a population of over 700 million people in over 43 countries, one South African business paper states: "Even by the standards of developing countries, Africa is a backwater, accounting for just 11.3% of developing country exports and 8.6% of developing country GDP, according to the IMF World Economic Outlook of May 1997" ("The Last African Frontier," August 30, 1998). Despite the fact that sub-Saharan Africa has vast deposits of gold and diamonds which it exports along with "large quantities of copper, bauxite, iron ore, uranium, phosphate rock and manganese; smaller quantities of asbestos, beryllium, cadmium, chromite, cobalt, germanium, lead, lithium, nickel, platinum, tantalite, tin, tungsten, nickel, vanadium, [and] zinc," prices in world markets for African products "have been falling sharply since 1950, with only an exceptional blip for oil and most minerals in the early 1970s" (Brown & Tiffen, 1992, pp. 3, 66). Negative economic performance is both cause of and caused by detrimental political performance, but while certain African governments are partially responsible for this current state of economic and political decline, Brown and Tiffen argue that "Africa's political disaster has to be understood in context." Specifically, they note that analysts must understand the following three elements in order to understand African economic and political stagnation: 1) "the brutalisation to which Africa has been subjected from outside since the beginning of the age of colonialism"; 2) "the artificial nature of the state structure which colonialism first imposed on Africa and then bequeathed to its new rulers"; and 3) "exploration of Africa first by colonists and later by the large transnational corporations has been accompanied by corruption," by rewarding local allies and suborning or eliminating those who get in the way (Brown & Tiffen, 1992, p. 7). Opposed by South African President Nelson Mandela, the Congress of South African Trade Unions (COSATU), the AFL-CIO, and others, the African Growth and Opportunity Act nonetheless had its corporate supporters in the likes of Chevron, Texaco, Mobil, Caterpillar, as well as the administration of President Bill Clinton, amongst others. Africa's underdevelopment may explain in part why consolidating a free trade regime for the continent had not been at the top of U.S. government priorities and took five years to pass, but the logic of capitalism for a constantly expanding market for its products necessitates, as Marx and Engels long ago argued, that this system "must nestle everywhere, settle everywhere, establish connexions everywhere" (Marx & Engels, 1848/1948/1998, p. 12).[147]

Further, though by no means last, the World Bank has begun implementing a fundamental transformation in its operational procedures designed to shift funding away from national governments to direct project assistance. Posturing itself as "a lender of last resort," the World Bank, since its inaugural meeting in 1946 following the Bretton Woods Conference, has lent money to countries to improve their creditworthiness on international capital markets.[148] Once a country's economy was stabilized, it was expected to "graduate" and stop borrowing from the World Bank. But the key aspect of this lending is that money was lent to the national government of the borrower country, which also received significant conditionalities over how such money could be spent. Nevertheless, its new operational plan implicitly, though not directly, calls for the bypassing of national governments. Designated as the Strategic Compact, this new plan developed in 1997 by World Bank President James D. Wolfensohn and approved by the Executive Board of the Bank in March of that year, calls for "refocusing the development agenda" to conform to "the rapidly changing global economy—where private capital flows are five times greater than official assistance."[149] In particular, the "Strategic Compact" calls for "decentralizing activities to the field in order to better customize country assistance strategies, design more appropriate conditionality, and build local ownership of development programs" (Strategic

Compact, 1997). As well, the World Bank heralds its strong cooperation with Non-Governmental Organizations (NGOs) who "are involved in half the Bank-assisted projects approved in fiscal 1997" and calls for "strengthening operations and dialogue with NGOs" (Strategic Compact, 1997). In effect, this new World Bank plan constitutes another attack on developing nations' sovereignty, many of whom are too powerless to resist the obvious undermining of the basic principle of sovereignty by which the international system has operated, at least in principle, since the 1648 Treaty of Westphalia.[150]

Another key institutional structure upon which this globalized New World Order is being built is an enlarged and more activist and interventionary International Monetary Fund (IMF). As an additional byproduct of the 1944 Bretton Woods Agreements, the IMF was established "largely in reaction to widespread inconvertibility and related exchange problems" which precipitated the worldwide depression of the 1930s (Driscoll, July 1997, p. 1). Beginning operations in 1946 with an initial membership of 39 countries, the IMF today has 181 member countries which, according to one IMF proponent,

> have voluntarily joined because they see the advantage of consulting with one another in this forum to maintain a stable system of buying and selling their currencies so that payments in foreign money can take place between countries smoothly and without delay (Driscoll, July 1997, pp. 1 & 3).[151]

IMF members are assigned annual "quota subscriptions" (reviewed every five years) which act as membership fees. It is from this pool of money that the IMF lends to member countries in financial difficulty. From an initial sum of $7.6 billion in 1945, the IMF lending pool had grown to more than $200 billion by 1997. The amount member countries may borrow from the IMF in periodic allocations known as SDRs (special drawing rights) is proportional to the amount they contribute. As well, members' voting power is directly linked to their annual financial contributions, giving the biggest contributors the strongest voice in determining IMF policies. Thus, for example, the U.S., with the world's largest economy, "contributes most to the IMF, providing about 18 percent of total quotas (around $38 billion)," garnering it "about 265,000 votes, or about 18 percent of the total." On the other hand, the Marshall Islands has the smallest quota, totaling about $3.6 million, giving it 275 votes (Driscoll, July 1997, p. 4). And contrary to Driscoll's claim that "[f]ar from being dictated to by the IMF, the membership itself dictates to the IMF the policies it will follow," it is clear from the vote allocation procedures that an asymmetry exists as to which IMF members do the dictating and which are forced to comply with the "will of the majority" (Driscoll, July 1997, p. 5). The recent IMF imposition of strict austerity measures (i.e. deflating of economies in conjunction with demands for reduced spending on social welfare measures) combined with directives to open up the economies (i.e. demands that governments sell off public enterprises and privilege production for export rather than for domestic consumption) of South Korea, Indonesia, Thailand, and the Philippines to foreign direct investment—measures emphasized by subsequent U.S. coercion—spell out the hierarchical nature of the IMF. Moreover, even though convertibility rates have, since the early 1970s, been determined by the market mechanism, the IMF has increased its monitoring of members' economies penetrating "beyond the exchange value" and examining "all aspects of the member's economy that cause the exchange value to be what it is." States Driscoll:

> The IMF calls this activity "surveillance," or supervision, over members' exchange policies. Supervision is based on the conviction that strong and consistent domestic economic policies will lead to stable exchange rates and a growing and prosperous world economy (Driscoll, July 1997, p. 7).

Concomitant to this surveillance role for the IMF, however, is also the power to be the final word on the health and stability of a country's economy and economic performance, thus centralizing such tasks in an institution which carries out the will of its most prosperous members, particularly the U.S.[152] During the 1980s and 1990s, the IMF has pumped billions of dollars into the international economy in the form of loans to prop up the existing LIEO and the international lenders who profit from it (Wessel, December 26, 1997, p. A2). The IMF lent member countries $28 billion in the early '80s to fend off threats of default on loans. And in 1995 alone, the IMF extended over $17.8 billion of credit to Mexico and more than $6.2 billion to Russia. The poor performance of the Russian economy required another $10 billion in IMF loans in 1996. This was followed by an initial agreement in July 1998 for an additional $22.6 billion in IMF loans which later fell through as, just four weeks later, on August 17, 1998, the Russian government defaulted on billions of dollars of debt and effectively devalued the rouble from around six to the dollar to 25 in a matter of weeks while 90 percent of shares on the Russian stock market were wiped out. Intense anti-Americanism amongst Russian citizenry during the 79-day US/NATO war on Yugoslavia between March and June, 1999 threatened to end relations with the West, which perhaps explains why the IMF came up with another $4.8 billion in loans in April of 1999. And in Asia, as these economies came under severe hardship in meeting their debt payments in 1997 and 1998, the IMF lent $21 billion to South Korea, $10 billion (with an additional $1 billion in IMF loans approved in March of 1999) to Indonesia, $4 billion to Thailand, and lesser amounts to other Asian countries ("IMF Bail Outs...," January 12, 1998, pp. 3-5). The number and size of these loans indicates that far from being just a supervisory "institution for coordinating efforts to achieve greater cooperation in the formulation of economic policies" (Driscoll, July 1997, p. 9), the IMF—despite its disavowals—has become in fact the capitalist world's central bank. And, as Wade notes in the wake of the Asian financial crisis of 1997-98, the IMF tended to agree with the U.S. that this crisis had "home-grown" causes, the so-called "crony capitalism" of "particularly corrupt national banking systems that promoted the misallocation of resources away from their most efficient uses." Consequently, the IMF "made further capital opening [i.e. liberalization] a condition of its huge bailout loans for Indonesia, South Korea, and Thailand" (Wade, Winter 1998-99, p. 43).

Since 1962, the IMF has extended a line of credit to a number of governments and banks throughout the world. This line of credit, known as the General Arrangements to Borrow (GAB) with a capitalization of about US $24 billion, has been recently supplemented by the New Arrangements to Borrow (NAB) adopted by the IMF Executive Board in January 1997 with a capitalization of US $48 billion ("IMF Adopts...," January 27, 1997, p. 1). While the NAB does not replace the GAB, the latter which remains as a lender pool, "the NAB will be the facility of first and principal recourse in the event of a need to provide supplementary resources to the IMF" ("IMF Adopts...," January 27, 1997, pp. 1-2). In effect, NAB is a response to the volatility in the international system, requiring the IMF to obtain resources from wealthy countries "in the form of loans up to specified amounts when supplementary resources are needed to forestall or cope with an impairment of the international monetary system or to deal with an exceptional situation that poses a threat to the stability of that system" ("IMF Adopts...," January 27, 1997, p. 4).

In the case of the 1997-98 Asian crisis, the IMF, states Wade, "had a near monopoly on the rescue effort and has been steered, in turn, by the U.S. Treasury." IMF-directed policy changes enforced on loan-recipient countries are of two kinds: 1) policies "to restrict domestic demand using higher interest rates, lower government spending, and stiffer taxes, the objective being to stabilize the currency and make it easier for countries to repay foreign debts," and 2) policies designed "to undertake liberalizing reforms in finance, corporate governance, and labor markets." In the latter case, adds Wade, "the IMF has pressed the governments involved to keep making it easier for financial capital to move in and out of their countries (in other words, to liberalize their capital account) ..." (Wade, Winter 1998-99, p. 44). Capital liberalization is "at the top of the U.S. foreign economic-policy agenda," remarks Wade, because the U.S. "needs to tap the rest of the world's savings, which is much easier to do if world financial markets are highly integrated." The U.S. pursues this policy, argues Wade, in order for it "[t]o maintain its high levels of consumption and investments"; the alternative of "financing investments via higher domestic savings," he adds, "would require a sharp cut in consumption (to allow the extra savings), causing massive recession" (Wade, Winter 1998-99, p. 45).[153]

In summation, by the actions described above, it is clear that the U.S. under President Clinton, "is carrying out the most important and ambitious international economic agenda of any President in nearly half a century." As Under Secretary for Economic and Agricultural Affairs, Joan E. Spero, stated in 1994: "The Cold War is over, and with it has gone our traditional frame of reference for looking at our international involvement. It is almost a cliché now to say that our future will be described in economic terms." And yet, she cautions: "We may be the world's only political and military superpower, but when it comes to economic and business matters, we have a lot of competition" (Spero, March 7, 1994, pp. 123-5). While Spero may be correct in both the ubiquity and/or intensity of world competition for control of markets, it is the unevenness of this competition which captivates the rest of the world, which intensely focuses on the U.S.'s political and military superpower status.

Demonstrating its resolve in the post-Cold War era, the U.S. secured control over Gulf oil resources for the foreseeable future with its victory over Iraq in 1991, where it was the driving force of a UN-sanctioned coalition of states. Through political and economic leverage, it has pacified and coopted Russia and most of the Soviet Union's former East European allies. More recently, and perhaps most demonstratively in exhibiting its resolve, given the lack of UN international sanction and violation of the sacred principle of state sovereignty, the U.S. has been the driving force behind the ongoing dismemberment of socialist Yugoslavia—a role which became obvious with the 79-day NATO bombing campaign against Yugoslavia (a military campaign which did not even attempt to obtain UN sanction beforehand and which violated defensive provisions in the 1949 NATO treaty itself) in the spring of 1999, effectively ending with the de-facto severing of the province of Kosovo-Metohija by June 10.[154]

While these military campaigns and the political and economic leverage over Russia and Eastern Europe do indicate U.S. intentions to clearly assert its domination, one side of Gramsci's prescription for hegemonic rule, it is the need to shore up its political leadership which will likely concern U.S. leaders more fully in this one-superpower era. Indeed, one new indication of this U.S. concern for how its political leadership is perceived—and which is likely a response to the less than enthusiastic support it received during the US/NATO war on Yugoslavia—is witnessed in the recent establishment by the Clinton administration in July, 1999 of a new International Public Information group, whose purpose is to "'influence foreign audiences' in support of U.S. foreign policy and to counteract propaganda by enemies of the United States." Intending to coordinate all overseas information among the various branches of the U.S. government, the aim of the IPI grouping, according to the IPI Core Group Charter, is "'to enhance U.S. security, bolster America's economic prosperity and to promote democracy abroad'." With a stated objective to "'synchronize the informational objectives, themes and messages that will be projected overseas...to prevent and mitigate crises and to influence foreign audiences in ways favorable to the achievement of U.S. foreign policy objectives'," Barber remarks that numerous clauses in the IPI Charter "have an Orwellian ring that gives the impression of a vast, coordinated propaganda operation" (Barber, July 28, 1999). While it is too soon to fully assess what success the U.S. will achieve in this endeavor, it is nonetheless evident that its goal is to project U.S. international leadership and, with it, the leadership of the capitalist world, through the vehicle of the U.S. national state. Exactly this sort of leadership from the U.S. was called for in early 1999 by the foreign affairs columnist for *The New York Times*, Thomas Friedman, who proclaims that globalization is the new international system that has replaced the cold-war system and that the driving idea behind globalization is free-market capitalism. For globalism to work, argues Friedman, "America can't be afraid to act like the almighty superpower that it is." Managing globalization "is a role from which America dare not shrink." Highlighting his article for the March 28, 1999 *New York Times Magazine* is a full-cover fist painted with red, white and blue stars and stripes of the U.S. flag. Calling for a global enforcer, Friedman argues: "The hidden hand of the market will never work without a hidden fist—McDonald's cannot flourish without McDonnell Douglas, the builder of the F-15. And the hidden fist that keeps the world safe for Silicon Valley's technologies is called the United States Army, Air Force, Navy and Marine Corps" (Friedman, March 28, 1999, pp. 84, 96).

    As is evident with the recent US/NATO-led war on Yugoslavia, the U.S. is willing to bypass established international institutions—institutions established in the wake of WWII—at least temporarily, to achieve its aims. It is unlikely, however, that U.S. hegemonic rule can long afford to ignore existing international institutions and agencies and, more likely, it will, as in the case of the International Criminal Tribunal for the Former Yugoslavia—established in May, 1993 to prosecute violators of international humanitarian law committed in the territory of the former Yugoslavia since 1991—utilize its leverage to direct these agencies to pursue activities in accordance with overall U.S. foreign policy objectives.[155] The withholding of U.S. dues to the United Nations until it undertakes U.S.-directed reforms is also another form of pressure utilized to effect its will on an international agency.[156] Providing a leadership role in the establishment of the WTO while continuing to shore up the IMF and the World Bank, promoting worldwide economic integration by supporting the establishment of free trade areas in the Americas, Asia, and Africa, while assisting in European Union consolidation, it is arguable that a two-track policy is being pursued, one which promotes the authority of (pro-U.S.) international institutions, and one which maintains U.S. domination in the international order, both tracks to be pursued by the lifting and/or removing of national restrictions on trade.

But is the world ready for barrier-free world trade—i.e. *laissez-faire* on the grand scale—albeit under the rubric of an international trade regime? Former Deputy Director of the GATT from 1987 through 1993, Charles R. Carlisle, answers in the negative. "Whatever the appeal of global free trade," he asserts, "the political support for the idea is just not there" (Carlisle, November/December, 1996, p. 115). Pointing out that no major initiative of the WTO stands a chance of success without both U.S. and E.U. cooperation, Carlisle recollects how the Uruguay Round of GATT talks nearly broke off over U.S.-European differences over agricultural subsidies and protection. Also, he notes that protectionist sentiment is still very high in both the U.S. and Europe not only in the area of agriculture (this sentiment is shared also by Japan, South Korea, and many other countries) but also in the areas of services, textiles, and especially labor. Indeed, whether the WTO will adopt internationally recognized labor rights is, states Carlisle, the "most highly contested question" (Carlisle, November/December, 1996, p. 114). And while, argues Carlisle, the extent to which increased international competition has contributed to job losses can be debated; nonetheless, he writes, "[t]here can be little doubt, however, that it is a significant factor, and political objections to job losses are being raised in Europe and America." He continues:

> The burden of adjustment tends to fall most heavily on those least able to handle it—those who have few skills and little education, or lack job mobility because of their age, health, or economic circumstances. In short, the burden falls on those unable to move into high-paying export-related jobs (Carlisle, November/December, 1996, pp. 116-17).

Noting also that China is not yet a member of the WTO, he cautions that requiring it "to commit to opening its markets completely to foreign competition would be as unwise as it would be futile" (Carlisle, November/December, 1996, p. 117). Russia also has not as yet been admitted to the

WTO, and Carlisle extends this same cautionary advice as regards China to Russia as well. Carlisle concludes by noting that "[f]ree trade world-wide is a distant goal, fraught with difficulties," but, he says, "regional trading arrangements have been somewhat easier to attain" (Carlisle, November/December, 1996, p. 118).

Arguably, given the above developments since 1990, the market for capital (financial or otherwise) is more globally oriented than ever before, though it is clear that the U.S. remains the driving force of this global capitalist system. The consolidation of the E.U. and the establishment of several free trade areas caught organized labor off-guard, partially owing to the disorientation associated with the Soviet Union's collapse and that of its Warsaw Pact allies, as well as labor's lack of strong international organizational ties and/or differences between the interests a nd capabilities (i.e. owing to technological variances) of labor in developing countries from that of labor in the so-called developed world.[157] With the establishment of the WTO in 1995, the mechanisms for regulating global free trade are in place, though their legitimacy and enforcement power remain to be fully tested. Moreover, policies which tend to undermine national sovereignty a nd self-determination a re being p ursued by t he WTO, the IMF, and the World Bank, which appear to have as their common rallying cry: "Privatization". The decentering of national state power (i.e. other than the U.S.) appears to be the aim of many of these policies which, in turn, is wreaking havoc over the social safety net of many countries' economies, which likewise impacts consumer demand, as millions of workers around the globe find scant security in their new-found economic condition.

Preliminary caution and alarm resulting from this crisis produced by globalization was uttered by financier George Soros in the wake of the 1997-98 Asian crisis when he stated that if the crisis were "left unchecked," it would "lead to the disintegration of the global capitalist system...[and] permanently transform the world's attitude toward capitalism and free markets." Morover, Soros added, "[w]hat makes this crisis so politically unsettling and so dangerous for the global capitalist system is that the system itself is the main cause." Dismissing criticism of the crisis as being wholly attributed to "crony capitalism," "Confucian capitalism," or "the Asian model," Soros remarks that "[t]he inescapable conclusion is that the crisis is a symptom of pathologies inherent in the global system." Singling out blame for unrestrained international financial markets, he writes:

> More precisely, the origin of this crisis is to be found in the mechanism that defines the essence of a globalized capitalist system: the free, competitive capital markets that keep private capital moving

unceasingly around the globe in a search for the highest profits and, supposedly, the most efficient allocation of the world's investment and savings (Soros, Winter 1998-99, p. 55).

Contrary to free market ideology which states that "financial markets are supposed to act in the long run like a pendulum, always swinging back toward equilibrium," Soros concludes that in the absence of public-policy measures enacted on the flow of international finance, then "[i]nstead of acting like a pendulum, financial markets can act like a wrecking ball, swinging from c ountry to country and d estroying everything that stands in their way" (Soros, Winter 1998-99, p. 58).

It is in this context of economic globalization that many question whether the U.S. emphasis on 'civil society' and its comcomitant private institutions can fill the socioeconomic void, service the needs of affected populations, and stave off political disorder while legitimating a new international political compact. Theoretically, what may follow, if the U.S. is successful in this complex and long-term endeavor, is a single global state as well as the internationalization of civil society. In this respect, the export of U.S. "democracy" may constitute the preliminary groundwork for the subsequent development of this eventuality. However, if policies and/or instruments designed to govern the global economy fail to check the system's excesses, global economic collapse along with global political disruption could likely result.

The Imperative of the Market & Its Democratic Cover

To analyze these international economic developments in a Marxian framework, a basic model of a capitalist enterprise will be presented followed by a Marxian class analysis which attempts to specify the complex fundamental and subsumed class positions comprising this new international or globalized social formation. This will be followed by an analysis of whether the export of U.S. democracy through the NED will contribute t o or detract from the expansion of capital and, hence, the extension of U.S. hegemony.

Utilizing the categories of "fundamental" and "subsumed" class positions, I have herein chosen a marxist analysis based upon that depicted by Resnick and Wolff (1987) which understands Marx as clearly distinguishing between different types of capitalists, as, for example, between the "functioning capitalist" who is engaged in the extraction of unpaid labor directly from the laborers as opposed to the merely property-owning capitalist, merchants, or moneylenders. In this sense, the "productive" or "industrial" capitalist exists within the production process, referred to as the fundamental class process, and is "directly involved in the appropriation of suplus labor in the form of suplus value" (Resnick & Wolff, 1987, p. 143). So-called "unproductive" capitalists, who are not directly engaged in appropriating surplus labor and who are outside of the production process, such as merchants or moneylenders, provide the conditions of existence for the fundamental capitalist class process as, for example, either in selling off excess inventory or extending money or credit so that a profit is realized for the industrial capitalists. In this regard, such unproductive capitalists occupy a subsumed class position *vis-à-vis* those productive capitalists engaged in the fundamental extraction of surplus value. And because Marx understands capital as "self-expanding value", each type of capitalist realizes an expansion in one's initial capital. In a successful circuit of capital expansion, the industrial capitalist realizes a profit, that is, value over and above his or her initial outlay for land, labor, machinery and materials for commodity production. Likewise, the merchant or moneylender will receive a share of the surplus value either as "merchants' discounts or interest payments" which "permit the values they dispose of to be expanded" (Resnick & Wolff, 1987, pp. 142-3). Subsumed class payments by industrial capitalists are made, therefore, in order to ensure the continued existence of the fundamental class process.

As well, Resnick's and Wolff's marxian analysis takes as its epistemological entry point the concept of "overdetermination" drawn from Freud (1895/1957, 1900/1950), Lukács (1923/1976), and Althusser (1970). To say a theory is overdetermined is, for Resnick and Wolff, to assert that "its existence, including all its properties or qualities, is determined by each and every other process constituting that society. Theory is the complex effect produced by the interaction of all those other processes. As such an effect, the process of theory embodies the different influences of its many determinants" (Resnick and Wolff, 1987, p. 2).[158] In addition, this marxist model is antiessentialist in that it rejects the notion that "complexities are reducible to simplicities of the cause-and-effect type. Instead," note Resnick and Wolff, "the presumption is that every element in the context of any event plays its distinctive role in determining that event." To wit:

> Every cause is itself also an effect and vice versa. An antiessentialist or nonreductionist theory refuses to look for the essential cause of any event because it does not presume that it exists. An antiessentialist theory understands every theory (including itself) to be inherently partial, a particularly focused intervention in social discourse (Resnick and Wolff, 1987, p. 3).

In addition to the previously described aspects of this marxian analysis, another basic component in its theorization of society is the entry-point concept of class, understood, as "the economic process of performing and appropriating surplus labor" (Resnick and Wolff, 1987, p. 26). Marxian theory, from this vantage point

> begins its analysis of any society by initially specifying the forms of the class process existing within that society. It proceeds to elaborate how such forms are overdetermined by all the nonclass processes existing within the social totality and how they participate in overdetermining all those processes (Resnick and Wolff, 1987, p. 26).

These aspects of the marxian analysis depicted above set off and distinguish this analytical approach from others which either do not differentiate amongst the different types of capitalists, do not distinguish themselves from the Hegelian dialectic, are essentialist in that they point to some simplicity which lies at the core of any apparent complexity, or which utilize the entry-point of class to function as an essence. This understanding of marxian analysis will be utilized in the example which follows.

In his book *One World, Ready Or Not: The Manic Logic of Global Capitalism* (1997), William Greider, commenting on the apparent discreditation of the Communist system "by human experience," remarks to the contrary: "but the ghost of Marx hovers over the global landscape, perhaps with a knowing smile." This is so, he adds, because: "The gross conditions that inspired Karl Marx's original critique of capitalism in the nineteenth century are present and flourishing again." And then as now, he writes, "[t]he fundamental struggle...is between capital and labor. That struggle is always about control of the workplace and how the returns of the enterprise shall be divided" (Greider, 1997, p. 39).

Though Greider recognizes that inequality characterizes the present condition of peoples subjected to globalizing capital, it is precisely because of the development of the global marketplace that he rejects the Marxian solution of the socialization of capital and property with the production and distribution of the surplus to be decided upon by the direct producers. For Greider, the global marketplace is shifting "opportunities for wealth and incomes from the older, richer societies to the poorer ones." And, while this transition is accompanied by ugly and "exploitative aspects," nonetheless, he predicts:

> the process of productive dispersal has the potential to produce a dramatic departure from the past, an opening for greater equality on a global scale (Greider, 1997, p. 42).

Projecting the metaphor of a seesaw, Greider sees a unique development emerging in human history, that the general prosperity of one side of the seesaw can only be defended by attending to human conditions at the other end. In sum, he argues: "For masses of people in the global market-place, economic self-interest is converging with altruism" (Greider, 1997, p. 43).

While the validity of Greider's harmonious prognostications remain to be seen, his basic model of a capitalist enterprise can serve as a useful heuristic device to examine the fundamental mechanism of capitalist economic development. Paraphrasing Thorstein Veblen, who taught that the problem of capitalist enterprise is always the problem of supply, i.e. "managing the production of goods in order to maximize profit and the return on invested capital," Greider states that "the present economic upheaval revolves around old-fashioned questions that have always been the basics of capitalism." Specifically, he notes: "The challenge of managing supply to match the market demand and to maintain profit levels is the heart of what preoccupies every business manager from the corner shop to the largest industrial corporation" (Greider, 1997, pp. 44-5). To explain this, he lays out his basic model of capitalist production by focusing on a localized, self-contained market in which an enterprise attempts to produce just enough to meet visible consumer demand. He writes:

> As demand rises and a firm's productive capacity is eventually exhausted, then the company invests in building more plant capacity to increase its output. In the meantime, its rate of profit should increase because, as rising demand exceeds the supply of goods, a firm is able to raise its prices, restrained only by competing firms that might capture the new sales by keeping their prices a bit lower.

On the contrary, Greider notes, when demand is weak and the company's returns are threatened by its production consistently outrunning the market of available buyers, this forces the firm to

> limit its supply of goods or else be struck with unsold inventories, surpluses that must be disposed of at discount or perhaps a dead loss. Excess production threatens to drive down prices and thus narrow the profit margins on the company's output. When a firm's profits decline, owners of capital typically respond by moving their investment capital elsewhere, dumping the company's stock and searching for others that will deliver a better return.

Eventually, in order to "halt the damage," Greider writes,

> the company has to shrink supply and even its productive capacity—closing the factory, either temporarily or permanently. In simplified terms, these are the main variables that managers try to keep in

balance as they respond to changing conditions in the market (Greider, 1997, p. 45).

Heralding as a "great virtue of capitalism" its ability to yield more from less, this expanding potential to produce more goods, he notes, "also poses the enduring contradition for capitalist enterprise: how to dispose of the surplus production." "You can make more things," he says, "but can you sell them?" He explains:

> An undisciplined expansion of productive capacity will be self-defeating, even dangerous for a firm, if all it accomplishes are continuing supply surpluses that degrade prices and undermine the rate of return. The problem of surplus capacity drives not only the competition among firms for market shares but also the imperative to discover new markets (Greider, 1997, p. 45).

The global revolution towards a one world market, Greider argues, "has deranged the logic of standard business calculations." Globalization, he argues, accelerates decision-making while technological innovation works to reduce costs and increase output on "an exponential scale." The new machines, he writes, "have given capital wings and allowed firms to disperse globally, going after shares in markets that were once securely local." In addition to expanding potential supply, he notes, "the breakout of new production methods and products creates pervasive downward pressures on prices." Consequently, he states:

> The old standard logic is thus destabilized: the imperative to modernize must be heeded lest a company lose out in the price competition, but the modernizing process also makes the supply problem worse. When companies adopt the technologies that reduce costs and protect their market shares, the inescapable result is to enlarge productive capacity. They do this to keep up, though it means supply surpluses will steadily accumulate somewhere in the marketplace— goods that can't be sold, plants that can't be operated at full capacity. Someone somewhere will have to eat the losses. Business people hope it is not their company (Greider, 1997, p. 46).

This scramble to avoid being left holding the surpluses is, argues Greider, now a major threat to the functioning of the current international economic system. Companies may attempt to protect themselves by closing factories or unloading excess goods below prevailing prices, but they are caught in the logic of the system which "compels them to keep doing more of the same: more cost reduction and price-cutting and, in turn, more expansion of potential supply." "The circle continues," he concludes, "with its destructive element concealed by the fabulous expansion of the system" (Greider, 1997, p. 46). Noting that the supply problem "is not the only way global revolution upends standard practices," he argues nonetheless: "but it is the one most central to everything else that happens" (Greider, 1997, p. 46).

While Greider's primary focus above is on the problems of the capitalist enterprise and of its basic contradiction found in its tendency for supply to outpace available demand, an analysis is also required of the basic class structure of civil society which upends the enterprise and makes capitalist production of commodities possible if we are to more fully understand the potential social and, hence, political disruptions which may undermine the NED's implantation of liberal democracies abroad. Quoting Marx, Resnick and Wolff understand the "class process" as that "'in which unpaid surplus-labor is pumped out of direct producers'" (Resnick & Wolff, 1987, p. 115). In demonstrating the exploitation inherent in capitalist production, Marx distinguished between necessary and surplus labor, with the former referring to the "quantity of labor time necessary to produce the consumables customarily required by the direct producer to keep working. Surplus labor," on the contrary, is "the further, the *extra* time of labor the direct producer performs beyond the necessary labor" (Resnick & Wolff, 1987, p. 115). Writes Marx:

> In the present state of production, human labour-power not only produces in a day a greater value than it itself possesses and costs; but with each new scientific discovery, with each new technical invention, there also rises the surplus of its daily production over its daily cost, while as a consequence there diminishes that part of the working day in which the labourer produces the equivalent of his day's wages, and, on the other hand, lengthens that part of the working day in which he must present labour *gratis* to the capitalist (Marx, 1849 & 1865/1933 & 1935/1985, p. 12).

The quantities of necessary and surplus labor vary depending on technological innovation, political strength or weakness of the workers or owners (i.e. the class struggle), the market for the specific commodity (-ies) the firm produces, the market of available labor, etc. In sum, the process of extracting surplus labor in capitalist production is a determination of many other aspects in the firm and society at large or rather, as Resnick and Wolff refer to it, it is *overdetermined* (Resnick & Wolff, 1987, p. 115). What is useful in this approach, for the purposes of this analysis, is the understanding that 1) the extraction of surplus labor is "the creation of 'unpaid value'" from the direct producer who is paid only a wage equivalent to her or his necessary labor, and this has its counterpart in 2) the "industrial profit 'as appropriation of other people's labor' (meaning their surplus labor)" (Resnick & Wolff, 1987, p. 116) for the firm and, hence, for those who own such enterprises—ownership being sanctified in the legality of private property in a capitalist social formation. The class process described above, pending no major disruptions, reproduces the two primary classes which comprise any particular capitalist social formation: i.e. capitalist and worker.

Resnick and Wolff refer to the above process where the direct producers perform necessary and surplus labor while capitalists extract or appropriate surplus labor as, outlined previously, the fundamental class process. The theoretical category of the fundamental class process, they emphasize, does not refer to any essential function as the final determinant of social change, but rather it is a conceptual category utilized to distinguish the production and extraction of surplus labor and the class of persons corresponding to this process, the productive laborers and the industrial capitalists, from other persons who occupy, what Resnick and Wolff refer to as, subsumed class positions, that is, persons who distribute the already appropriated surplus labor or its products. The purpose of the subsumed class distributors and recipients of surplus value is to "provide specific conditions of existence of the capitalist fundamental class process" (Resnick & Wolff, 1987, p. 119). Thus, for example, a portion of the surplus value may need to be paid to a landowner so that surplus value may be produced and appropriated. In this respect, the private landowner occupies a subsumed class position in that the landowner provides a specific condition of existence necessary for the capitalist fundamental class process to occur. Resnick and Wolff provide other examples of subsumed classes, for example, the necessity of private moneylenders to provide "access to quantities of money capital" so as to satisfy a specific condition of the capitalist fundamental class process. "Government, too," they argue,

> provides conditions of existence under certain social conditions, for example, a judicial apparatus for adjudicating and enforcing contractual relations. The existence of the capitalist fundamental class process may then require that a distribution of surplus value to the government be accomplished (in the form of taxes on capitalists) (Resnick & Wolff, 1987, pp. 119-20).

It is possible, they add, for the government to defray its costs in other ways without levying a tax on surplus value, that is, by providing a judicial condition of existence without requiring a subsumed class distribution, though it is not readily apparent how this might occur. Other than by taxing the direct producers for such costs, perhaps the authors are referring to state plunder and booty from war or other imperial "taxes" extracted in a hegemonic interstate relationship which allows a government to defray its costs without a subsumed class distribution for judicial or other conditions of existence necessary for the operation of the fundamental class process? Suffice it to say that whether through government taxing authority or private expenditures of surplus value, the conditions of existence for the fundamental class process to operate will vary in form and content relative to the population and geographical parameters either extant or foreseen in the near future in any particular capitalist social formation. "In general terms," they state,

> the interaction between the capitalist fundamental class process and all the other processes occurring within any particular social formation will overdetermine which conditions of existence of that fundamental class process require a subsumed class process to exist. Subsumed classes are then the persons occupying the positions of distributors or receivers of the portions of surplus value allocated to secure the provision of those conditions of existence. The overdetermination of both fundamental and subsumed class processes implies that both are contradictory and constantly changing (Resnick & Wolff, 1987, p. 120).

Viewed within this Marxian framework, the operatives of the National Endowment for Democracy in pursuing its mission of exporting liberal democracy abroad can be seen as occupying a subsumed class process. In this regard, the political arrangements the NED seeks to establish and support worldwide are geared towards establishing specific conditions of existence (e.g. electoral democracies based on two or more market-oriented parties, with apolitical and anticommunist trade union movements, support for collective bargaining arrangements, privatization of public enterprises, civilian control of national militias and defense forces, etc.) for capitalism's fundamental class process to operate on a global scale under U.S. hegemony. And all of these efforts of the NED are enabled through subsumed c lass payments o f surplus value through the taxing authority of the U.S. government utilized to fund this endeavor. Given the necessity for capitalists to balance their potential supply of commodities with available consumer demand, the necessity for workers—the direct producers—to earn enough in wages to cover the costs of their daily reproduction, coupled with the necessity of any capitalist social formation to expend surplus value in order to provide specific conditions o f existence for its fundamental class process to occur (such a s maintaining its class domination and hegemonic rule in that social formation), it is apparent that these necessary tendencies will continue to interact, contradict one another, and overdetermine each other in the developing globalized capitalist world economy. As well, it is arguable that if large sections of the globe are to be organized in a transnational social formation under the direction of one national segment of the international extracting class, then the particularity of such a universal arrangement will likely generate the universality of a particular opposition. National jealousies and resentment towards the U.S. hegemon for what most assuredly will be perceived as the usurpation of the rights of self-determination of nations are unlikely to be contained under present conditions and understandings. Traditional (i.e. since WWII) reliance upon either military dictatorships in Latin America, authoritarian dictatorial rulers in Asia, military strongmen or racial extremists in Africa, or Emirs, Sheikhs, Sultans, Crown Princes, and Shahs in the Middle East worked adequately for the Bretton Woods LIEO and for U.S. hegemonic ascendancy since WWII. With the collapse of the Soviet Union and, hence, the departure from the scene of the U.S.'s main protagonist representative of what anti-soviet partisans referred to as "imperial" communism, then—short of the revitalization of the "communist threat"—a new ideological framework is definitely a logical necessity for the maintenance and expansion of U.S. post-Cold War hegemony.

That "democracy" and its particular development under the conditions present in the U.S. capitalist social formation, and especially as a response to democratic developments elsewhere in the world in the last two centuries, has become the primary organizing mantra in the construction of this post-Cold War hegemony is understandable, given the apparent acceptance of its contradictory aspects and definitions by successive generations of the U.S. populace, or so we are to believe by those promoting this policy. The degree to which actual implantation of this form of capitalist democracy can be established and sustained abroad is, arguably, of limited duration, however, though perhaps sufficiently so as to allow for (re)organization of existing or new international organizations (e.g. the IMF, the World Bank, the WTO, etc.), the establishment and/or consolidation of new regional economic regimes (e.g. NAFTA, APEC, FTAA, the EU, etc.) in conjunction with the diminishing of existing state bureaucracies through the opening up of countries to the unfettered flow of trade and investment, and the standardization of business practices in order to take advantage of the political void opened up by the collapse of the Soviet Union and its allies.

Some notable contradictory effects contrary to the U.S. goal of democracy p romotion, however, c an be witnessed with g overnmental power either remaining with or reverting back to communist party leadership in Cuba, Belarus, Mongolia, and Romania. In Cuba, for example, Fidel Castro continues to rule over a one-party communist state with a socialized economy despite numerous attempts by the U.S. and the NED to oust and/or undermine the Cuban Communist Party's rule. Indeed, lopsided votes in the United Nations calling on the U.S. to end its embargo against Cuba for the past eight years suggests that many countries support Cuba in order to spite the U.S. for its perceived hegemonistic policies. As a Pepperdine School of Public Policy study stated: "The 1999 vote [for ending the Cuban embargo] was 152-2, with only the U.S. and Israel voting against engagement." The study concludes that "America has been acting essentially unilaterally against Cuba, while many of its allies have established formal diplomatic ties and enjoy extensive trade relationships with Cuba" (McCormally & Skandera, April 2000). Another example of outcomes contrary to NED goals can be seen in Belarus, a former province of the Soviet Union which became an independent state in 1991. Since his landslide election victory in 1994, President Alexander Lukashenko has ruled Belarus as a soviet-style communist state despite attempts by NED supported groups to bolster a viable opposition in the interim. As Radio Free Europe/Radio Liberty reporter Tony Wesolowsky writes: "For years there's been little reason for hope for the opposition in Belarus, where President Alyaksandr Lukashenka has kept the country locked in the repressive Soviet pass" (Wesolowsky, October 11, 2000). And, on July 3, 2000, in Mongolia, the communist controlled Mongolian People's Revolutionary Party (MPRP) swept back into power winning 72 of 76 seats in Mongolia's unicameral Parliament ousting the free market oriented "democrats" who had taken power in 1996 under the banner of the Democratic Union from office. And, indeed, a 19-member delegation organized by the International Republican Institute—a core NED recipient—did "not observe any instances of systematic fraud or widespread voting irregularities" in the Mongolian vote (Nicholson, September 1, 2000, p. 1). The MPRP, which had ruled for seven decades and had received patronage from the Soviet Union, stated the *South China Morning Post*, "was riding a wave of popular anger against political gridlock under the Democratic Union coalition government and economic austerity measures imposed by the International Monetary Fund (IMF), which have plunged many of Mongolia's 2.4 million people into poverty" in this landlocked nation the size of Western Europe ("Former Communist Rulers Swept Back Into Power", July 4, 2000; Rennie, July 4, 2000). And on December 9, 2000, former Communist Ion Iliescu won Romania's presidential election garnering over 70 percent of the vote in this country of 23 million people. Facing an ultranationalist rival, Corneliu Vadim Tudor, Iliescu secured the backing of many "mainstream groups" who "pledged to back the former communist functionary, fearing that Romania could become an international pariah if Tudor won" ("Polls Show Ex-Communist Wins Romanian Vote", December 10, 2000). These anti-capitalist reactions to the pro-capitalist

NED agenda possibly foreshadow the limits of this U.S.-led crusade or, at the very least, indicate that the NED's path will have outcomes at times contrary to the intentions of its "democratic activists".

In this latter regard, the question arises as to the possible formation of hegemonic and counterhegemonic blocs, in the Gramscian sense, of either a broad unification of intellectuals and masses in support of NED-style democracy or, on the contrary, a widespread movement organized in opposition to this perceived "foreign" import. In the case of the ouster o f President M ilosevic in Yugoslavia in October 2000, Z oran Djindjic, Democratic Party President and campaign manager for the NED-backed successor to the Yugoslavian presidency, Vojislav Kostunica, was able to unite 18 opposition parties which garnered Kostunica an initial electoral majority which united into a successful demand for Milosevic's ouster when the latter attempted to hold a run-off election. Suffering from ten years of war and western economic sanctions, the U.S. had created the material conditions within Yugoslavia which had given rise to ideologies contrary to Milosevic and his Socialist Party rule. Previous opposition leaders such as Vuk Draskovic and Zoran Djindjic himself had been unable to rally the masses behind the pro-democratic anti-socialist rhetoric of the NED. Kostunica, however, presented himself as a Serbian nationalist, even though he was an ardent advocate of western conceptualized democracy and liberal economics. A 56-year-old former legal scholar, Kostunica strongly supported Serbian troops in Kosovo and is opposed to NATO interference in the traditional Yugoslavian province. In fact, during the 2000 presidential campaign, one CNN reporter wrote that "his disdain for Milosevic was matched only by his contempt for the United States" (Ratnesar, October 6, 2000). Kostunica's nationalism combined with his anti-U.S. rhetoric and the depressed economic conditions of a war-weary Yugoslavian population had produced the conditions for what Gramsci refers to as a historical bloc, "[t]hat is to say the complex, contradictory and discordant *ensemble* of the superstructures" reflecting "the *ensemble* of the social relations of production" (*PN*, p. 366). In this linkage of form and content, ideologies and material forces, Gramsci echoes Marx's idea that "a popular conviction often has the same energy as a material force" and writes:

> To the extent that ideologies are historically necessary they have a validity which is "psychological"; they "organise" human masses, and create the terrain on which men move, acquire consciousness of their position, struggle, etc. (*PN*, p. 377).

The historical bloc is that wielding together of an ideological unity by the class of intellectuals of the would-be dominant group. It is the intellectuals of the "historically (and concretely) progressive class" who end up "subjugating the intellectuals of other social groups," argues Gramsci. In this manner, "they thereby create a system of solidarity between all the intellectuals, with bonds of a psychological nature (vanity, etc.) and often of a caste character (technico-juridical, corporate, etc.)." At first manifesting itself "'spontaneously'" in its progressive period, when the bloc "really causes the whole society to move forward," eventually, notes Gramsci,

> [a]s soon as the dominant group has exhausted its function, the ideological bloc tends to crumble away; then "spontaneity" may be replaced by "constraint" in ever less disguised and indirect forms, culminating in outright police measures and *coups d'état* (*PN*, pp. 60-1).

Though it is still too early to tell whether the social group which has formed around Kostunica is 100% homogeneous on the level of ideology, an extreme which Gramsci utilizes only to emphasize the very real "existence of the objective conditions for the revolutionising of praxis" and, hence, the creation of an historical bloc, Kostunica's stunning v ictory nonetheless indicates that the intellectuals around him have, at least for the near-term, supplanted the intellectual moral leadership of Milosevic's Socialist Party (*PN*, p. 366). One month later, on November 25, however, Milosevic was reelected to lead his Yugoslavian Socialist Party, which is now in opposition. To c reate a c ounterhegemonic bloc, the task f or Milosevic is to link Kostunica with U.S. funding through the NED and to denigrate the latter's Serbian nationalism as contrary to Yugoslavia's best interest and indeed as a pretense for continued U.S. transgression of Yugoslavian so vereignty. G aging the su ccess of such hegemonic or counterhegemonic blocs would require a protracted long-term study which is not undertaken here. Suffice it to say that the formation of such historical blocs will require more than a few years to solidify, though nascent examples of such development exists, as in the case of Yugoslavia. As well, it is also noteworthy that in the Yugoslavian case above, the initial success of the NED-backed candidate is, in part, due to his exhibition of a virulent anti-U.S. rhetoric and determined Serbian nationalism, elements which, in the long term, may undermine the very democracy the U.S. seeks to create in Yugoslavia.

The push for capitalist "democracy" as the expected, normal, developed and desired form of government—the apex of human achievement in social relations—and t he institutions and practices a ssociated with this catchword by the NED represents a U.S. attempt at providing intellectual and moral leadership in this New World Order and serves to provide a normative trajectory of how social and political development in much of the world should proceed. Backed up by its status as the singular most powerful superpower (both militarily and technologically), some would argue that the current U.S. effort to promote "democracy" abroad falls within the prescription for hegemonic rule outlined by Gramsci (in the formula of intellectual leadership protected by the armor of coercion), and on this criteria alone they would be correct. Such leadership, however, is likely to suffer from its grounding in one particular state of the international system, and charges of cultural chauvinism, elitism, racism, sexism, and imperialism may grow proportionally with every instance of the use of force made necessary by the U.S. hegemon (e.g. the 1999 Kosovo conflict). It is in recognition of this likelihood that the political tendency for the further development and enhancement of international governing institutions will—in the absence of any systemic dysfunction or failure or major alteration of the developing globalized capitalist social formation— likely gain momentum and further political efficacy amongst the members of the international extracting class and its subsumed class participants. That such a development is possible follows from the capabilities of the forces at work in the present international system and eclipses the logic not only of a single hegemonic center (i.e. the U.S.) but as well will bring to the forefront basic questions of political obligation of the citizen to the national state.

Notes

[1] Webster's defines *democracy* as: "**1 a** : government by the people; *esp* : rule of the majority **b** : a government in which the supreme power is vested in the people and exercised by them directly or indirectly through a system of representation usu. involving periodically held free elections" (*Webster's Ninth New Collegiate Dictionary*, 1898/1984, p. 338). *Hegemony* is defined by Webster's as: "preponderant influence or authority esp. of one nation over others" (*Webster's Ninth New Collegiate Dictionary*, 1898/1984, p. 561).

[2] One notable example of U.S. chauvinism is that expounded in the late 1800s after the U.S. conquest of the Philippines by the-then senator from the state of Indiana, Senator Albert J. Beveridge, in a speech before his senatorial colleagues (cf. Beveridge, *Imperialism At Its Height*, in Barlett, 1947, pp. 385-8).

[3] The International Freedom of Expression Exchange Clearing House, Action Alert Service writes that Freedom House's current activities include surveys and programs aimed, amongst other things, at: "Promoting an engaged U.S. foreign policy" (IFEX web site, <http://www.ifex.org/org/fh/>). Former U.S. U.N. Ambassador Jeane J. Kirkpatrick praised Freedom House for having "demonstrated through decades since its founding [in 1941] a most extraordinarily consistent, clearheaded commitment to the democratic politics in free societies" (Freedom House web site: <http://www.freedomhouse.org/>). In addition to managing the regional networking component of USAID's Democracy Network program, its American Volunteers in International Development (AVID) program, its Center for Religious Freedom which defends "persecuted Christians worldwide", its Cuba Democracy Project (CDP), and numerous other projects, Freedom House proudly announces its support for democratic change by proclaiming:

> With support from foundations, corporations, labor unions, private donors, and the U.S. government, Freedom House's international democratization programs are advancing the remarkable worldwide expansion of political and economic freedom (Freedom House web site: <http://www.freedomhouse.org/>).

For criticisms of Freedom House's *Annual Survey* and how the *Survey* is seen as supporting U.S. foreign policy by unfairly glossing over the disparaging human rights policies of U.S. allies, see also Scoble and Wiseberg, 1981, p. 160 and Schoultz, January-March, 1980, pp. 94-6. In the 1986-1987 *Survey*, Raymond D. Gastil responded to criticisms which purported that Freedom House's Survey of Freedom "is really a propagandistic attempt to generate support for American foreign policy, or the capitalistic economic system" by asserting: "The author would like to take this opportunity to assure readers that he serves no such masters, and that his judgments can be as unpalatable to many within the Freedom House organization as to these critics" (Gastil, 1987, pp. 80-1).

Freedom House utilizes three categories of freedom: "Free", "Partly Free", and "Not Free". Its *Survey* groups two sets of characteristics under political rights and civil liberties. Free and fair elections and their mechanics are the primary concern of the *Survey*'s focus on political rights, while freedom "to develop views, institutions and personal autonomy apart from the state" characterize the *Survey*'s focus on civil liberties (McColm, 1991, pp. 49-51).

[4] By the beginning of 1993, 75 countries and 48 related territories were designated as "Free", or 25% of the world's estimated population of 5.446 billion people, with 31% of the population living in 38 states and 12 related territories falling under the "Not Free" categorization (McColm, 1993, p. 4). In its 1996 survey, out of an estimated world population of 5.7015 billion people, Freedom House rated 76 countries and 44 related territories as "Free" with 62 states and six related territories labeled "Partly Free" (i.e. with some constraints on political rights and civil liberties) while 53 countries and 8 related territories were designated as "Not Free" (i.e. in which basic rights are denied) (Karatnycky, 1996, p. 4). This latter figure in the "Not Free" category, one should note, represented a jump from 1990 to nearly 39% of the world's population. The report does note a rise in the number of "formal democracies," with up to 117 of the world's 191 countries and 57 related territories or 61% as compared to 42% or 41 of the world's countries just ten years ago. This translates into 3.1 billion people out of a 1996 world population of 5.7 billion living under "democratically elected governments." The report notes, however, that "[d]emocracy is not synonymous with freedom," and, hence, designates only 76 of the world's 117 democracies as "Free", with 40 classified as "Partly Free", and only one—Bosnia—as "Not Free" (Karatnycky, 1996, pp. 4-5).

[5] Socialist countries known as "Peoples' Democracies" like the People's Republic of China, Republic of Cuba, Socialist Republic of Vietnam, or the Democratic People's Republic of Korea fall, according to the Freedom House classification, under the "Not Free" category. Indeed, the latter three regimes were listed by Freedom House as members of "The Most Repressive Regimes of 1998" (1998).

As Adam Watson stated in reference to Spartan and Athenian support for oligarchy or democracy: "they did it because they saw advantage to themselves in doing so." "Similarly the British government in its nineteenth-century heyday and the United States government today have encouraged democracy in the different sense in which we now understand it. Intervention in internal affairs, to the degree necessary to ensure that the government of another community is friendly to the intervening power, has the effect of integrating the system, of shifting it in practice further towards the imperial end of the spectrum" (Watson, 1992, p. 53).

[6] The idea of establishing nongovernmental organizations to provide overt funding to private sector groups engaged in international programs was first proposed by the Johnson Administration after public disclosure of the CIA's covert funding of overseas activities of private organizations in the late 1960s. This idea was not acted upon until, in 1979, the leaders of the Democratic and Republican parties created the American Political Foundation (APF) as a nonprofit, bipartisan organization designed to undertake political exchanges with their counterparts abroad. It was the APF which formulated a research proposal to examine how the U.S. could support democratic forces abroad and sought and received President Reagan's support for these efforts. In his 1982 British Parliament speech, President Reagan also referred to the examples of the German and other European parties which had programs to assist democratic forces abroad (U.S. General Accounting Office, 1984, GAO/NSIAD-84-121, pp. 1-2). [NOTE: All General Accounting Office Reports are listed herein by their GAO classification and found in the Bibliography under the heading: U.S. General Accounting Office.]

[7] That U.S. world hegemony is a fully articulated policy, however, can be argued on the basis of a 46-page 1992 Pentagon planning document which described itself as "'definitive guidance from the Secretary of Defense' for preparation of defense budgets for fiscal 1994 through 1999" (Gellman, March 11, 1992, p. A1). Drafted under the supervision of Paul Wolfowitz, undersecretary for policy, the "Defense Planning Guidance" (DPG) received little publicity, yet declared that the political and military mission of the U.S. in the post-cold war era will be "to insure that no rival superpower is allowed to emerge in Western Europe, Asia or the territory of the former Soviet Union." As Patrick Tyler of *The New York Times* stated, "the Pentagon document articulates the clearest rejection to date of collective internationalism." He continues: "The classified document makes the case for a world dominated by one superpower whose position can be perpetuated by constructive behavior and sufficient military might to deter any nation or group of nations from challenging American primacy" (March 8, 1992, *The New York Times*, p. A1 & A14). As regards the authority of this DPG document, Barton Gellman, *Washington Post* National Correspondent, communcated to me in personal correspondence the following:

> [T]he [1992 Pentagon] document was Dick Cheney's last Defense Planning Guidance for the Bush administration. In itself it represented the culmination of a formal mechanism within DOD to define the fundamental security interests and strategy of the United States.

It was not a draft or a proposal, but, as the story said, the standard against which military planners should measure their work. In bureaucratic practice, the DPG is the narrative that explains and justifies the choices made in the DOD budget. There would be no requirement for Congress to endorse it, though the legislative history o r committee r eports of the associated b udgets might comment.

...You're right t o say t he policy w as adopted b y publication o f Cheney's DPG, which required interdepartmental approval (Scowcroft, Baker) in the B ush administration (Personal correspondence with Barton Gellman on November 26, 2000).

[8] One underlying assumption in this analysis is that the accentuation of capitalist economic structures, practices, laws, etc. in other countries does benefit U.S. national interests given the history of uneven colonial and neo-colonial development which has resulted in an asymmetrical relationship between a dominant U.S. state versus all other states and which, because of their relative weakness *vis-à-vis* the U.S. hegemon, are unable to set the terms of trade, and, hence, often are the recipients of disadvantageous trade regimes and/or political alliances. Furthermore, unless and until some world state transcends the current U.S. hegemon, it is unlikely that any other capitalist state will be able to take advantage of "free market" conditions, given their subordination to the U.S. hegemon, and their dependence upon it to maintain system stability and order.

[9] Notes Cohn: "In 1995, President Clinton called democracy promotion 'one of the central pillars of the United States security strategy.' But democracy needs to be promoted for its own sake, not simply as an instrument to further U.S. security or economic interests." Not dismissing a U.S. role entirely in supporting democratic processes, Cohn nonetheless argues that such U.S. assistance can be supported "only if democracy assistance is delinked from furthering U.S. security and economic interests. One way to accomplish this is for U.S. democracy assistance to be channeled through multilateral and regional organizations" (Cohn, July 9, 1999, p. 4).

[10] As Weaver and Barnes point out in regards to the 1990 electoral defeat of the Sandinista Front for National Liberation (FSLN) by the United Nicaraguan Opposition (UNO), which was heavily financed with $5.2 million by the NED between 1984 and 1989 and with an estimated $15 million by the CIA plus an additional $5.9 million from a congressional package approved in October 1989:

> The FSLN pointed to UNO's heavy U.S. financing, to UNO's ex-Somocistas on UNO's candidate lists as proof that UNO was simply a new form of U.S.-sponsored counterrevolution....
> UNO's electoral victory did achieve Washington's goals of unseating the FSLN, defeating uncompromising Nicaraguan nationalism, and bringing back into power leaders who know their place in the U.S.

backyard. That, however, is not the same thing as promoting democracy (Weaver and Barnes, 1991, pp. 138-40).

[11] US isolationism in the inter-war years, writes Coker,

> derived much of its legitimacy in the eyes of the American people from the wish to keep the country's virtue intact. Unable to expand any further once the frontier had been reached, unwilling to follow up Theodore Roosevelt's imperial mission which for a brief moment in the United States' history had extended the frontier into the Pacific, the Americans felt 'trapped in time'. In this supreme moment of introspection, of 'sectarian withdrawal', many Americans felt the need to maintain their exceptional standing by contracting out of a corrupting world which had little or nothing to offer the United States, or the American people (Coker, 1989, p. 8).

[12] Watson uses the term hegemony to refer to "some power or authority in a system [which] is able to 'lay down the law' about the operation of the system, that is to determine to some extent the external relations between member states, while leaving them domestically independent." Though he notes that some scholars usually reserve the term hegemony to describe the exercise of this authority by a single power, he argues: "The difficulty there is that in fact the authority can be exercised either by a powerful individual state, or as is often the case by a group of such states" (Watson, 1992, p. 15).

The distinction between internal and external realms is a common dichotomy utilized by state theorists which both allows and delimits which forms of behavior are considered appropriate, in their view, to each realm. Whereas this debate in international relations once centered on theories of human nature and then shifted to the condition of anarchy and the distribution of power in the states-system, both otherwise subsumed under the concept of "structure", Wendt (1992) has recently moved the debate onto the question of "process" involving the interaction of participants in the system and the learning attained thereby. He argues that there is no essential feature to the anarchical condition of the states-system such as to give rise necessarily to self-help and power politics in the international arena.

[13] "As a legal construct," write Kegley and Wittkopf, "states are assumed to possess a relatively permanent population, a well-defined territory, and a government possessing sovereignty (that is, supreme authority over its inhabitants as well as freedom from interference by others)" (Kegley & Wittkopf, 1981/1989, p. 36).

[14] Other recurrent dichotomies along these lines include the relationship between liberty and equality (Hadley, 1925/1969; Nielsen, 1985; Robbins, 1977; Paul, Miller, and Paul, 1985), liberty and justice (Day, 1987; Smith and Murphy, 1965; Bollier, 1982) and freedom and equality (Dixon, 1986; Sjöstrand, 1973; Oddo,

1979).

[15] Der Derian posits the relationship of order to anarchy, arguing that international societies, institutions, and regimes having been historically constructed "out of the desire for order and the fear of anarchy." International theory and critical investigations both share this recognition yet differ over "the degree to which anarchy is conceived as the threat and order as the task; or put less charitably," he states, "whether the will to order produces the very effect of anarchy" (Der Derian, 1995, p. 4).

[16] Hansen states: "First, *demokratia* was both a political system and a set of political ideals. Second, the ideals singled out by the Athenian democrats were liberty (*eleutheria*) and equality (*isonomia* and other compounds with *isos*, the adjective meaning "equal") (Hansen, 1989, p. 3).

    Aristotle's focus on various constitutions for comparative political analysis is somewhat indicative of a particular reverence the ancient Greeks had for constitutions, believing them to be the foundation of society's happiness or misery. As one noted Greek historian stated: "Now in all political situations we must understand that the principal factor which makes for success or failure is the form of a state's constitution: it is from this source, as if from a fountainhead, that all designs and plans of action not only originate but reach their fulfilment" (Polybius, c. 200-118 B.C.E./1979/1986, pp. 302-3).

[17] Writing about a century and a half after Aristotle, the Greek statesman and historian Polybius (c. 200-118 B.C.E.) also delineates six kinds of government, but for Polybius these six forms naturally develop in a cycle of political revolution with *kingship, aristocracy*, and *democracy* rightfully describing the virtuous forms of government while *one-man rule, minority* or *oligarchic rule*, and *mob rule* aptly descriptive of their defective and degenerative forms which leads to a transition to a different form. As regards democracy, Polybius states: "In the same way a state in which the mass of citizens is free to do whatever it pleases or takes into its head is not a democracy. But where it is both traditional and customary to reverence the gods, to care for our parents, to respect our elders, to obey the laws, and in such a community to ensure that the will of the majority prevails—this situation it is proper to describe as democracy." It is interesting to note that Polybius states that the *best* constitution is "one which includes elements of all three [i.e. kingship, aristocracy, and democracy] species," for, he adds, "this has been proved not only in theory but in practice by Lycurgus, who was the first to construct a constitution, that of Sparta, on this principle" (Polybius, c. 200-118 B.C.E./1979/1986, pp. 303-4).

[18] When Cleisthenes (c. 572 - c. 485 B.C.E.), thought by Athenians to be the principal founder of their democracy*, first implemented his reforms, Martin notes, "he made the preexisting villages of the countryside and the neighborhoods of the city of Athens (both called 'demes,' *demoi*) the constituent units of Athenian political organization." The demos were the people who resided in these units, which were mostly country villages. The wealthy landowners resided

mostly in the city, though many had country houses as well. "Organized in their demes, the male citizens participated directly in the running of their government: they kept track in deme registers of which males were citizens and therefore eligible at eighteen to attend the assembly to vote on laws and public policies." Concludes Martin: "Cleisthenes' rearrangement of the political map of Athenian government meant that local notables no longer could easily control election results just by exercising influence on the poorer people in their immediate area." Furthermore, "the idea that persuasion, rather than force or status, should constitute the mechanism for political decision making in the emerging Athenian democracy fit well with the spirit of the intellectual changes which were taking place during the late Archaic age. That is, the idea that people had to present plausible reasons for their recommendations corresponded to one of the period's new ways of thought" (Martin, 1996, pp. 87-8).

* In his *Histories* (written in the middle of the 5th century), Herodotus states that Cleisthenes "instituted the democracy in Athens" (Herodotus, c. 490 B.C.E.-425 B.C.E./1954/1987, Book Six, Para. 132, p. 435). Sealey states: "The history of Herodotus is the earliest extant work in which the word *dēmokratia* occurs" (Sealey, 1987, p. 100). Aristotle, in his *Politics* (written in the middle of the 4th century B.C.E.), states that Solon (c. 640-c. 558 B.C.E.) "established the traditional Athenian democracy by mixing the constitution well." In particular, for Aristotle, the opening of the judiciary aspect of the state to all citizens is the essential aspect of Solon's reforms. Writes Aristotle: "by setting up courts drawn from the entire body of citizens, he [i.e. Solon] did establish democracy at Athens" (Aristotle, 384-323/1962/1984, Book II, Ch. XII, Para. 1273b35, pp. 160-1). Ostwald quotes Aristotle to the effect that Solon furthered the cause of the common people through three populist measures: 1) "the prohibition against giving loans on the security of the person of the debtor, [which] created the minimal social and economic prerequisite for the common man's exercise of citizenship," 2) "the extension to any person of the right to take legal action in behalf of an injured party, [which] constituted a major step toward the advancement of popular power: it enabled any citizen, regardless of social status, to contribute to the enforcement of Solon's laws by initiating legal action," and, 3) "the institution of an appeals procedure, *ephesis*, and of a new court, the *hēliaia*, to hear appeals, [which] provided—at least theoretically—a check against the arbitrary administration of justice on the part of the aristocratic establishment. It made the people the court of last resort" (Ostwald, 1986, pp. 14-15). Noting that Solon's reforms of the administration of justice were left untouched by Cleisthenes, Ostwald states that the identification of Cleisthenes as the one who instituted democracy in Athens "can, however, be justified only as a retrospective inference drawn from effects to origins. The origins themselves, as described by Herodotus and Aristotle, show that Cleisthenes' aim was not to place the decisive power of governing the state (*kratos*) into the hands of the *dēmos*, but rather to ameliorate conditions that had first brought about tyranny in Athens and had resulted in political strife as soon as

the Peisistratids had been expelled in 511/10 B.C. Cleisthenes was, in other words, no ideological democrat but a practical statesman and politician concerned with eliminating the roots of internal conflict from the society in which he lived" (Ostwald, 1986, pp. 15-6).

[19] In his funeral oration, Pericles points out the numerical essence of democracy as well as its meritocratic virtue as follows: "'Our constitution is called a democracy because power is in the hands not of a minority but of the whole people. When it is a question of settling disputes, everyone is equal before the law; when it is a question of putting one person before another in positions of public responsibility, what counts is not membership of a particular class, but the actual ability which the man possesses. No one, so long as he has it in him to be of service to the state, is kept in political obscurity because of poverty'" (Pericles, quoted in Thucydides, c. 460-404 B.C.E./1954/1985, Book II, Para. 37, p. 145).

[20] Major General Smedley D. Butler quoted from a U.S. military publication, *Training Manual No. 2000-25*, which stated: "The United States is a republic, not a democracy. Democracy is a government of the masses...results in mobocracy...the attitude toward property is Communistic...the attitude toward law is that the will of the majority shall regulate, whether it be based upon deliberation, or governed by passion, prejudice and impulse...it results in demagogism, license, agitation, discontent, anarchy" (quoted in Butler, 1935, Part I, p. 9).

[21] As the left wing of the English bourgeois revolution of 1640-1660, the Levellers fought against the remnants of feudalism but also resisted the rise of capitalism. With a large following amongst the London poor, the Levellers represented those groups being torn asunder in the transition to capitalism. Their political program, radical for its day, included the demand for the separation of church and state, together with demands for religious tolerance for Catholics, Jews, and atheists, as well as demands for annual elections, universal male suffrage, and the redistribution of wealth ("The Levellers and Irish Freedom," 1997).

[22] Following the U.S. Civil War (1860-65), the ratification of the fifteenth amendment to the U.S. Constitution in 1870 legally ensured Black American males with the right to vote. With the passage of the twentieth amendment to the U.S. Constitution in 1920, women in the U.S. gained the right of suffrage. On June 2, 1924, the American Indian Citizenship Act was passed by Congress granting all non-citizen Indians born within the territorial limits of the United States citizenship.

[23] As one commentator wrote regarding the present relationship between wealth and political power in the world, particularly as played out in the World Trade Organization:

> The Group of Seven (G-7)—the U.S., Britain, France, Germany, Japan, Italy and Canada—had a gross national product of close to $20 trillion in 1997. That is 64 percent of the world's production coming from countries with only 11.8 percent of the world's population. Of

the top 500 corporations in the world, only six are from countries outside the U.S., Europe, Canada or Japan. Of the 100 largest banks in the world, all are from the imperialist countries. As of 1997 the imperialist countries exported close to $5 trillion and imported a similar amount—controlling the vast majority of world trade. In the same year, the oppressed countries were in debt to the tune of $2.2 trillion to the imperialist banks and governments of the world. The underdeveloped countries are truly prisoners in the WTO. The WTO processes are carried out behind closed doors among the rulers of the organization, whose proposals are brought to the General Council. The governments of the Third World basically sit outside waiting to hear what the G-7 proposes (Goldstein, December 9, 1999).

The most notable instance of official deception by the U.S. government was its increasing, yet undisclosed, involvement in Southeast Asia during the Vietnam War revealed by the "Pentagon Papers" released to *The New York Times* by psychiatrist and government employee Daniel Ellsberg in 1971. As the *Columbia Encyclopedia* (Sixth Edition) states:

> The study revealed a considerable degree of miscalculation, bureaucratic arrogance, and deception on the part of U.S. policymakers. In particular, it found that the U.S. government had continually resisted full disclosure of increasing military involvement in Southeast Asia— air strikes over Laos, raids along the coast of North Vietnam, and offensive actions by U.S. marines had taken place long before the American public was informed (2000 <http://www.bartleby.com/65/pe/PentPap.html>).

[24] Flathman points out that "the practice of political obligation is not a necessary part of a political order. Political societies sometimes achieve a degree of order and uniformity of behavior by force, deception, and manipulation; other political orders are marked by a degree of order and uniform behavior owing to the habitual, unthinking conformity of their subjects." Flathman's conception of 'political obligation', as a conscious political order not characterized by force, deception, and manipulation, implies a normative concept. As such, he argues, "in point of fact reason and choice are an integral part of the practice of political obligation" (Flathman, 1972, pp. 64-5). As he writes elsewhere, "having an obligation to do X is not the same as being under compulsion to do it, and that acting to discharge an obligation is not the same as being compelled. If compulsion has the force of necessity the question of justification simply has no place. One does not do X, he suffers or experiences it." And further: "Insofar, then, as doing an action involves discharging an obligation, there is logical room for a well-grounded decision on *B's* part to do the action or not" (Flathman, 1976, p. 77).

[25] Though Macpherson considers the Levellers to be part of the newly emergent

162

bourgeoisie, others take a different view which sees them as the first segment of an emergent working class or proletariat (cf. Brockway, 1980, p. 98).

[26] The "effective use of 'obligation' to guide conduct," states Flathman, "presupposes a considerable degree of commonality in the society or social group and contributes to stable patterns of conduct." "Commonality and stability," he maintains, "are threatened by unreflective conformity to particular legal rules and the general rule [i.e. 'an established rule to the effect that there is an obligation to obey the laws and other authoritative commands of the state' (p. 48)]. They are best maintained when the conviction of the value of these rules is continuously renewed through critical examination of their content and the consequences of accepting and obeying them (Flathman, 1972, p. 63). While idealistic in his focus, Flathman's interpretation of political obligation attempts to avoid legal positivism (i.e. that law is whatever the ruler says it is) by arguing that societies which operate upon a basis of political obligation do so without constraint upon reason and choice. [For an in-depth analysis into his "formal-procedural theory of authority", see Flathman (1980).]

[27] Disunity of the dispossessed, however, would continue to fragment working-class political power in the U.S. so long as women, Africans Americans, Native Americans, Asian Americans, and others remained disenfranchised—victories which awaited twentieth-century struggles which further exposed the weakness (if not limits) of and eroded support for liberal democracy. The weight of centuries of gender- and racially-biased laws and cultural attitudes will likewise hinder working-class unity into the unforeseen future.

[28] Coker writes that "Churchill was quite right to interpret the arrival of the American era not so much a threat to British power as the conclusion of one phase in the history of the English-speaking peoples and the beginning of the next" (Coker, 1989, p. 40). However, we see a much more contested perspective from Canadian sociologist John A. Hall who writes:

> Geopolitical exhaustion played a decisive role in [Britain's] decline. Britain was faced in the modern world by Germany, a geopolitical rival beyond appeasement. The waging of two world wars resulted in the loss of external balances and inability in 1945 to protect itself against America's almost brutal insistence on becoming the world's leader (Hall, 1997, p. 8).

Gamble (1981/1994) notes that the "uneasy relationship" between Britain and the United States began in 1917 as a consequence of the first world war which led to the deterioration of Britain's traditional naval prominence, the undermining of her financial strength, and Britain's inability "to establish and maintain the conditions for a liberal world economic order." Reconciling itself to a subordinate role to the U.S., particularly after the new order emerged in the 1940s, Gamble explains:

The negotiated transfer of hegemony which took place between these two Great Powers w as unprecedented a nd by n o means s mooth. Britain at many points resisted American demands and fought for its own interests, and the preservation o f its Empire (Gamble, 1981/ 1994, pp. 27-8).

And Woodcock in his *Who Killed the British Empire?* (1974) remarks that "the United States has consistently applied pressure tending to the diminution of the Empire from the time of the Washington Treaty [of 1922] fifty years ago" (p. 329).

James (1994) notes the American usurpation of Britain's position in the Middle East beginning in 1945 with the American rejection of the British proposal to have the Turkish army placed under its command, the luring of Ibn Saud of Saudi Arabia into the American orbit, followed by the American takeover of Operation Boot, renamed Ajax by the CIA, to overthrow Iranian leader Mussadiq and replace him with Shah Mohammed Reza Pahlevi in 1953, and the removal of Britain from influence over Egypt and the Suez Canal in the 1950s. As contrasted with Britain's traditional dominance of the Middle East, James writes: "Now it was being hustled out, humbled, and forced to comply with the wishes of the United States, which seemed poised to usurp its old position" (James, 1994, pp. 568-77).

And of the three causes Mann (1988) assigns for the decline of Britain's role in world affairs, it is the second cause—"murder by other powers"—of which he says: "social scientists tend to downplay the importance of the second [cause] because most are uncomfortable at handling geo-political and military power." As to the specificity of this "murder", Mann writes:

> Amid these events we can find a few murderous acts committed by the rising power, the United States, against Britain. The terms of US entry into the Second World War and the terms of the settlement of 1945-6 were both designed to weaken British post-war power. Thus US goods now had equal access to the Empire; thus the crippling burden of dollar debt in 1945 was to be paid for by the import of US goods; thus the US insistence on the convertibility of the sterling. In 1946 a rush to convert sterling holdings into dollars depleted Britain's gold and dollar reserves and caused a crisis. Convertibility was suspended in 1947 after a demonstration, satisfactory to American eyes, of sterling's vulnerability. This was calculated to finish off Britain's remaining global rivalry to the United States. It was not nice behaviour, even if it was typical of a Great Power on the make (as Britain itself had earlier been) (Mann, 1988, pp. 212-215).

[29] On August 5, 1964, alleged attacks (later discounted) by North Vietnamese

gunboats against U.S. destroyers were reported as motive for U.S. retaliatory bombing against North Vietnam. President Johnson used the alleged attacks to greatly escalate U.S. involvement in the Vietnam War. Two days later, on August 7, the U.S. Congress approved the Gulf of Tonkin Resolution which provided the President with authorization to take whatever means deemed necessary to repel such "attacks" against the United States and thus began the momentous escalation of the war which led to over fifty thousand U.S. casualties and millions of Vietnamese casualties (cf. Well, 1994).

The Pentagon Papers were a 7,000 page top-secret Defense Department history completed in January 1969 analyzing how the decisions of four U.S administrations during the period from WWII to 1968 led to a deeper and more intractable commitment by the U.S. in Southeast Asia, little of which had been previously made public. On June 13, 1971, *The New York Times* began publishing a series of articles exposing these papers which heretofore had been kept from public knowledge. Immediately, the Nixon Administration's Justice Department asked for, and was granted, a court order blocking further publication of the series based on what they felt was an immediate threat to U.S. national security. This was the first attempt ever made by the Federal Government to impose a prior restraint on the press in the name of national security. The Supreme Court eventually ruled that the government cannot block publication of a controversial story before the public even sees it (cf. Sheehan, et al., 1971).

On June 17, 1972, the office of the Democratic National Committee in the Watergate Hotel in Washington D.C. was burglarized by a secret White House special investigation unit referred to as the "Plumbers", set up by President Nixon and the Committee to Re-elect the President (CREEP), because their job was to stop the leaks to the press from the Nixon White House by investigating the private lives of Nixon's critics and political enemies. Five members of the Plumbers were arrested during the Watergate Hotel break-in and their subsequent trial led to revelations exposing a secret taping system in the White House, legal battles over "executive privilege", firing of the special prosecutor, the near-impeachment of President Nixon, and Nixon's early resignation, amongst other controversial and/or criminal allegations.

The Iran-Contra affair involved the covert selling of arms to Iran (through Israel) by the Reagan Administration against his stated policy of neutrality (and thus resulting in release of American hostages in Iran), utilizing the profits from these arms sales to fund a civil war in Nicaragua in direct violation of the 1984 act of Congress, the Boland Amendment, which forbade United States agencies from giving aid to the Nicaraguan contra rebels. As R.W. Apple wrote in *The New York Times*: "Governments, meantime, have continued to conceal and, on occasion, to prevaricate. The Iran-contra affair, almost certainly illegal, was conceived and carried out by the Reagan Administration in total secrecy, and no one involved blew the whistle—any more than anyone had done so during the months and years as the nation stumbled ever deeper into the Vietnam quagmire" (Apple, June 23,

1996; cf. Kornbluh & Byrne, 1993).

[30] Career CIA officer, Ralph McGehee, a 25-year employee of the CIA, stated how U.S. government deception works:

> I want to reveal to those who still believe in the myths of the CIA what it is and what it actually does.... My view backed by 25 years of experience is, quite simply, that the CIA is the covert action arm of the Presidency. Most of its money, manpower, and energy go into covert operations that, as we have seen over the years, include backing dictators and overthrowing democratically elected governments. The CIA is not an intelligence agency. In fact, it acts largely as an anti-intelligence agency, producing only that information wanted by policymakers to support their plans and suppressing information that does not support those plans. As the covert action arm of the President, the CIA uses disinformation, much of it aimed at the U.S. public, to mold opinion. It employs the gamut of disinformation techniques from forging documents to planting and discovering "communist" weapons caches. But the major weapon in its arsenal of disinformation is the 'intelligence' it feeds to policymakers. Instead of gathering genuine intelligence that could serve as the basis for reasonable policies, the CIA often ends up distorting reality, creating out of whole cloth 'intelligence' to justify policies that have already been decided upon. Policymakers then leak this 'intelligence' to the media to deceive us all and gain our support. Now that President Reagan, in his Executive Order of December 4, 1981, has authorized the Agency to operate within the United States, the situation can only worsen" (McGehee, 1983, p. xi).

[31] One aspect of this contest over control of the modern state can be seen in the discourse of political obligation. Lister (1997) notes that "an increasingly influential 'duties discourse' is, in various guises, supplanting the dominant postwar [i.e. post-WWII] social rights paradigm. Most importantly," she writes, "both the new right (in particular neo-conservatives) and communitarians have deliberately challenged the 'rights discourse' so as to shift the fulcrum of the citizenship paradigm which dominates contemporary politics in the UK and the US...." Citing two such examples (Lawrence Mead's *Beyond Entitlement: The Social Obligations of Citizenship* (1986) and Michael Novak's, et al.'s, *The New Consensus on Family and Welfare* (1987)), Lister states that: "Both emphasize citizenship obligations over rights and both appeal to the common good in identifying as the prime obligation engagement in paid work by welfare recipients to support their families" (Lister, 1997, pp. 18-19). It is interesting to note in these neoconservative admonishments of the poor regarding welfare recipients' failure to adhere to what they consider the poor's political obligations [*viz.* get a job] the absence of any reciprocal political obligations for the wealthy. Janoski argues that the "chronic avoidance of obligations is puzzling because not only do rights

require obligations for their fulfillment, since no right may exist without an obligation to help make the right exist, but obligations must also constrain each person's bundle of citizenship rights to make any system of rights workable." And yet, he notes, "little is known about what citizens in advanced-industrialized countries believe their obligations to be, and what factors lead to those beliefs" (Janoski, 1998, pp. 53-4).

[32] Cohn writes that "the Clinton administration was the first to use the term 'market democracies.' However," she adds, "this definitional linkage of free market policies with political democracy is often more theoretical than real. Economic globalization,privatization, and free trade tend to widen the gap between rich and poor, and this can exacerbate crime, corruption, and instability, thus undermining efforts to build democratic institutions. As a result, U.S. democracy programs may have a negative impact on a country's political democratization processes" (Cohn, July 9, 1999, p. 3).

[33] The term "Amphictyonic" refers to the league of the twelve leading states of ancient Greece who formed "a league of good neighbours" (Trend, 1951, p. 170).

[34] Interest articulation is the act of giving utterance or expression to political needs of either all or part of a community. Interest aggregation is the act of galvanizing and organizing individuals for the purposes of collectively advancing shared political interests. Together, these activities are sometimes referred to as lobbying.

[35] Cartledge notes that: "Like all ancient Greek states, the Athenian democracy did not, and would not have wanted to, recognise the modern theoretical notion of the 'separation of powers' of government and public administration. In the Athenian *demokratia* of the fifth century B.C., both in constitutional theory and in everyday political praxis the *demos* (People) exercised the *kratos* (sovereign power) in all three spheres of legislation, executive action and jurisdiction." He attributes the institutional basis of this civic ideology to the reforms of Ephialtes and Perikles carried out in the late 460s and 450s B.C.E. So complete, says Cartledge, was the association of citizenship with the taking part in the administration of justice in ancient Athens, e.g. serving as a judge and juror on the annually recruited panel of 6,000 *dikastai* "who staffed at need the various People's Courts", that "in 423 Aristophanes (*Clouds* 206-8) could make one of his comic characters pretend not to recognize a map of Athens because he could see no *dikastai* depicted on it" (Cartledge, et al., 1990, pp. 42-4).

[36] "[I]n today's terms," says Cartledge, "Athens would fail to constitute a relevant 'community'. Classical Athens, in Phillips' (1993) estimation, scored highly with regard to common history and shared values, widespread political participation, strong bonds of solidarity (civil society, voluntary associations, family, property rights, mitigation rather than elimination of class stratification, sufficient separation of private from public domains). But these admitted successes were achieved only by means, and at the severe costs, of excluding and exploiting women and slaves for the benefit of a small minority of male citizens.

No doubt, all closely knit communities almost always breed an opposition of insiders and outsiders, but on these grounds it would be hard to set Athens up as a moral-philosophical standard, let alone as a practicable model for us to imitate..." (Cartledge, et al., 1998, p. 9).

[37] And, yet, for all of Doyle's praise of Athenian "spirit," it was Athens which suffered final defeat to Sparta in 405-4 B.C.E. thus ending the Peloponnesian War (cf. Sagan, 1991, p. 126).

[38] Doyle makes no explicit definition of what he means by a "differentiated society", but in other references in this work, he refers to "socioeconomic differentiation" as a basic element of empire (Doyle, 1986a, p. 344), speaks of the "conquering tribe" which "becomes socially differentiated and centrally directed in order to retain empire" (Doyle, 1986a, p. 106), and says that "[t]ribal societies were both highly undifferentiated and thoroughly integrated. They lacked a centralized state—the political life of the society was not differentiated from its social life, nor was it organized in a central coercive institution..." (Doyle, 1986a, p. 132), and perhaps the most explanatory definition he provides is when he speaks about the primary weakness of the tribal societies of the west, which, he claims, did not lack internal unity, "[r]ather, their primary weakness was a lack of social differentiation and thus their small scale. Social roles were mixed together, familial ties shaped commerce and religion, and political leaders were, indistinguishably, both public and private figures" (Doyle, 1986a, p. 89).

[39] With the Spartan defeat of Athens in 405/404 B.C.E. and, hence, the collapse of the latter's empire, it should be noted that for the next 81 years, as Sagan notes, Athens enjoyed amazing stability for, he states: "No class or social brutality, from either oligarchs or lower-class economic radicals, broke the civil peace." Calling this period from 403-322 B.C.E. "The Golden Age of the Radical Democracy," Sagan argues:

It was a remarkably vibrant democratic era. It was also the greatest age of philosophy ever, giving us Plato and Aristotle, and, therefore, the basis of 2,500 years of Western thought (Sagan, 1991, p. 11).

[40] See Gramsci's *Prison Notebooks* [referred to throughout as *PN*] (1929-35/ 1971/1987). Due to the prison censors, Gramsci would sometimes use the word 'group' in place of the marxist term 'class'. I shall utilize Gramsci's terms as faithfully as possible and leave it up to the reader's insight to determine the difference.

[41] The bourgeois revolution against feudalism, i.e. against the power of landlords and the state bureaucracy of the feudal state, is a revolution which replaces feudal monarchical and landed estate rule with the rule of the capitalist class, the bourgeoisie, in which commodity production is the predominant mode of production and where wage-labor replaces serfdom and the corvée or the system of labor rent. Recognizing itself as a social class, the bourgeoisie fights for freedom of trade and

competition, security of property and fruit of enterprise, free play in energies, markets, profit. As Otto Rühle stated: "It is the historical task of the bourgeois revolution to overcome the absolutism of the feudal era and to procure for capitalism, as the new economic system, legal recognition and social acceptance in the framework of the bourgeois-liberal state order.... The success alone of the revolution, which consists in the creation of the capitalist economic order and the social order appropriate to it, determines its nature as a bourgeois revolution" (Rühle, 1924/1970/1974).

[42] "The big bourgeoisie, the landowners, and the factory owners, ..." Lenin argued, "... owing to their class position they are incapable of waging a decisive struggle against tsarism; they are too heavily fettered by p rivate property, by capital and land to enter into a decisive struggle. They stand in too great need of tsarism, with its bureaucratic, police, and military forces for use against the proletariat and the peasantry, to want it to be destroyed. No, the only force capable of gaining 'a decisive victory over tsarism', is the *people*, i.e., the proletariat and the peasantry, if we take the main, big forces, and distribute the rural and urban petty bourgeoisie (also part of 'the people') between the two. 'The revolution's decisive victory over tsarism' means the establishment of the *revolutionary-democratic dictatorship of the proletariat and the peasantry*" (Lenin, 1905/1972, p. 56).

[43] States Machiavelli: "The parable of this semi-animal, semi-human teacher is meant to indicate that a prince must know how to use both natures, and that the one without the other is not durable" (Machiavelli, 1532/1935/1952, Ch. 18, p. 92).

[44] The Jacobins (named for the monastery in which these political activists met; Jacobins was the Parisian name for the Roman Catholic Order of Preachers, otherwise known as the D ominicans after its founder D ominic Guzman, a ka: St. Dominic) were a radical political club, comprised mostly of bourgeois elements, which heavily influenced the French Revolution of 1789.

[45] In an August 9, 1999 radio interview with Gennadiy Andreyevich Zyuganov concerning Russian President Boris Yeltsin's replacement (the fifth prime minister change in 18 months) of Prime Minister Sergey Stepashin with Vladimir Putin, the Russian Communist Party leader derisively stated:

> As for [newly-appointed Prime Minister Vladimir] Putin, there is no real difference between Putin and Stepashin. Both are from Leningrad; both are from the same *democratic gang*; both unreservedly support Yeltsin and his policy; both are from power-wielding ministries; neither has any experience of the economy; neither has any party or movement base, or any solid support anywhere. Both are forced to serve a man who is not in control of himself (Buntman, August 9, 1999)(italics are mine).

In Bulgaria, the main recipient of NED aid is the anti-communist political coalition which calls itself the United Democratic Forces whose members are referred to colloquially as "democrats" (see "Hoods Against Democrats" by Robert D. Kaplan in the December 1998 *Atlantic Monthly*). Or see "The Case Of Yugoslavia: Why The Democrats Failed" by Miljenko Dereta in *Uncaptive Minds* (Summer-Fall 1997, vol. 9, nos. 3-4) published by the Institute for Democracy in Eastern Europe (IDEE), an NED recipient. One of the most virulent denouncements of western-sponsored "democrats" can be seen in Yugoslav President Slobodan Milosevic's speech to the nation on October 2, 2000, in which he asserted:

> A grouping has for a long time now been present in our midst which, under the guise of opposition political parties of democratic orientation, represents the interests of governments which are the protagonists of pressures against Yugoslavia, and especially against Serbia. That grouping appeared in these elections under the name Democratic Opposition of Serbia. Its true head is not its presidential candidate. Its head for many years has been the president of the Democratic Party and collaborator of the military alliance which waged a war against our country. He could not even conceal his collaboration with that alliance. In fact, our entire public knows of his appeal to NATO to bomb Serbia for as many weeks as necessary to break its resistance. The grouping organized in this manner for these elections therefore represents the armies and governments which recently waged war against Yugoslavia.... At this moment ahead of the run-off elections, because the Democratic Opposition of Serbia doubts it can achieve the result it needs, leaders of the Democratic Opposition of Serbia with money introduced into the country are bribing, blackmailing and harassing citizens and organizing strikes, unrest and violence in order to stop production, all work and every activity (Federal Ministry of Foreign Affairs, Yugoslav Daily Survey, October 2, 2000 Belgrade <http://tanjug.co.yu/Arhiva/2000/Oct%20-%2000/03-10e04.html>).

This was followed by another strident speech denouncing Yugoslavia's pro-democratic leaders as "traitors" following ex-President Milosevic's reelection as head of the Yugoslavian Socialist Party on November 25, 2000 in which he "described those who sought his removal as 'paid Western spies' who are aiding the 'occupation' of the country ("Defiant Milosevic Re-Elected Party Leader", Associated Press & Reuters, November 25, 2000, CNN.com <http://europe.cnn.com/2000/WORLD/europe/11/25/yugoslavia.milosevic.02/index.html>).

[46] Burbach, Núñez, and Kagarlitsky see globalization, not as part of the extension of U.S. hegemony—which they assert is in decline, but rather as "the integration of the global economy under capitalist hegemony." Occurring simultaneously with the accelerated pace of technological advancement, the end result, they assert, is both an "increasing concentration of money and capital in the hands of the rich and powerful" which "is leading to misery and marginalization for ever-

increasing numbers of the world's population." To survive, they assert, capital must move globally, but in so doing, it is leading to global disorder and instability (Burbach, et al., 1997, pp. 53-4).

[47] Protests against the WTO, the World Bank, the IMF, and the G8 Summits have been occurring around the world for the last several years. "Street parties" against globalization, for example, were celebrated in 35 cities across the globe during the G8 Summit in Birmingham from May 15-17 of 1998. Some of these protests witnessed WTO symbols being burned in Hyderbad, thousands of landless and homeless people marching against the WTO in Brasilia, and similar actions in Sydney, Toronto, Prague and elsewhere. Recent actions against globalization include protests against the WTO at its meeting in Geneva on November 17, 1999; protests of over 40,000 at the WTO's Third Ministerial meeting in Seattle—the so-called "Battle in Seattle"—from November 30 through December 3, 1999 with similar protests during this same time period around the world in Holland, Canada, Columbia, Bolivia, Bangladesh, Pakistan and elsewhere; protests of over 30,000 in Washington, DC from April 15-17, 2000; protests on May 31, 2000 of IMF austerity programs by 80,000 people in Buenos Aires; protests of 50,000 persons in Millau, France against globalization and in support of José Bové and his ten collaborators on trial for the tearing down of a McDonald's restaurant in the town, as the U.S.-based restaurant was said to symbolize the American dominance of and main force behind globalization; and protests of over 25,000 persons at the July 21-23, 2000 G8 Summit in the Kyushu-Okinawa region of Japan which included not only anti-WTO slogans but as well calls for the removal of U.S. military bases from Okinawa. Newer targets for anti-IMF, anti-WTO, anti-World Bank, and anti-G8 protests include the U.S. Republican National Convention in Philadelphia from July 31 to August 3, 2000 where over 430 protesters were jailed; the U.S. Democratic National Convention in Los Angeles from August 14-17, 2000; the September 6-8 United Nations Millenium Summit in New York city; and the September 26-30, 2000 55th annual conference of the IMF and World Bank in Prague. In addition, many web sites have sprung up on the internet in opposition to this capitalist-oriented globalization including, amongst others, <http://www.a16.org/>, <http://www.globalexchange.org/wbimf/links.html>, <http://www.50years.org/>, and <http://www.jubilee2000uk.org/main.html>.

[48] "'Direct investment'," states Dicken, "is defined as the investment by one firm in another with the intention of gaining a degree of control of that firm's operations. 'International' or 'foreign' direct investment is simply direct investment which occurs across national boundaries, that is, where a firm from one country buys a controlling investment in a firm in another country or where a firm from one country sets up a branch or subsidiary company in another country" (1992, p. 87). Foreign Direct Investment is channeled primarily through transnational corporations; in fact, he argues, "the TNC is the single most important force creating global shifts in economic activity" (Dicken, 1992, p. 47).

[49] Wight states that "international theory may be supposed to be a tradition of

speculation about the society of states, or the family of nations, or the international community." Noting that "speculation of this kind was formerly comprehended under International Law," Wight writes of the paucity of international theory and pejoratively asks: "What international theory, then, was there before 1914?" (Wight, 1966a, p. 18).

[50] As part of the Protestant Reformation, the German princes' claim to dictate a religion to their subjects came to be known as the *jus reformandi*, and gave rise to the maxim, *cujus regio ejus religio*: where the idea was that the one who had the power had the right to say which was the right religion, which at the time was a choice between Catholicism or Lutheranism (*New Catholic Encyclopedia*, 1967, V. I, p. 1040). With the 1648 Treaty of Westphalia, this maxim received a more formal kind of imperial sanction, with the establishment of the principle of *cujus regio illius et religio*: "the lord of the land shall be also lord of religion. And accordingly territorial limits became religious limits within which the inhabitant had to profess and practise the faith imposed on him by the ruler" (*New Catholic Encyclopedia*, 1967, V. XIV, pp. 886-888; *New Advent Catholic Encyclopedia*, 1913/1996, <http://www.knight.org/advent/cathen/07256b.htm>.

The 1555 Peace of Augsburg was concluded between Holy Roman Emperor Charles V (1500-1558) and the princes of the Lutheran southern German principalities, which, emboldened by the Protestant Reformation initiated by Martin Luther, sought autonomy for their states. The 1552 Peace of Passau allowed the Lutheran states the exercise of their religion, and this was reaffirmed in the 1555 Peace of Augsburg (*New Catholic Encyclopedia*, 1967, V. I, p. 1040). However, and as indication that this was not to be the final battle on the matter, Schiller noted:

> Whatever may be said of the equality which the peace of Augsburg was to have established between the two German churches, the Roman Catholic had unquestionably still the advantage. All that the Lutheran Church gained by it was toleration; all that the Romish Church conceded was a sacrifice to necessity, not an offering to justice. Very far was it from being a peace between two equal powers, but a truce between a sovereign and unconquered rebels (Schiller, 1901, p. 17).

[51] This religious war was fought between Protestant German princes against the Catholic sovereigns of the Austrian Habsburg empire. Begun in 1618, the war officially ended on October 24, 1648 with the signing in Munster of the Peace of Westphalia. The 1648 Peace of Westphalia enlarged upon the 1555 Peace of Augsburg by allowing Calvinist states, in addition to Lutheran and Catholic states, to practice their own religion. As such, the Peace of Westphalia ended the Holy Roman emperor's wish to restore the hegemony of Catholicism throughout the empire. Indeed, the empire itself fragmented into a number of virtually indepen-

172

dent states.

[52] Noting the description given the Peace of Westphalia as "marking an epoch in European history," a disagreeable Wedgwood writes that the Peace "is supposed to divide the period of religious wars from that of national wars, the ideological wars from the wars of mere aggression." This "demarcation," she asserts, "is as artificial as such arbitrary divisions commonly are. Aggession, dynastic ambition, and fanaticism are all alike present in the hazy background behind the actual reality of the war, and the last of the wars of religion merged insensibly into the pseudo-national wars of the future." And though she notes that "[t]he war hastened the development by leaving the princes as the only power to whom the disorganized people could turn," Wedgwood is unable to link this shattering of dynastic empire and the feudal system it rested upon with a growing diversity in freedom of speech and thought reflecting the growing diversity of private capital in competition, along with the growing dominance of the new capitalist mode of production (Wedgwood, 1938/1969, pp. 501, 505).

[53] Hedley Bull limits the essential aspects of the states-system to three: 1) a plurality of sovereign states; 2) a degree of interaction among them, in respect of which they form a system; and 3) a degree of acceptance of common rules and institutions, in respect of which they form a society (Bull, 1977, p. 233).

[54] "Essentialism," as Resnick and Wolff point out, is a specific presumption which characterizes many theories in that it "holds that any apparent complexity—a person, a relationship, a historical occurrence, and so forth—can be analyzed to reveal a simplicity lying at its core. In relation to conceptualizing causality, essentialism is the presumption that among the influences apparently producing any outcome, some can be shown to be *inessential* to its occurrence while others will be shown to be *essential* causes.... The goal of analysis for such an essentialist theory is then to find and express this essential cause and its mechanism of producing what is theorized as its effect" (Resnick and Wolff, 1987, pp. 2-3).

[55] "A society of states (or international society) exists," states Bull, "when a group of states, conscious of certain common interests and common values, form a society in the sense that they conceive themselves to be bound by a common set of rules in their relations with one another, and share in the working of common institutions" (Bull, 1977, p. 13). Wight uses the terms 'society' and 'community' interchangeably because, he argues, "[s]ociologists have not agreed on a satisfactory distinction in usage between the words" (Wight, 1966b, p. 92).

[56] Stated Kubálková and Cruickshank (1980):

> At present, as attempts to build a general theory of international relations in the West have apparently been abandoned[,] this abandoned direction has coincided, oddly enough, with the shift to behaviouralism. The choice of level of abstraction or generality and the role played by models in the analysis of an historical situation are

basically of a sociological nature, but international relations theorists
in the West appear at present to lack a global sociological account of
the nature of social phenomena in general, comparable to that fur-
nished by Marxism-Leninism (p. 9).

[57] Wæver states that this fourth debate remains either unnumbered or is referred
to by some as the "third" debate and cites the following sources: Lapid 1989;
Neufeld 1993; and Holsti 1993 (Wæver, 1997, p. 8).

[58] The revolution in communications technology has allowed for the instanta-
neous transfer of information and finances on an unprecedented scale. "One of the
advantages of digital cash," writes Mikkelsen (Summer 1998/99), "is that transactions could take place without the need for banks to intermediate in international
transactions. Instant transfer of money would not only encourage the development of a free worldwide market, by removing the present significant barriers to
transacting, but also reduce the ability of governments to impose taxation and
disclosure obligations on banks (such as withholding tax)" (p. 14). "Twenty-four
hours a day," notes Burbach, Núñez, and Kagarlitsky, "365 days a year, trillions
of dollars in capital are transferred by electronic processes from one point of the
globe to another. In effect," they argue, "capitalism and technology are collapsing
time and space" (1997, p. 13).

[59] The UN Conference on Trade and Development *World Investment Report 1999*
estimates the existence of about 60,000 transnational corporations (TNCs) currently extant, with no less than 89 percent of these companies headquartered in
the "Triad" consisting of the European Union countries (principally France, the
UK, Germany, Sweden, Italy, the Netherlands, and Belgium), North America (i.e.
the U.S. and Canada), and Japan (Ch. 3, pp. 6-8). "Overall," states the report,
"stability predominates within the world's largest TNCs" with "[a]pproximately
85 per cent of the top 100 TNCs list ... dominated by firms that have been in the
top 100 ranking during the past five years" with "a substantial part of these TNCs
originat[ing] in the European Union, United States and Japan." In 1997, states the
report, General Electric held the top position as the largest non-financial TNC
followed by Ford Motor Company and then Royal Dutch Shell. Only two TNCs
from developing countries made it into the top 100 in 1997 and these were Petroleos
de Venezuela (PDVSA) and the Daewoo Corporation (World Investment Report
1999, 1999, Ch. 3, p. 1).
Dicken (1992) states his preference for:

the term 'transnational corporation' to the more widely used term
'multinational corporation', simply because it is a more general, less
restrictive, term. The term 'multinational corporation' suggests operations in a substantial number of countries whereas 'transnational
corporation' simply implies operations in at least two countries, including the firm's home country. In effect, all multinational corpora-

tions are transnational corporations but not all transnational corporations are multinational corporations (pp. 47-8).

[60] Although the colonization of Africa and Asia resulted in states which were formally referred to as nation-states, it must be noted that many of these state boundaries transgressed and divided traditional tribal and/or ethnic areas.

[61] The concept of the tragedy of the commons refers to the depletion or degradation of a resource, usually referred to as a common property resource, to which people have free and unmanaged access. It is a concept derived from a 1968 article in *Science* magazine by Garret Hardin that was entitled simply "The Tragedy of the Commons".

[62] Frank has since switched his adherence from Dependency Theory to World-Systems Theory with, initially, his *The World System: Five Hundred Years or Five Thousand?* edited with Barry Gills (1993) but most recently with his work *ReOrient: Global Economy in the Asian Age* (1998), the latter which challenges the Eurocentric origins of the modern world-system asserting instead that Europe's subsequent domination of the world-system did not occur until the eighteenth century and was preceded by an Afroeurasian world-economy which revolved around China.

[63] In an interview published in the *Chicago Tribune* on January 5, 1879, Marx spoke of international relations as arising between workers when asked by the reporter: "What has socialism done so far?" "Two things," he replied.

> "Socialists have shown the general universal struggle between capital and labor…and consequently tried to bring about an understanding between the workmen in the different countries, which became more necessary as the capitalists became more cosmopolitan in hiring labor, pitting foreign against native labor not only in America, but in England, France, and Germany. *International relations* sprang up at once between workingmen in the three different countries, showing that socialism was not merely a local, but an international problem, to be solved by the international action of workmen" (Marx, January 5, 1879, *Chicago Tribune*) (italics mine).

[64] See Chapter 5 below "The Imperative of the Market & Its Democratic Cover" for a discussion on the distinction of Marx's dialectic from that of Hegel.

[65] For a fuller explanation of "fundamental" and "subsumed" class processes as well as distinctions between various types of capitalists, see Chapter 5 below "The Imperative of the Market & Its Democratic Cover".

[66] In his classic defense of the pacific nature of capitalism, Schumpeter (1951) argues to the contrary and asserts that modern imperialism is merely a residual effect from the precapitalist autocratic state. "Imperialism," he argues, "is atavistic in character" (p. 84). Modern capitalism's detrimental aspects including "export monopolism", the use of force to break down customs barriers or to secure

control over foreign markets, or overt colonization and the suppression of native labor, are all the product not of the present but, rather, of past relations of production. In particular, he argues, this atavism "in the social structure, in individual, psychological habits of emotional reaction...must gradually disappear" with the fuller development of capitalism (p. 85). Modern imperialism, he argues, is "a heritage of the autocratic state, of its structural elements, organizational forms, interest alignments, and human attitudes, the outcome of precapitalist forces which the autocratic state has reorganized, in part by the methods of early capitalism" (p. 128). "A purely capitalist world," he writes, "can offer no fertile soil to imperialist impulses." Indeed, Schumpeter argues, "we must expect that anti-imperialist tendencies will show themselves wherever capitalism penetrates the economy and, through the economy, the mind of modern nations" (pp. 90-91). "[M]odern pacificism," he writes, "in its political foundations if not its derivation, is unquestionably a phenomenon of the capitalist world" (p. 92).

[67] Carlo Cipolla dates this agricultural revolution from the eighth millenium B.C.E. and states that it, along with the eighteenth century Industrial Revolution, "created deep breaches in the continuity of the historical process" (1962/1964, p. 29).

[68] To this starting point list should be added the fight against racism as well.

[69] Dependency theory has historically catalogued how much of the asymmetries resulting from the internationalization of capitalism has played out and been understood by many, especially by those theorists from the world's periphery whose countries have suffered the most from core domination of developing economies.

[70] A cogent example of such expansionist language can be seen in President McKinley's description to a group of Methodists of how he had agonized over the disposition of the Philippines claiming to have prayed to "Almighty God" every night until:
"And one night late it came to me this way...that there was nothing left for us to do but to take them all [the Philippine archipelago], and to educate the Filipinos, and uplift and civilize and Christianize them, and by God's grace do the very best we could by them, as our fellow-men for whom Christ also died. And then I went to bed, and went to sleep and slept soundly..." (*Christian Advocate*, January 22, 1903, New York; quoted in Bailey, 1040/1946, p. 520).
The U.S. purchase of Louisiana in 1803, East Florida in 1819, the 1853 Gadsden Purchase, and the 1867 purchase of Alaska in addition to earlier and subsequent forcible acquisitions or divisions of territory were all arrangements with either European state powers or the government of Mexico, territories bought, sold, conquered, or divided which—save for the seldom honored Indian Treaties—never seriously consulted the opinions of nor recognized as binding the rights of the indigenous tribal occupants of these lands.

[71] Wilson was alluding to those citizens who followed the authority of those leaders the U.S. recognized.

[72] Slater further elaborates on modernization theory as follows:

> In contrast, the countries of Africa, Asia and Latin America were defined by the prevalence of traditional culture, undeveloped divisions of labour, the lack of utilization of their own resources, over-population, pre-democratic structures, and the predominance of rites, rituals and primitive customs. Above all, they were characterized in terms of *lack*—lack of capital, technology, entrepreneurship, advanced social and political institutions and modern values. In the early 1950s, a prominent US academic argued that the United States had interests in the welfare of foreign peoples that went beyond national security and commercial prosperity; we want these people to have some participation in the good material things of life which we enjoy in the United States. Viner (1952: 176) commented that 'we want the common man and his wife and his children to have not only Coca-Cola and chewing gum and ice cream, not only modern plumbing, automobiles, refrigerators and electric lighting, but also good health and good diet, good education' ... and 'the benefits and virtues ... of political democracy and social security'. The West was constructed as the model and prototype for the non-West—the future destination for traditional societies willing and able to make the transition to modernity. As one political scientist presciently observed in the 1970s, a little over a decade before the term 'end of history' became so famous, — 'the idealized vision of modernity has an American face' ... 'this ideal type is in effect the end of history, the terminal station at which the passengers to modernization can finally get out and stretch their legs (Cruise O'Brien 1979: 53)' (Slater, 1997, p. 642).

[73] Allen Haden, an observer of U.S. foreign policy in Latin America in the period of the second world war commented that: "Latin America is in effect a laboratory in which much of the application of foreign policy can get its first workout..." (Haden, 1945, p. 48).

[74] Greene writes:

> Webster traces the noun filibuster to the Dutch *vrijbuiter* (*vriz*, free; *buit*, booty) and gives this definition: "A freebooter or soldier-of-fortune who aids a revolution in a foreign country in order to enrich himself; first applied to buccaneers in the West Indies, who preyed on the Spanish commerce to South America, and later to such adventurers as followed López to Cuba, and Walker to Nicaragua, in their expeditions of conquest" (Greene, 1937, Introductory *Note*).

[75] The term "Manifest Destiny" was invented by John L. O'Sullivan, leader of the Young America movement in the 1830s and 1840s. O'Sullivan coined the term as "warrant for the country's westward expansion" (Wills, January 31, 1999, p.

15).

[76] The "Democrats, who were strong in the Southern states, put themselves on record in their platform of 1856 as approving Walker's efforts 'to regenerate' Nicaragua. The British not unnaturally felt that this prince of filibusters was but 'the advance guard of Manifest Destiny,' and that he was engaged in a covert attempt to secure territory for the United States in Central America, in violation of both the letter and the spirit of the Clayton-Bulwer Treaty" (Bailey, 1940/1946, p. 294).

[77] "Whether [filibustering] was wrong or right was a question answerable only after the filibuster had failed or succeeded. Successful, he was a hero; unsuccessful, he was an outlaw contemned by all of his fellows" (Greene, 1937, p. 27).

[78] By the treaty of December 10, 1898, Spain relinquished sovereignty over Cuba and ceded the Philippines, Puerto Rico, and Guam to the U.S. The U.S. took possession of Wake Island on January 17, 1899 while the Samoan Islands were divided up between the U.S. and Germany later that same year. The Hawaiian Islands had just previously been annexed by the U.S. on July 7, 1898 (Bailey, 1940/1946, pp. 466-530).

[79] Fejes points out the "control of communications, first point-to-point, and later the mass media" was an important element in the establishment of U.S. power in Latin America. "[F]irst film, then newspapers and magazines, and lastly radio broadcasting—were integrated into the media structure of the United States. By 1945, United States hegemony in hemispheric communications was complete" (Fejes, 1986, p. 4).

[80] Kennan himself has maintained that he only called for 'political' containment of the Soviet Union and not 'military' containment or, what is referred to as, rollback. Taking blame for his policy recommendation's misinterpretation, Kennan states: "I should have explained that I didn't suspect them [i.e. the Soviet Union] of any desire to launch an attack on us. This was right after the war, and it was absurd to suppose that they were going to turn around and attack the United States. I didn't think I needed to explain that, but I obviously should have done it" (Kennan, April 18, 1996).

[81] As the U.S. State Department states regarding the 1954 Senate censure of Senator Joe McCarthy:

> The hunt for subversives started during the war itself, and was furthered by congressional committees that often abused their powers of investigation to harass people with whom they differed politically. Then in February 1950, an undistinguished, first-term Republican senator from Wisconsin, Joseph McCarthy, burst into national prominence when, in a speech in Wheeling, West Virginia, he held up a piece of paper that he claimed was a list of 205 known communists currently working in the State Department. McCarthy never produced documentation for a single one of his charges, but for the next four

years he exploited an issue that he realized had touched a nerve in the American public <http://www.usinfo.state.gov/usa/infousa/facts/democrac/60.htm>.

[82] Sr. Toriello, Foreign Minister in the Arbenz government, commenting shortly before the 1954 CIA-backed *coup d'etat* on U.S. Secretary of State Dulles's anti-communist resolution adopted at the 1954 Tenth Inter-American Conference in Caracas, Venezuela, characterized U.S. policy as amounting to "cataloguing as 'Communism' every manifestation of nationalism or economic independence, any desire for social progress, any intellectual curiosity, and any interest in progressive or liberal reforms" such that: "any Latin American government that exerts itself to bring about a truly national program which affects the interests of the powerful foreign companies, in whose hands the wealth and the basic resources in large part repose in Latin America, will be pointed out as Communist; it will be accused of being a threat to continental security and making a breach in continental solidarity, and so will be threatened with foreign intervention." Connell-Smith notes that even though Toriello was given an ovation for standing up to what was widely interpreted as a pretext for U.S. intervention, only Mexico and Argentina abstained on the U.S.-backed resolution—the rest of the Latin American countries fearing a cut-off of U.S. economic aid (Connell-Smith, 1966, pp. 162-63).

As Schlesinger and Kinzer (1982) describe Arbenz: "He was a nationalist hoping to transform an oligarchic society" (p. 49).

[83] It was also in 1954 that a Presidential Commission issued a top secret report calling "on the CIA to be 'an aggressive covert psychological, political and paramilitary organization more effective, more unique and, if necessary, more ruthless than that employed by the enemy'" (Weiner, August 29, 1993, *The New York Times*).

[84] In a secret document prepared by the CIA and Armas, communists were singled out for either "Executive action" (i.e. murder) or imprisonment or exile. Under the subject heading "Guatemalan Communist Personnel to be disposed of during Military Operations of Calligeris" (the code-name for the disposal operation), Category I listed 58 people for disposal while Category II listed 74 people for either imprisonment or exile (Doyle and Kornbluh, "CIA and Assassinations: The Guatemala 1954 Documents." *National Security Archive Electronic Briefing Book No. 4*, Document 4).

[85] CIA historian Nick Cullather in his 1994 in-house secret account of the 1954 coup in Guatemala wrote that the political repercussions from the coup saw "Guatemala's political center...vanished from politics into a terrorized silence. Political activity simply became too dangerous as groups of the extreme right and left, both led by military officers, plotted against one another." In the mid-1960s, the "United States responded by sending military advisors and weapons, escalating a cycle of violence and reprisals that by the end of the decade claimed the lives of a U.S. ambassador, two U.S. military attachés, and as many as 10,000 peasants.

In 1974, the Army stole another election, persuading another generation of young Guatemalans to seek change through intrigues and violence. Increasingly, Indians and the Catholic Church—which had formerly remained aloof from politics—sided with the left, isolating the Army on the far right" (Cullather, 1994, pp. 90-91).

[86] *Labor-power*, not labor, is, as Marx stated in *Wage-labor and Capital*, the worker's commodity which is sold to the capitalist in exchange for a wage in the form of money. In exchange for a specified wage, the worker expends her/his labor under the direction of the capitalist for a specified period of time, i.e. "so much money for so long a use of labor-power." As Marx writes: "Labor-power, then, is a commodity, no more, no less so than is the sugar. The first is measured by the clock, the other by the s cales." Why does t he worker s ell this c ommodity? Simply put, states Marx, "in order to live." Labor, or the actual exercise of human productive powers to alter the use-value of commodities and thus to add value to them, cannot be bought and sold in the same sense that labor-power can be bought and sold. The worker sells the power to labor under the direction of the capitalist or his agents in exchange for a wage, but she/he does not sell her/his labor. Moreover, it is important to understand that the sell of labor-power to the capitalist for a wage precedes production and the emergence of a value in the product, and that this is the basic mechanism by which surplus value is appropriated in the capitalist mode of production. If the capitalist fails to exact more productive value from the worker in the process of production than he pays the worker in the form of a wage, then the capitalist will reap no profits.

[87] It is interesting to note in the initial organization of this anti-communist labor program in Europe the role played by ex-Nazis and other intelligence operatives. The operations set up in Italy, Greece, Germany, Britain, Turkey, Portugal, Holland, Belgium, Denmark, Luxembourg, as well as in ostensibly neutral countries such as Sweden and Austria were organized on the avowed basis of so-called "stay-behind units" which were "to undertake resistance operations or sabotage against Soviet troops" in the event of a Soviet invasion of Western Europe. In fact, the head of the German unit was none other than General Reinhard Gehlen, Hitler's chief intelligence officer on Soviet and East European affairs. Gehlen, who directed the stay-behind units in Europe for nearly two decades during the Cold War, worked closely during the war with former Waffen SS Colonel Otto Skorzeny, a fierce Hitler loyalist. Together, they arranged for the training and equipping of five-man cells known as "Werewolves." These Werewolf units "had access to buried depots of food, radio equipment, weapons, explosives, and other liquidation devices." And like the medieval lore for which they were named, these stay-behind units were to operate as normal citizens by day while "meting out death and destruction to their enemies under the cover of darkness" (Lee, Martin A. 1997. *The Beast Reawakens*. New York, NY: Little Brown Publishers, pp. 24). These operations were instructed to link up with the "Romanian Iron Guard, the Vanagis of Latvia, the Croatian Ustaše, the Organization of Ukranian Nationalists,

Polish quislings, and an army of Russian defectors led by General Andrei Vlasov..."
(Lee, 1997, p. 23). Similar European-wide stay behind units were set up by the
CIA after the war. With names like "GLADIO," "Column 88," "Gray Wolves,"
and the "Gehlen Operation" or simply "the Org", these operations recruited
heavily from former SS officers, Mussolini's secret police, and from other fascist
organizations. In addition to their extermination and destruction campaigns, their
methods also included the making of payments to unionists, identified by AFL
operatives as "potential scabs," the organization of goon squads to attack strikers,
and collaboration with the Sicilian mafia (Gibson, Richard. 1992. "CIA Leaders
and the NEA-AFT Merger Plans." From *ACTIV-L* listserv, the *Activists Mailing
List*).

[88] Godson writes that in the immediate post-WWII period, the AFL "utilized a
variety of channels to provide moral, material, and organizational support to
European trade unionists who were resisting engulfment by and within Communist-dominated labor organizations" (Godson, 1976, p. 104). To aid in this endeavor, the AFL, in 1944, created two multi-million-dollar organizations, the Free
Trade Union Fund (FTUF) and the Free Trade Union Committee (FTUC) in order
"to fight the Russians and rebuild democratic trade unions" in Europe. As Scott
notes:

> The FTUC became the official foreign policy vehicle of the Federa-
> tion while war was still raging and communists were still allies in war.
> While the organization had the declared aim of assisting unionists who
> were in the anti-Nazi underground resistance, the dispensers of aid
> were deliberately selective, funnelling assistance to anti-communist
> socialists and making life difficult for those who were suspected of
> sympathising with communism (Scott, 1978, p. 194).

In 1945, the International Federation of Trade Unions (IFTU), which had been
dominated by reformist socialist leaders before the war, joined with the Congress
of Industrial Organizations (CIO) and with Soviet trade unions to form the World
Federation of Trade Unions (WFTU). As Godson notes, the Russian and European communists, as participants in the WWII victory, "enjoyed enormous pres-
tige" and "many workers saw little reason to oppose the Communists." Fearful of
European trade leaders cooperation with the communists, the AFL reasoned that
the rank and file would likewise "see little reason not to elect and appoint Communists to positions of power and accept them as brothers" (Godson, 1976, p. 105).
In a move to divide the WFTU, the AFL encouraged American unions to join any
one of the 27 International Trade Secretariats (ITS), which were autonomous
subsidiaries of the IFTU. In so doing, the AFL refused to become associated with
the WFTU, encouraged the development of anti-communist unions in Europe, and
continued to press the dangers of communist infiltration and control of trade
unions.

As one of the methods used to provide moral and psychological support to European anti-communist labor groups, "the AFL issued a continuous stream of policy resolutions and statements stressing the tyrannical nature of communism and the fate that befell workers when the Communists came to power" (Godson, 1976, p. 107). Also, in 1946, the FTUC began the monthly publication of *the International Free Trade Union News* in English, French, German, and Italian. In addition to featuring AFL resolutions and policy statements, Godson notes, "the publication carried analyses and details of the suppression of free trade unionism in Communist countries and in such noncommunist dictatorships as Spain." In addition to publications, the AFL also brought a number of anti-communist European labor leaders to the United States in the late 1940s, while AFL leaders "repeatedly visited most of the European countries and gave numerous speeches" (Godson, 1976, p. 109). Food packages were also shipped to non-communist trade unions in Europe by the AFL. While in Germany, these packages amounted to an essential program of material assistance, due to the devastation caused by war, in France "they were a further demonstration of the AFL's support for the democratic elements," especially, notes Godson, for those anti-communist workers in the mining regions "where Communist militants received assistance from the Communist party" (Godson, 1976, p. 110). Another AFL initiative was the organization of a series of Marshall Plan trade union conferences which, states Godson, "were catalytic in the processes that eventually split the WFTU." One London conference, notes Godson, had important symbolic effects, in that it "gave the stamp of trade union approval to the Marshall Plan, it officially established a permanent administrative organization to ensure organized labor a role in the execution of the ERP [i.e. the European Recovery Plan, a.k.a. the Marshall Plan], and it marked the first time that both the AFL and the CIO participated in an international meeting of trade union organizations." By the late 1940s, it should be noted, "the CIO was in the process of expelling Communists from its ranks" (Godson, 1976, pp. 112-14). Largely on this anti-communist basis were the two unions to merge into the AFL-CIO in 1955 (cf. Morris, 1967, pp. 57-8). With this merging of the two largest union groupings in the United States, states Scott, dominant union opinion regarding foreign policy "was that the United States must act decisively to prevent the extension of communism in the world, in order to protect the economic and strategic military security of the country" (Scott, 1978, pp. 197-8). Also, believing that France was the key to the control of Western Europe in the immediate postwar period (due to the prostration of Germany and the defeat of Italy), the AFL utilized funding through the FTUC to weld together the anti-communists labor groups into the Force Ouvrière (FO), as a counter to the communist-dominated Confédération Générale du Travail (CGT). Not only was financial assistance provided to these French anti-communist labor activists, but, as well, office equipment—including typewriters and mimeograph machines—was provided to FO offices throughout France. Also, in a campaign to "neutralize what it believed to be Communist terror and intimidation," the FTUC hired "strong-arm men" to work alongside dock workers, so that when a strike was called, "professional and occasional dockers" who refused to join the strike would be "protected". "Thus," states Godson, "the Communists would have to tangle with men experienced in the techniques of violence" (Godson, 1976, p. 121).

[89] For an insightful account and subsequent consequences of Office of Strategic Services (OSS) and Central Intelligence Agency (CIA) collaboration with the Sicilian Mafia and Corsican gangsters to limit the political gains of the Italian and French Communist parties after WWII, from recruiting thugs to battling union strikers to breaking up leftist political rallies, see McCoy (especially Chapter 1), *The Politics of Heroin in Southeast Asia* (1972).

[90] The American Federation of Labor (AFL) was founded in 1886. The Congress of Industrial Organization (CIO) dates from 1935. The AFL organized craft and trade unions and ignored the conditions of unskilled and semi-skilled, i.e. 'industrial', workers. After the CIO emerged as a national federation of industrial unions in the mid-1930s, the AFL responded by working to enhance the economic status of both trade and industrial workers. In 1955, the two labor federations merged into the AFL-CIO.

[91] For a thoroughgoing account of U.S. covert activities in Latin America from WWII to the early 1990s, including the extensive role played by Nelson and David Rockefeller in using the Cold War as a cover to expand their vast financial and mineral-rich land holdings in South and Central America, to the funding and usage of missionary societies to educate tribal natives in the Amazon and elsewhere to obey national governments (which claimed jurisdiction over tribal territory) and to fear "communism," and the widespread use of terror, torture, and occasional genocide to promote U.S. economic interests and development policies, see Colby and Dennett, *Thy Will Be Done* (1995). Also, see Penny Lernoux, *Cry of the People: The Struggle for Human Rights in Latin America* (1982) for an account of U.S. persecution and murder of missionaries in Latin America who aligned themselves with the peasantry and workers. See also William Blum, *The CIA: A Forgotten History, US Global Interventions Since World War 2* (1986) for a grim account of the role played by the CIA "in overthrowing governments, perverting elections, assassinating leaders, suppressing revolutions, manipulating trade unions and manufacturing 'news'" in more than 50 countries since World War II.

[92] Prior to 1963, the Southern Command was known as the Caribbean Command. Note also that the School of the Americans is often referred to by the term given it by anti-SOA political activist and Catholic priest Father Roy Bourgeois as the "School of the Assassins." Designated originally since its opening in 1946 as the U.S. Army Caribbean Training Center in Panama, its name was changed to the School of the Americas in 1963 under JFK's Alliance for Progress. On December 15, 2000, in an attempt to distance itself from public criticism and repeated protests, its name was again changed to the Defense Institute for Hemispheric Security Cooperation with command shifting from the U.S. Army to the Department of Defense.

[93] An example of this can be witnessed by the guilty plea on January 27, 2000 by Laurie Anne Hiett, the wife of Colonel James Hiett, the former head of U.S. anti-drug operations in Bogota, to drug charges in a scheme to smuggle $700,000 worth of heroin into the United States from her husband's post in Colombia (Hays, January 28, 2000).

[94] Currently serving a 40 year sentence in a U.S. federal prison, Noriega failed to convince U.S. courts that the 1989 invasion of Panama violated international treaties and principles of customary international law. In *United States of America v. Manuel Antonio Noriega* (U.S. District Court of Southern Florida, 1990, 746, Fed. Supp. 1506), the Court ruled that Noriega, as an individual, lacked standing to challenge violations of international law; only sovereigns could. And since the new Panamanian regime of Guillermo Endara (installed and strongly backed by the U.S.) did not issue a protest on Noriega's behalf, the Court refused to entertain the question of whether international treaties had been violated by the U.S. military action in Panama (Slomanson, William R. 1990/95. pp. 412-14).

Both Saunders and Missick had been lured to Miami, Florida by U.S. DEA agents when they were arrested in 1985.

[95] The Torricelli Law was denounced in the UN General Assembly on a vote of 59 to 3 with 71 abstentions in November of 1992.

The Helms-Burton Act was denounced by the Organization of American States by a vote of 32 to 2 in June of 1996 and condemned by the European Commission. On September 6, 1996, the Inter-American Juridical Committee of the Organization of American States unanimously declared that the Act "is not in conformity with international law."

[96] Pursuant to the Foreign Affairs Reform and Restructuring Act of 1998, the United States Information Agency (USIA) was integrated into the Department of State on October 1, 1999. The Broadcasting Board of Governors (BBG), now part of USIA, and which includes the Voice of America (VOA) and surrogate broadcasting, has become a separate federal entity. The United States Agency for International Development (USAID) has remained a separate agency, though the 1998 legislation stipulated that on April 1, 1999, the USAID Administrator would report to and be under the direct authority and foreign policy guidance of the Secretary of State. As such, USAID, for the first time, became an independent statutory agency within the Executive Branch of the U. S. government as of April 1, 1999 (Foreign Affairs Reorganization Fact Sheet, December 30, 1998).

It is important to note that the authorizing legislation did not officially "create" the NED but, rather, "merely recognized the existence of the Endowment as a private, non-profit organization already incorporated in the District of Columbia and authorized funding for Endowment activities." As a General Accounting Office report notes:

The director of the Democracy Program told us that this significant change in the character of the Endowment was made because the

Board members were not willing to accept a presidentially appointed board that they found would be necessitated if C ongress were t o create the Endowment (GAO/NSIAD-84-121, 1984, p. 10).

[97] The first two goals were: 1) a commitment to "a more peaceful, secure world" so that s tates may pursue "peaceful change and to realize t heir political and economic aspirations," and 2) "to restore order and stability to the international economic system" by coordinating U.S. domestic and foreign economic policies in order to "achieve sustainable, non-inflationary growth" (Shultz, 1983, p. 2).

[98] Then-USIA director Charles Z. Wick testified that American ideals and values were "under attack by a potent Soviet propaganda and disinformation campaign" (Wick, 1983, p. 116).

[99] Cohen states that *democracy-building* "refers generally to information and training programs that support the growth of participatory government, publicly accountable institutions, and the rule of law" (Cohen, 2000, p. 846).

[100] See, for example, the Helsinki Final Act, Sections I, II, III, IV, and, especially, VI: *Non-Intervention in Internal Affairs*, in Henkin, et al., 1987/1993, pp. 262-264; UN Charter, Art. 1 (2), Art. 2 (1-7), in Henkin, et al., 1987/1993, p. 2; and UN General Assembly Definition of Aggression Resolution of 1974, in Henkin, et al., 1987/1993, p. 333.

[101] In response to an April 1993 National Security Council request for information on democracy promotion activities of the U.S. government, the State Department provided other agencies the following list of purposes or activities to serve as a guide for identifying what constitutes "democracy promotion":

civic education; civic organization; civic-military relations; conflict prevention/resolution; ethnic, racial, and religious diversity programs; human rights education and training; information exchange; legislative training/development; media training and development; political party development; public administration development; rule of law; support for elections/election reform; and trade union development (GAO/NSIAD-94-83, 1994, p. 10).

[102] In Marxist theory, the superstructure refers to social institutions (legal, political, and cultural) that are erected upon the economic base.

[103] Prior to 1997, the AFL-CIO's Free Trade Union Institute (FTUI) represented organized labor's NED core recipient. But as of 1997, the FTUI has been redesignated as the American Center for International Labor Solidarity ('the Solidarity Center' for short) representing the merger of the four international institutes of the AFL-CIO, i.e. the American Institute for Free Labor Development (AIFLD), the Asian American Free Labor Institute (AAFLI), the African American Labor Center (AALC), and the Free Trade Union Institute (FTUI).

[104] The URL for the NED website is as follows: <http://www.ned.org/>.

[105] This researcher is thankful to NED librarian Allen Overland at the Democracy Resource Center for overcoming this obstacle by sending me via the Internet the entire grant file database for years 1990-97 and for Jane Riley Jacobsen at NED who sent me hard copies of the NED's grant database for years 1998-99. Thanks also are extended to UMass OIT Data Analysis Services for their help in sorting the 1990-97 data, particularly Scott Evans, Eva Goldwater and Trina Hosmer.

[106] It should be noted that ACILS's (which before 1997 was known as the FTUI) web page is supported solely on the NED server whereas each of the other core institutes host their own fully developed web sites. The nonexistence of a separate web site for ACILS has been noted by Scipes who writes that one ACILS critic pointed out that there is also no notice of ACILS on the AFL-CIO's own web site <http://www.aflcio.org/> (Scipes, July 8, 1999). This omission raises the question of the possibility of the AFL-CIO's reluctance to admit its collusion with both corporate and U.S. government agencies.

[107] Titles of NED conferences include: The 1999 Elections and the Future of Nigeria (October 1999), International Relations and Democracy (March 1999), Democratic Consolidation in South Africa: Progress and Pitfalls (February 1998), India's Democracy at Fifty (September, 1998), Institutionalizing Horizontal Accountability: How Democracies Can Fight Corruption and the Abuse of Power (June, 1997), Democracy in South Asia (September, 1997), Five Years into the Transition: Where is Russia Headed? (May, 1997); Consolidating Democracy in Taiwan (March, 1997); Democracy in East Asia (December, 1996); Constructing Democracy and Markets: East Asia & Latin America (July 1996); Stability and Reform in Egypt (May 1996); Mexico: the Challenge of Political Opening (December 1995); Civil-Military Relations and the Consolidation of Democracy (June 1995); Democracy's Future (April 1995); Nigeria's Political Crisis: Which Way Forward? (February 1995); The Prospects for Political Change in China (December 1994); and The Unfinished Revolution (April 1991).

This March 23, 1996 presidential election represented Taiwan's first election since Chiang Kai-shek and his Kuomintang party (KMT) fled mainland China in 1949, after losing the civil war with the communists, and set up a dictatorial government on the island of Formosa. Democratic opposition to the KMT-led government coalesced around the Democratic Progressive Party (DPP) which was able to successfully push for the lifting—for the first time since 1949—of Martial Law in 1987. The DPP's success in pushing for a political opening in Taiwan, however, was not rewarded in the 1996 elections, which was won by the ruling KMT party candidate, Lee Teng-hui.

[108] See Chapter 3 above on the enlistment of the U.S. labor movement in America's fight against communism.

[109] Formally known as the Cuban Democracy Act of 1992, the Torricelli bill (named after Robert Torricelli (D.-NJ)) forbids overseas subsidiaries of U.S. corporations from doing business with Cuba, threatens reprisals against any country trading with the island, and prevents foreign ships that visit Cuban ports from

docking in U.S. harbors.

The 1996 Helms-Burton Act (the Cuban Liberty and Democratic Solidarity (LIBERTAD) Act) allows lawsuits in U.S. courts against foreigners who use property seized by Castro's government from U.S. companies or citizens, including people who were Cuban citizens at the time of confiscation but whom are now U.S. citizens. The Act also bans executives from companies investing in such properties from the U.S. by denying them visas.

[110] Elian Gonzalez was a six-year-old Cuban boy who was brought illegally to the U.S. by his mother in November of 1999, the latter who drowned along with ten other Cuban immigrants in the crossover to the Florida coast from Cuba. His Cuban father later won a custody battle to repatriate his son to Cuba on July 6, 2000, albeit in defiance of Miami-based anti-Castro activists who filed numerous lawsuits to prevent the boy's return.

[111] In 1997, the Center for Public Integrity identified CANF as not only "'the most potent voice on U.S. policy toward Cuba'" but as well "'dollar for dollar, arguably the most effective'." The Center's report notes that CANF funneled approximately $3.2 million into the U.S. political system from its founding in 1981 until 1997. As *Washington Post* reporter Karen DeYoung writes, CANF "claims credit for the current pillars of sanctions policy—Radio and TV Marti, a $28 million-a-year taxpayer-financed system broadcasting into Cuba, along with the embargo-tightening Cuban Democracy Act in 1992 and the 1996 Helms-Burton Act" (DeYoung, February 21, 2000, p. A02).

Mas Canosa died unexpectedly on November 23, 1997. As the front man for U.S. policy towards Cuba for the previous decade and a half, his death has arguably altered the previously beligerent manner in which U.S. policy towards Cuba is carried out.

[112] In 1987, Fascell was the recipient of the NED's first Democracy Award which, since 1991, is a small-scale replica of the so-called "Goddess of Democracy" statue constructed by students for use during the Tiananmen Square protests in Beijing, China in May and June 1989.

[113] It should be noted that in its 1996 report, the GAO chose not to include any projects undertaken by the Center for International Private Enterprise (CIPE) in its review on U.S. democratic development assistance to Russia stating that "the primary focus of the Center's projects was to promote privatization and promarket reforms, two areas outside the scope of our review" (GAO/NSIAD-96-40, 1996, p. 10). Commenting on the GAO's omission of CIPE projects, NED President Carl Gershman argued that the GAO "erroneously categorized CIPE's efforts as business development" rather than, he argued, as "strengthening the capacity of private groups to build a constituency for free market democratic reforms through advocacy and educational programs" (GAO/NSIAD-96-40, 1996, p. 63).

[114] In the midst of the 1999 US/NATO war on Yugoslavia, instigated on the pretext of "preventing a humanitarian catastrophe," with the stated intent to bring democracy to that country or, at the very least, to its Kosovo-Metohija region,

and following the bombing of the Chinese embassy in Belgrade, the Chinese *People's Daily,* in an article entitled, "On New Development of US Hegemonism," stated, as regards the US armed intervention in Yugoslavia:

> It is an important measure taken by the United States to step up implementation of its global strategy of seeking hegemony at the turn of the century, and a major indication of the new development of US hegemonism....
>
> Flaunting the banners of "freedom", "democracy" and "human rights", the United States wantonly interferes in the internal affairs of the developing countries. The United States has tabled, year after year, motions concerning other nations' human rights at the UN human rights meetings, attempting to act as the "human right judge" and conduct "trials" of developing countries ("On New Development...", *People's Daily Online,* May 27, 1999).

[115] With the appointments of Warren Christopher, as the 63rd Secretary of State on January 20, 1993, and his successor, Madeleine Albright, the first female Secretary of State, who was sworn in on January 23, 1997, Clinton may be said to have gotten the type of Secretaries of State he wanted. In his Senate confirmation remarks on January 13, 1993, Secretary-designate Christopher stated:

> Democracy cannot be imposed from the top down but must be built from the bottom up. Our policy should encourage patient, sustained efforts to help others build the institutions that make democracy possible: political parties, free media, laws that protect property and individual rights, an impartial judiciary, labor unions, and voluntary associations that stand between the individual and the state. American private and civic groups are particularly well suited to help. In this regard, we will move swiftly to establish the Democracy Corps, to put experienced Americans in contact with foreign grassroots democratic leaders, and to strengthen the bipartisan National Endowment for Democracy.
>
> We must also improve our institutional capacity to provide timely and effective aid to people struggling to establish democracy and free markets....
>
> These three pillars for our foreign policy—economic growth, military strength, and support for democracy—are mutually re-enforcing. A vibrant economy will strengthen America's hand abroad, while permitting us to maintain a strong military without sacrificing domestic needs. And by helping others to forge democracy out of the ruins of dictatorship, we can pacify old threats, prevent new ones, and create new markets for US trade and investment (Christopher, January 13, 1993).

And as Secretary-designate Albright stated in her prepared confirmation remarks before the U.S. Senate Foreign Relations Committee on January 8, 1997:

> Mr. Chairman, we have reached a point more than halfway between the disintegration of the Soviet Union and the start of a new century. Our nation is respected and at peace. Our alliances are vigorous. Our economy is strong. And from the distant corners of Asia, to the emerging democracies of Central Europe and Africa, to the community of democracies that exists within our own hemisphere—and to the one impermanent exception to that community, Castro's Cuba—American institutions and ideals are a model for those who have, or who aspire to, freedom.
>
> All this is no accident, and its continuation is by no means inevitable. Democratic progress must be sustained as it was built—by American leadership....
>
> And we will continue to promote and advocate democracy because we know that democracy is a parent to peace, and that the American constitution remains the most revolutionary and inspiring source of change in the world (Albright, January 8, 1997).

[116] NED's annual budget of approximately $32 million "is 0.2 percent of America's $16 billion foreign operations budget and just 0.01 percent of its $300 billion defense budget" (Cohen, 2000, p. 848).

[117] From 1995 to December, 1998, the Organization for Economic Cooperation and Development (OECD), a Paris-based invitation-only secretariat that includes 29 member countries, including all of the world's wealthiest nations, had been negotiating a pact "aimed at setting investment ground rules in the world's richest nations, to remove limits on foreign ownership of certain industries, and allow the free movement of capital across international borders" (*Multilateral Agreement on Investment...*, March 5, 1998, pp. 1-2). According to the testimony of Lori Wallach, director of Public Citizen's Global Trade Watch, the U.S.-based public interest watchdog group, the goal of the MAI "is to expand the same extreme multinational corporate agenda of undermining countries sovereignty and disempowering even legitimate government action which is found in the GATT-WTO" (*Multilateral Agreement on Investment...*, March 5, 1998, p. 58). Public Citizen's Global Trade Watch Backgrounder notes that the proposed MAI would "legally limit how and when nations, states or communities can set investment policy," "would require 'national treatment' for all member countries meaning foreign investors must be treated equal to domestic investors in all instances," "would ban 'performance requirements,' such as employment, reinvestment or other conditions used to regulate multinationals investing in some communities," and it "would grant legal standing to investors and corporations so that they can directly sue governments in international tribunals for failure to deliver all of the MAI's benefits." In short, the proposed MAI "would accelerate economic globalization while at the same time greatly restricting the power of democracies to control investment policy." It

"would greatly hinder the ability of governments to combat the worst consequences of economic globalization: increased disparity of wealth and income, growth of national and global monopolies and loss of democratic control of a wide range of policies, from human rights to the environment, from labor rights to welfare policy" ("The Alarming Multilateral Agreement on Investment (MAI) Now Being Negotiated at the OECD"). As a U.S. Congressional committee hearing underscored the opposition's arguments: "one of the critical concerns about the MAI" is the "infringement on national sovereignty" (*Multilateral Agreement on Investment...*, March 5, 1998, p. 2). In an official statement released on December 3, 1998, the OECD stated: "Negotiations on the MAI are no longer taking place" (*Official OECD Statement*, December 3, 1998). However, as De Brie points out, learning from the temporary failure of MAI, "big business and technocrats are trying to force through a decision before the end of 1999" either through the Transatlantic Economic Partnership (TEP) or the Millennium Round of the World Trade Organisation scheduled to take place in Seattle in December 1999 "that will remove the final obstacles to the free play of 'market forces' and require countries to submit to the unfettered expansion of the multinationals." So far, however, neither of these meetings was able to revive the MAI. However, the TEP, with its lobby of big businesses on both sides of the Atlantic known as the Transatlantic Business Dialogue (TABD), continues to seek to dissolve the European Union in a free trade area with the United States. As regards the WTO meeting in Seattle, De Brie writes: "The idea is to convert the meeting of the ministerial conference of the 131 WTO member countries in Seattle in December 1999 into an enormous globalisation fair, where the removal of the final obstacles to capital's freedom of action would be negotiated pell-mell" (De Brie, May 1999). But with the enormous protests galvanized by this 1999 Seattle meeting, the WTO has temporarily been stalemated in attempting to move forward in this regard.

[118] Driscoll notes that during the 1930s: "The relation between money and the value of goods became confused, as did the relation between the value of one national currency and another. Under these conditions the world economy languished. Between 1929 and 1932 prices of goods fell by 48 percent worldwide, and the value of international trade fell by 63 percent" (Driscoll, July 1997, p. 3).

[119] From 1945 to 1971, the U.S. dollar was said to be "as good as gold," for countries were indeed allowed to trade in their U.S. dollars for gold. Exchanged at the rate of one ounce of gold for every $35, the U.S. government backed up this arrangement, exchanging gold for dollars at the above rate on demand. Moreover, as Kegley and Wittkopf note: "Dollars earned interest, which gold did not; they did not entail storage and insurance costs; and they were needed to buy imports for survival and postwar reconstruction" (Kegley & Wittkopf, 1981/1989, pp. 187-9). However, in 1971, the gold standard was abandoned, as countries, resentful over U.S. policies in Vietnam and fearing American instability due to chronic deficits in the U.S. balance of payments (necessary to keep the war going), in-

creasingly demanded gold instead of dollars. The resulting depletion of U.S. gold reserves forced the transition to a free floating currency market not based on gold convertibility. Since then, each countries' money has been worth whatever it can fetch on the world's markets.

[120] The two central propositions of the hegemonic stability thesis as outlined by Keohane are: 1) "that order in world politics is typically created by a single dominant power. Since regimes constitute elements of an international order, this implies that the formation of international regimes normally depends on hegemony. The other major tenet of the theory of hegemonic stability is that the maintenance of order requires continued hegemony" (Keohane, 1984, p. 31).

[121] The tendency of capitalism to lead to an excess supply of commodities relative to available consumer demand (and this situation's resulting consequences of driving down prices and profits, leading to capital flight, closure of industries, etc.) indicated to governments in the 1930s the political inadvisability of waiting for "self-regulating" markets to correct their imbalances, amidst massive unemployment, demands for protecting national trade and, hence, the proliferation of world tariff barriers, and other distortions. The British economist John Maynard Keynes proposed addressing the counterpart to the problem of overproduction, *viz.* inadequate demand, through governmental interventionist policies designed to spur consumer purchasing power. This was done in the U.S., for example, through FDR's New Deal programs such as the Works Progress Administration, the Civilian Conservation Corps, the Federal Emergency Relief Administration, and the Civil Works Administration, etc. (Leuchtenburg, 1963). As Greider notes:

> Keynes argued that markets cannot extricate themselves from permanent stagnation, high unemployment and underutilized capacity without the artificial demand stimulus of government spending. The new spending creates market demand for goods and labor; governments promote rising wages and schemes that redistribute incomes downward to those who will spend the money (Greider, 1997, p. 51).

The consensus around the success of the Keynesian solution to the capitalist crisis of oversupply lasted well into the decade of the 1970s until free market purists gained a political upperhand and began demanding the shrinkage of government while heralding the benefits of unregulated markets.

[122] As of 1998, the U.S. Treasury Department notes that the term "Most Favored-Nation (MFN)" has been changed to "Normal Trade Relations (NTR)" status. The name was changed, the department states, "because the term Most Favored-Nation status was deceiving since most nations have this trade status except for a handful of rogue nations that have been refused this normal trade relationship." Like MFN, "[u]nder NTR both parties agree not to extend to any third party nation any trade preferences that are more favorable than those available under the agreement concluded between them unless they simultaneously

make the same provisions available to each other" (International Trade Data System [ITDS], June 4, 1999).

[123] Using World Bank figures, Madeley (1992) writes that trade barriers used by industrialized countries to keep out Third World goods "cost poor countries anything between $50 billion and $100 billion a year" (p. 56). Industrialized countries either use a *tariff*, which is basically a tax levied on a product at the port of entry into a country which has the effect of increasing the cost of the product and hence reduces its sale or, most expecially since the 1980s, protectionist measures of industrialized countries have included the usage of non-tariff barriers such as the *quota*, which restricts the quantity of a particular product which is allowed to be imported into the market of a country. By 1990, states Madeley, "nearly a quarter of protectionist measures were in the form of non-tariff measures" (Madeley, 1992, p. 132). Though "the MFN clause might be more accurately called the 'equal treatment' clause," "[w]hatever its name, the clause has frequently been ignored by Western countries in their dealings with developing countries" (Madeley, 1992, p. 132).

[124] Title IV, of the U.S. Trade Act of 1974, sets out the conditions and procedure for restoring MFN status to any of the "nonmarket economy" (NME) countries. The two key conditions of Title IV are: "(1) conclusion of a bilateral trade agreement containing a reciprocal grant of the MFN status and additional provisions required by law, and approved by the enactment of a joint resolution; and (2) compliance with the freedom-of-emigration requirements ('Jackson-Vanik amendment'). These requirements can be fulfilled either by a Presidential determination that the country in question places no obstacles to free emigration of its citizens, or, under specified conditions, by a presidential waiver of full compliance" (Pregelj, June 10, 1998).

[125] Currently, the Non-Aligned Movement consists of 112 mostly developing nations.

[126] Currently, there are 132 member countries of the G-77.

[127] "[T]he North-South system is one of disparity and inequality," writes Spero. "In 1977, the developed market economies had an average gross national product of $7,317 per capita whereas the underdeveloped countries had an average gross national product of $573 per capita" (Spero, 1981, p. 14).

[128] "The Organization of Petroleum Exporting Countries (OPEC) was formed at a conference held in Baghdad on September 10-14, 1960. There were five original members: Iran, Iraq, Kuwait, Saudi Arabia, and Venezuela. Between 1960 and 1975, the organization expanded to 13 members with the addition of Qatar, Indonesia, Libya, United Arab Emirates, Algeria, Nigeria, Ecuador, and Gabon. Currently, OPEC consists of 11 member nations (Ecuador dropped out in December 1992 and Gabon withdrew effective January 1995)" ("OPEC FACT SHEET," January 1998).

[129] Krasner defines *regimes* "as sets of implicit or explicit principles, norms,

rules, and decision-making procedures around which actor's expectations converge in a given area of international relations" (Krasner, 1982, p. 186; see also Krasner, 1983). Ruggie defines "international economic regimes" as "governing arrangements constructed by states to coordinate their expectations and organize aspects of their behavior in such issue areas as trade and monetary relations" (Ruggie, 1984, p. 34).

[130] "A society of states (or international society) exists," states Bull, "when a group of states, conscious of certain common interests and common values, form a society in the sense that they conceive themselves to be bound by a common set of rules in their relations with one another, and share in the working of common institutions" (Bull, 1977, p. 13).

Though the Bretton Woods monetary and financial system collapsed in 1971, management of the LIEO remained in the hands of the U.S. which continued to sustain the free market principles of the Bretton Woods system. Nations could no longer exchange dollars for gold and fixed exchange rates were replaced by free-floating currency values determined by market forces, thus introducing uncertainty and unpredictability into international monetary relations while alerting other countries to the fact of U.S. inability to solely manage the existing LIEO (Kegley & Wittkopf, 1981/1989, p. 194).

[131] The initial signatories to the ECSC included France, Germany, Italy, the Netherlands, Belgium, and Luxembourg.

"In creating the EC its original six members set out on a more ambitious course, the essential aim of which was described in the 1950 Schuman [i.e. French Foreign Minister Robert Schuman] Plan as a federation" (Pryce in Duff, et al., 1994, p. 10).

[132] Denmark, Ireland, and the UK became EC members on January 1, 1973. Greece, Spain, and Portugal were admitted in the 1980s. Sweden, Finland, and Austria were admitted on January 1, 1995, bringing current EC membership to a total of 15 countries.

The European Parliament (EP) grew out of the representative assembly established with the ECSC, though prior to 1979, Members of the European Parliament (MEPs) were selected by their respective national parliaments (Laffon in Cafruny & Rosenthal, 1993, p. 45; Fontaine, 1997). The European Council, on the other hand, has been meeting since 1974. Here, "[H]eads of State or Government meet at least twice a year in the form of the European Council or 'European Summit'. Its membership also includes the President of the Commission. The President of the European Parliament is invited to make a presentation at the opening session" ("The Council of the European Union," 1997).

The Council of the European Union "is usually known as the Council of Ministers, and has no equivalent anywhere in the world. Here, the Member States legislate for the Union, set its political objectives, coordinate their national policies and resolve differences between themselves and with other institutions.... Each meeting of the Council brings together Member States' representatives, usually ministers, who are responsible to their national parliaments and public opinions. Nowadays, there are regular meetings of more than 25 different types of Council meeting: General Affairs (Foreign Affairs ministers), Economy and Finance, and Agriculture meet monthly, others such as Transport, Environment and Industry meet two to four times a year" ("The Council of the European Union," 1997).

[133] The treaty was passed by the national parliaments of the remaining EC states.

[134] One should note that the adoption of a single currency for the countries of Europe has its counterpart in the calls for the "dollarization" (i.e. adopting the U.S. dollar as legal tender in place of the national currency) of several economies in Latin America. In fact, in February of 1999, Argentine President Carlos Menem called for the abandonment of the Argentine peso and the adoption of the U.S. dollar as the country's official medium of exchange. And though one analyst states that this indicates how far nationalism has receded in Argentina compared to only ten years prior, he adds that, in actuality, Menem's proposal is not as radical as it sounds because, he states, "Argentina is effectively dollarized anyway, since 50 percent of the deposits in the country's financial system are already in dollars or dollar-denominated instruments" (Falcoff, April 1999). Opposition to dollarization, however, was witnessed in Ecuador in January 2000 when mass protests against Harvard-educated President Jamil Mahuad were followed by a coup d'etat by several of the countries' top generals—after Mahuad announced plans for dolarization of the Ecuadorian economy—forcing Mahuad to resign his office and replacing him with his vice president as the country's new leader. Economist Ross Mcleod, who is pushing a similar plan for Indonesia, says that the movement towards dollarization "is a legacy of the steady stream of financial crises that have beset the world over the last two decades." States Mcleod:

> In these crises, countries experienced sudden capital outflow driven by a widespread expectation that their currencies were likely to be markedly devalued. A striking implication of this is that if countries did not have their own currencies, they could never be subjected to destabilizing swings in capital flows resulting from exchange rate speculation. It follows that vulnerability to occasional, but severe, financial crises could be mitigated if countries were to abolish their own currencies (Mcleod, January 28, 2000, V. 26, No. 3, *CNN.com Asia Now*).

[135] EFTA was established on November 20, 1959, as Ministers from Austria, Denmark, Norway, Portugal, Sweden, Switzerland, and the United Kingdom (seven West European countries that were not members of the European Economic Community) approved in Stockholm the text of a Convention establishing the European Free Trade Association (EFTA), which entered into force on May 3, 1960. As an alternative method toward European integration, EFTA's goal "was: (a) to remove import duties, quotas and other obstacles to trade in Western Europe and (b) to uphold liberal, non-discriminatory practices in world trade."

"The membership of the EFTA has undergone significant changes since the inception of the organization. Iceland became a member in 1970; Finland, which had been an associate member from 1961, became a full member in 1986; and Liechtenstein became a full member in 1991. Of the original members, six have left to join the European Union (EU): the United Kingdom and Denmark in 1972; Portugal in 1986; and Austria, Finland, and Sweden, on January 1, 1995. Norway, however, decided against membership in the EU in a referendum in November 1994, after completing negotiations for accession to the EU along with the other three EFTA countries. The present members of EFTA are: Iceland, Liechtenstein, Norway, and Switzerland" (European Free Trade Association, April 10, 1997).

Only Iceland, Norway, and Liechtenstein (the latter which joined EFTA in 1991) remain as the sole EFTA members in the EEA.

[136] One notable aspect of the new treaty is that identity checks along internal borders will be abolished within five years of the signing of the treaty, except at the borders of Ireland and the United Kingdom.

[137] Philosopher Jacques Derrida, in his *Specters of Marx* (1993/1994), states that "the eschatological themes of the 'end of history,' of the 'end of Marxism,' of the 'end of philosophy,' of the 'ends of man,' of the 'last man' and so forth were, in the '50s, that is, forty years ago, our daily bread.... Thus," he notes, "for us, I venture to say, the media parade of current discourse on the end of history and the last man looks most often like a tiresome anachronism" (Derrida, 1993/1994, pp. 14-15). Referring to Fukuyama's thesis that "'liberal democracy remains the only coherent political aspiration that spans different regions and cultures around the globe'" as an "anhistoric (sic) *telos* of history," Derrida adds that not only is Fukuyama's model of a liberal state "that of Hegel, the Hegel of the struggle for recognition" but, moreover, "it is that of a Hegel who privileges the 'Christian vision'" (Derrida, 1993/1994, pp. 57-60). Expanding upon Fukuyama's admission that some countries might not be able to achieve the *ideal* of liberal democracy, Derrida argues that this failure to measure up characterizes not only "so-called primitive forms of government, theocracy, and military dictatorship" but as well characterizes "*a priori* and by definition, *all* democracies, including the oldest and most stable of so-called Western democracies. At stake here," he writes, "is the very concept of democracy as concept of a promise that can only arise in such a *diastema* (failure, inadequation, disjunction, disadjustment, being 'out of joint'). That is why we always propose," he adds, "to speak of a democracy *to come*...." Comparing the democratic promise to the communist promise, Derrida states that its effectivity "will always keep within it, and it must do so, this absolutely undetermined messianic hope at its heart, this eschatological relation to the to-come of an event *and* of a singularity, of an alterity that cannot be anticipated" (Derrida, 1993/1994, pp. 64-5). Noting that Fukuyama explicitly states his rejection of empirical evidence which contradicts the ideal state of existence to which liberal democracy has presumably brought in its wake, and quoting him to the effect that we can only judge "the goodness or badness of any regime or social system" by certain "trans-

historical standards," Derrida states that, on the one hand, Fukuyama "accredits the logic of the empirical event" whenever it is a question of certifying the defeat of "so-called Marxist States and of everything that bars access to the Promised Land of economic and political liberalisms," while on the other hand, "in the name of the trans-historic and natural ideal," he discredits the "so-called empirical event" in order, argues Derrida, "to avoid chalking up to the account of this ideal and its concept precisely whatever contradicts them in such a cruel fashion: in a word, all the *evil*, all that is *not going well* in the capitalist States and in liberalism..." (Derrida, 1993/1994, pp. 67-9). This author is in agreement with Derrida that Fukuyama's 'end of history' argument is ahistorical and a mere apologia in line with U.S. post Cold War triumphalism.

[138] In comparison with Middle Eastern OPEC countries, U.S. oil reserves of 22.4 billion barrels do not come close to Kuwait's reserves of 96.5 billion barrels, Iraq's 112 billion barrels, Saudi Arabia's more than 259 billion barrels, and Iran's 88 billion barrels of proven oil reserves (Energy Information Administration Country Analysis Briefs; <http://www.eia.doe.gov/emeu/cabs/contents.html>.

[139] The Gulf Cooperation Council (GCC) states include: Bahrain, Kuwait, the Sultanate of Oman, Qatar, Saudi Arabia, and the United Arab Emirates.

[140] A symbolic prelude to this collapse was the destruction, beginning in November 1989, of the wall which had divided East and West Berlin since 1961 in anticipation of the economic, monetary, and social union between East and West Germany, which was enacted in 1990.

[141] The term "full-court press," as described by Scheer, "is a basketball expression that describes an attempt to wrest the ball away from one's opponent in his own territory" (Scheer, 1982, p. 8). It was first used within the anti-Soviet context in a United Press International report by Helen Thomas which quoted a Reagan Administration official as stating that Reagan had "'approved an eight-page national security document that 'undertakes a campaign aimed at internal reform in the Soviet Union and shrinkage of the Soviet empire.' He affirmed that it could be called 'a full-court press' against the Soviet Union'" (Story by UPI White House correspondent Helen Thomas, May 21, 1982, quoted in Scheer, 1982, p. 7).

[142] International economic integration has been defined by economists specializing in international trade as denoting "'a state of affairs or a process which involves the amalgamation of separate economies into larger free trading regions'." El-Agraa comments that less specialized economists "have for quite a while been using the term to mean simply increasing economic interdependence between nations" (El-Agraa, 1997, p. 1).

[143] ASEAN is currently comprised of ten nations: Brunei, Cambodia, Indonesia, Laos, Malaysia, Myanmar, the Philippines, Singapore, Thailand, and Vietnam. Founded in 1967 to buttress U.S. efforts in the Vietnam War, ASEAN later expanded to include Brunei in 1984, Vietnam in 1995, and Laos and Myanmar in 1997, and Cambodia in 1999 (El-Agraa, 1997, pp. 27-9; Chalermpalanupap, June

1, 1999).

[144] The E.U. is a customs union whereas NAFTA and the FTAA are free trade areas. Customs unions have common external trade barriers whereas free trade areas do not. Member nations of free trade areas do "remove all trade impediments amongst themselves but retain their freedom with regard to the determination of their own policies vis-à-vis the outside world" (El-Agraa, 1997, p. 1).

[145] The San Jose Declaration, which served as the basis for the beginning of the hemispheric trade negotiations by heads of state and government at the Second Summit of the Americas in Santiago, Chile on April, 18-19, 1998, represents "the largest regional integration effort ever undertaken involving both developed and developing countries in a common objective to realize free trade and investment in goods and services, on a basis of strengthened trading rules and disciplines" (cf. FTAA web site, <http://www.alca-ftaa.org/EnglishVersion/view_e.htm>).

[146] Associated Press writer Sonya Ross notes: "The inclusion of Caribbean nations helps level the trade playing field that tilted in Mexico's favor after the North American Free Trade Agreement went into effect" (Ross, May 18, 2000).

[147] Walter Rodney, in his book *How Europe Underdeveloped AFRICA* (1982), states in regards to Africa's development situation:

> The question as to who, and what, is responsible for African underdevelopment can be answered at two levels. First, the answer is that the operation of the imperialist system bears major responsibility for African economic retardation by draining African wealth and by making it impossible to develop more rapidly the resources of the continent. Second, one has to deal with those who manipulate the system and those who are either agents or unwitting accomplices of the said system. The capitalists of Western Europe were the ones who actively extended their exploitation from inside Europe to cover the whole of Africa.
>
> In recent times, they were joined, and to some extent replaced, by capitalists from the United States; and for many years now even the workers of those metropolitan countries have benefited from the exploitation and underdevelopment of Africa (Rodney, 1982, p. 27).

[148] In its new Strategic Compact plan, the World Bank now states that its "basic mission" is one of "reducing poverty" (Strategic Compact, 1997).

[149] By tradition, the President of the World Bank is a U.S. national whereas the Managing Director of the International Monetary Fund (IMF) is a European (Driscoll, July 1997, p. 5).

[150] Achille Mbembe, Executive Director of the Dakar, Senegal-based Council for the Development of Social Science Research states that many African economies have been so hard hit by the imperatives of economic liberalization that some of them are likely to "simply be swallowed up by more fortunate neighbours." With Africa's debt now standing at $235 billion (which even the Archbishop of Canterbury, George Carey, urged the multilateral finance institutions to cancel) and promised foreign aid to those countries who implemented IMF and World Bank liberalization measures nonexistent, Mbembe adds: "The entanglement of Africa is likely to lead to the fragmentation of public authority and the emergence of private indirect government. Then, the bottom line is that many African countries would revert to the post-Atlantic slave trade era where trade by barter would replace monetised (sic) economy" (Mbembe, quoted in Njoku, January 27, 1998).

[151] The formerly centrally planned economies of Eastern Europe and the former Soviet Union have, since 1991, become IMF members.

[152] Running a distant second to the U.S. IMF quota of 18.25% are: Germany (5.67%), Japan (5.67%), France (5.10%), and the United Kingdom (5.10%) (Driscoll, July 1997, p. 4).

[153] Currently, the U.S. aggregate savings rate is the lowest among Organization for Economic Cooperation and Development (OECD) countries, with "gross domestic savings equal to 15 per cent of GDP, equal with the UK at the bottom of the scale—and its household savings rate of 1 per cent of disposable income is the lowest of any major industrial economy since the Second World War" (Wade & Veneroso, September/October 1998, pp. 17-18).

[154] Yugoslavia was the only country in Eastern Europe which steadfastly held on to its socialist economy, despite years of intimidation, economic sanctions, and political and military intrigue from the U.S. and other U.S. allies.

[155] Charges assailing the International Criminal Tribunal for the Former Yugoslavia and tribunal prosecutor Judge Louise Arbour for their lack of impartiality have been made by Professor Michael Mandel, a professor of law at York University in Toronto, and one of the complainants in a (so far unsuccessful) case brought against NATO leaders. Mandel notes that Judge Arbour appeared at two press conferences during the 79-day war, once with British Foreign Secretary Robin Cook and once with U.S. Secretary of State Madeleine Albright, both of whom have formal complaints against them before the tribunal, and each time the press conferences were highlighting alleged "Serbian war crimes." Further evidence substantiating his charge of bias in the international tribunal can be gleaned from the fact that Secretary Albright publicly announced at that press conference with Judge Arbour that the United States was the major provider of funds for the tribunal and had pledged even more money to it. "Within two weeks," of this press conference, writes Mandel, "indictments were issued against Yugoslav President Slobodan Milosevic and four other Serb leaders, in what seemed indecent haste, dictated not by the needs of justice, which certainly could have waited, but by flagging popular support for NATO's war effort in the face of mounting

'collateral damage'" (Mandel, July 20, 1999, p. A11).

[156] As Senator Charles S. Robb stated on June 17, 1997, "the political reality of the situation we find ourselves in is that a majority of this body [i.e. the U.S. Senate] is prepared only to pay our debts conditioned on comprehensive reforms being implemented at the U.N." (Robb, June 17, 1997). By 1999, U.S. arrears to the UN had exceeded $1.3 billion.

[157] The 1997 defeat of Fast Track legislation to expand NAFTA in the U.S. Congress indicates organized labor's growing strength as they were credited with largely engineering this defeat and as well signals the possible limits to the free trade euphoria reigning since the beginning of the decade. So-called "fast track" legislation would allow the President to negotiate trade agreements and write "implementing legislation" needed to change U.S. laws to adapt to the agreement. Under such power granted to the President, Congress must vote "yes" or "no" on the implementing legislation with no amendments within 60 legislative days.

Three main bodies currently exist which promote international organization ties among labor: the International Labor Organisation (ILO), the International Confederation of Free Trade Unions (ICFTU), and the (marxist oriented) World Federation of Trade Unions (WFTU).

[158] Althusser in *For Marx* (1965/1986) utilizes the category of overdetermination so as to distinguish Marx's conception of contradiction from Hegel's as depicted in the *Phenomenology of Spirit* (1807/1977). Referring to the experiences of consciousness and their dialectic, Althusser acknowledges that the further we progress into Hegel's dialectic, the more complex it becomes. "However," he states:

> it can be shown that this complexity is not the complexity of an *effective overdetermination*, but the complexity of a cumulative *internalization* which is only apparently an overdetermination. In fact at each moment of its development consciousness lives and experiences its own essence (the essence corresponding to the stage its has attained) *through all the echoes* of the essence it has previously been, and through the *allusive presence* of the corresponding historical forms. Hegel, therefore, argues that every consciousness has a suppressed-conserved (*aufgehoben*) *past* even in its present, and *a world* (the world whose consciousness it could be, but which is marginal in the *Phenomenology*, its presence virtual and latent), and that therefore it also has as its *past the worlds of its superseded essences*. But these past *images* of consciousness and these latent *worlds* (corresponding to the images) never affect present consciousness as *effective determinations different from itself*: these images and worlds concern it only *as echoes* (memories, phantoms of its historicity) of what it has become, that is, *as anticipations of or allusions to itself*. Because the past is never more than the internal essence (in-itself) of the future it encloses, this presence of the past is the presence to consciousness of

consciousness itself, *and no true external determination. A circle of circles, consciousness has only one centre*, which solely determines it; it would need circles *with another centre than itself—decentred circles—* for it to be affected at its centre by their effectivity, in short for its essence to be over-determined by them. But this is not the case (Althuser, 1965/1986, pp. 101-2).

* [NOTE on the Bibliography: References' dates of publication follow the author(s)'s or editor(s)'s names. In the case of ancient or classical texts, a prior date is listed which locates the work in its historical context followed by a slash and the date of the most recent publication which was used. Other works with previous publication histories will likewise be identified by the date of their first publication and the publication date from which current reference has been made. This author believes that placing texts in their historical context is imperative for understanding subsequent philosophical and political developments.]

Bibliography*

ABC of Dialectical and Historical Materialism. 1976. Trans. by Lenina Ilitskaya. Moscow: Progress Publishers.

Abu-Lughod, Janet L. 1989. *Before European Hegemony: The World System A.D. 1250-1350.* New York, NY: Oxford University Press.

Adorno, Theodor W. 1966/1973. *Negative Dialectics.* Trans. by E.B. Ashton. New York: Continuum Publishing Company.

Agee, Philip. 1975. *Inside the Company: CIA diary.* London: Allen Lane.

_____. October, 1990. "Producing the Proper Crisis." *Z Magazine: A Political Monthly.* Woods Hole, MA.

"Agenda 2000: Strengthening the Union and preparing enlargement." March 26, 1999. The European Commission Europe web site <http://europa.eu.int/comm/agenda2000/index_en.htm>.

"The Alarming Multilateral Agreement on Investment (MAI) Now Being Negotiated at the OECD." Public Citizen 's Global Trade Watch Backgrounder. Washington, DC: Public Citizen Global Trade Watch. <http://www.citizen.org/pctrade/mai/What%20is/maibg.html>.

Albrecht-Carrié, René. 1958. *A Diplomatic History of Europe Since the Congress of Vienna.* New York, NY: Harper.

Albright, Madeleine. January 8, 1997. "Secretary of State-Designate Madeleine K. Albright: Prepared statement before the Senate Foreign Relations Committee." Washington, DC: Office of the Spokesman, Department of State <http://secretary.state.gov/www/statements/970108a.html>.

_____. May 16, 2000. "Secreaty of State Madeleine K. Albright. Remarks at National Endowment for Democracy, Rayburn House Office Building." Washington, DC: Office of the Spokesman, U.S. Department of State <http://secretary.state.gov/www/statements/2000/000516.html>.

Alchian, Armen A. and Harold Demsetz. December 1972. "Production, Information Costs, and Economic Organization." *American Economic Review*, v. 62, no. 5, pp. 777-95.

Althusser, Louis. 1965/1986. *For Marx*. Translated by Ben Brewster. London: Verso.

_____. 1990. *Philosophy and the Spontaneous Philosophy of the Scientists & Other Essays*. Edited by Gregory Elliott. London & New York: Verso.

Althusser, Louis and Etienne Balibar. 1968/1987. *Reading Capital*. Trans. by Ben Brewster. London: New Left Books.

Ambrose, Stephen E. 1971/1979. *Rise to Globalism. American Foreign Policy: 1938-1976*. New York, NY: Penguin Books.

Amin, Samir. 1974. *Accumulation on a World Scale: A Critique of the Theory of Underdevelopment*. Translated by Brian Pearce. New York: Monthly Review Press.

_____. 1997. *Capitalism in the Age of Globalization: The Management of Contemporary Society*. London & Atlantic Highlands, NJ: Zed Books.

Amin, Samir, Giovanni Arrighi, Andre Gunder Frank, and Immanuel Wallerstein. 1982. *Dynamics of Global Crisis*. New York and London: Monthly Review Press.

Andrade, Manuel Correia de. 1967. *Espaco, polarizacao e desenvolvimento: a teoria dos polos de desenvolvimento e a realidade nordestina*. Recife, Brazil: Centro Regional de Administracao Municipal.

"APEC Economic Leaders Declaration: Strengthening the Foundations for Growth." November 18, 1998. Kuala Lumpur, Malaysia <http://www.apecsec.org.sg/virtualib/econlead/malaysia.html>.

"APEC Finance Ministers' Meeting: Joint Ministerial Statement." April 24, 1995. *U.S. Department of State Dispatch.* Washington, D.C.: Office of Public Communication, Bureau of Public Affairs, V. 6, N. 17, pp. 368-69.

APEC News Announcements. January 8, 1998. APEC Secretariat home page, URL: <http://www.apecsec.org.sg/whatsnew/announce/apecna.html>.

"APEC 1999 Summit - Aukland, New Zealand." 2000. Canadian Department of Foreign Affairs and International Trade < http://www.dfait-maeci.gc.ca/trade/canada-apec/history/auckland-e.asp >.

Aptheker, Herbert, ed. 1965. *Marxism and Democracy: A Symposium.* New York, NY: Humanities Press, Inc.

Aristotle. c. 335-322 B.C.E./1959/1976. *Aristotle's Politics and The Athenian Constitution.* Edited and Translated by John Warrington. London: J.M. Dent & Sons Ltd.

_____. c. 335-322 B.C.E./1962/1984. *The Politics.* Translated by T.A. Sinclair. New York: Penguin Books.

Augelli, Enrico and Craig Murphy. 1988. *America's Quest for Supremacy and the Third World: A Gramscian Analysis.* London: Pinter Publishers.

"A Year of Freedom." December 31, 1991. *The Wall Street Journal.*

Bailey, Thomas A. 1940/1946. *A Diplomatic History of the American People. Third Edition.* New York & London: Appleton-Century-Crofts, Inc.

Baker, James A., III with Thomas M. DeFrank. 1995. *The Politics of Diplomacy. Revolution, War And Peace: 1989-1992.* New York: G.P. Putnam's Sons.

Baloyra, Enrique A., ed. 1987. *Comparing New Democracies: Transitions and Consolidation in Mediterranean Europe and the Southern Cone.* Boulder & London: Westview Press, Inc.

Baran, Paul A. 1957/1968. *The Political Economy of Growth.* New York & London: Modern Reader Paperbacks.

Baran, Paul A. and Sweezy, Paul M. 1966. *Monopoly Capital: An Essay on the American Economic and Social Order*. New York: Modern Reader Paperbacks.

Barber, Ben. July 28, 1999. "Group will battle propaganda abroad." Washington, D.C.: *The Washington Times*.

Barber, Benjamin R. March 1992. "Jihad Vs. McWorld." *The Atlantic Monthly*, Vol. 269, No. 3.

_____. 1984. *Strong Democracy: Participatory Politics for a New Age*. Berkeley and Los Angeles, CA: University of California Press.

Barlett, Ruhl J. 1947. *The Record of American Diplomacy: Documents and Readings in the History of American Foreign Relations*. New York: Alfred A. Knopf.

Barnet, Richard J. and John Cavanagh. 1994. *Global Dreams: Imperial Corporations and the New World Order*. New York: Simon & Schuster.

Barnet, Richard J. and Ronald E. Muller. 1974. *Global Reach: The Power of the Multinational Corporations*. New York: Simon and Schuster.

Barry, Tom & Deb Preusch. January, 1990. *AIFLD In Central America: Agents As Organizers*. Albuquerque, NM: The Inter-Hemispheric Education Resource Center.

Berlet, Chip and Holly Sklar. April 2, 1990. "The N.E.D.'s Ex-Nazi Adviser: Harbinger of Democracy?" *The Nation*: 450-51.

Beschloss, Michael and Strobe Talbott. 1993. *At The Highest Levels: The Inside Story of the End of the Cold War*. Boston, Toronto, & London: Little, Brown and Company.

Bezold, Clement, ed. 1978. *Anticipatory Democracy: People in the Politics of the Future*. New York: Random House.

Bhagwati, Jagdish N. 1984. "Rethinking Global Negotiations." Jagdish N. Bhagwati and John Gerard Ruggie, eds., *Power, Passions, and Purpose: Prospects for North-South Negotiations*. Cambridge, MA: The MIT Press.

Biskupic, Joan. June 15, 1991. "House Bill Eliminates Funding For Democracy Endowment." *Congressional Quarterly*: 1594-95.

Blackburn, Robin. 1977. *Revolution and Class Struggle: A Reader in Marxist Politics*. New Jersey: The Humanities Press.

Blomstrom, Magnus and Hettne, Bjorn. 1984. *Development Theory in Transition*. London: Zed Books Ltd.

Blum, William. 1986. *The CIA: A Forgotten History, US Global Interventions Since World War 2*. London and New Jersey: Zed Books, Ltd.

_____. 1995. *Killing Hope: U.S. Military and CIA Interventions Since World War II*. Monroe, Maine: Common Courage Press.

_____. 2000. *Rogue State: A Guide to the World's Only Superpower*. Monroe, ME: Common Courage Press.

Bollier, David. 1982. *Liberty & Justice for Some: Defending a Free Society from the Radical Right's Holy War on Democracy*. Washington, D.C: People for the American Way; New York: F. Ungar Publishing Co.

Boswell, Terry and Christopher Chase-Dunn. 2000. *The Spiral of Capitalism and Socialism: Toward Global Democracy*. Boulder & London: Lynne Rienner Publishers.

Bottomore, Tom, Laurence Harris, V. G. Kiernan, and Ralph Miliband. 1983. *A Dictionary of Marxist Thought*. Cambridge, MA: Harvard University Press.

Bowles, Samuel and Herbert Gintis. 1982. "Crisis of Liberal Democratic Capitalism: The Case of the U.S." In *Politics & Society*: 11: 51-94.

_____. 1986. *Democracy and Capitalism: Property, Community, and the Contradictions of Modern Social Thought*. New York: Basic Books.

Branan, Karen. January 1990. "Making Dads Proud." *Mother Jones*: 14.

Braudel, Fernand. 1981, 1982, 1984. *Civilization and Capitalism: 15th-18th Century, Vols. 1-3*. New York, NY: Harper & Row.

Brockway, Fenner. 1980. *Britain's First Socialists: the Levellers, Agitators, and Diggers of the English Revolution.* London & New York: Quartet Books.

Brown, Michael Barratt and Pauline Tiffen. 1992. *Short Changed: Africa and World Trade.* London & Boulder, CO: Pluto Press.

Brown, Michael E., Sean M. Lynn-Jones, and Steven E. Miller, eds. 1996. *Debating the Democratic Peace.* Cambridge, MA: MIT Press.

Browne, Ray B. 1982. *Objects of Special Devotion: Fetishism in Popular Culture.* Bowling Green, OH: Bowling Green University Popular Press.

Budget of the United States Government: Fiscal Year 1993. 1992. Washington, D.C.: U.S. Government Printing Office.

Buchanan, Patrick J. "The Rise of Sovereignty Fears." The Official Buchanan Brigade Home Page <http://www.buchanan.org/fear.html>.

Bull, Hedley. 1966. "Society and Anarchy in International Relations." In Butterfield, Herbert and Martin Wight, eds. *Diplomatic Investigations: Essays in the Theory of International Politics.* London: George Allen & Unwin, Ltd., pp. 35-50.

_____. 1977. *The Anarchical Society: A Study of Order in World Politics.* New York, NY: Columbia University Press.

Buntman, Sergey. August 9, 1999. "Zyuganov Says Yeltsin 'has No Control Over Himself'." Moscow: Radiostantsiya Ekho Moskvy. [Translation via Center for Defense Information Russia Weekly <http://www.cdi.org/russia/>, Johnson's Russia List, #3432, 11 August 1999.]

Burns, James MacGregor, J. W. Peltason and Thomas E. Cronin. 1987. *Government By The People: Bicentennial Edition 1987-1989.* Englewood Cliffs, NJ: Prentice-Hall, Inc.

Bush, George. January 29, 1992. "Text of Bush's Message: Heating Up the Economy, and Looking Beyond." *The New York Times,* p. A16.

Butler, Smedley D., Major General. 1935-36. "America's Armed Forces." [A five-part article appearing from October 1935 to March 1936.] *Common Sense*.

Cafruny, Alan W. and glenda G Rosenthal. 1993. *The State of the European Community: The Maastricht Debates and Beyond, Vol. 2*. Essex, England: Longman Group UK Limited; and Boulder, CO: Lynne Rienner Publishers, Inc.

Cardoso, Fernando Henrique. 1973. "Associated-Dependent Development: Theoretical and Practical Implications." In *Authoritarian Brazil: Origins, Policies, and Future*, edited by Alfred Stepan. New Haven: Yale University Press, pp. 142-76.

Cardoso, Fernando Henrique and Enzo Faletto. 1979. *Dependency and Development in Latin America*. Translated by Marjory Mattingly Urquidi. Berkeley, CA: University of California Press.

Carlisle, Charles R. November/December, 1996. "Is the World Ready for Free Trade?" *Foreign Affairs*, V. 75, N. 6, pp. 113-126.

Cartledge, Paul and Paul Millett and Stephen Todd, eds. 1998. Kosmos: Essays in Order, Conflict, and Community in Classical Athens. Cambridge, England & New York: Cambridge University Press.

_____. 1990. *Nomos: Essays in Athenian Law, Politics, and Society*. Cambridge, England & New York: Cambridge University Press.

Cash for Violeta. October 7, 1989. *The Economist*: 28.

Chalermpalanupap, Termsak. June 1, 19999. "ASEAN-10: Meeting the Challenges." Paper presented at the Asia-Pacific Roundtable held in Kuala Lumpur, Malaysia <http://www.aseansec.org/secgen/articles/asean_10.htm>.

Chilcote, Ronald H. 1981. *Theories of Comparative Politics: The Search for a Paradigm*. Boulder, CO: Westview Press, Inc.

_____. 2000. *Imperialism: Theoretical Directions; Key Concepts in Critical Theory*. Amherst, NY: Humanity Books.

Chinchilla, Norma Stoltz. 1983. "Interpreting Social Change in Guatemala: Modernization, Dependency, and Articulation of Modes of Production." In Chilcote, Ronald H. and Dale L. Johnson. *Theories of Development: Mode of Production or Dependency?* Beverly Hills, London, & New Delhi: Sage Publications, pp. 139-178.

Christopher, Warren. January 13, 1993. "Statement at Senate Confirmation Hearing [of] Secretary-Designate Christopher: Senate Foreign Relations Committee." Washington, DC: Office of the Spokesman, Department of State <http://dosfan.lib.uic.edu/ERC/briefing/dossec/1993/9301/930113dossec.html>.

Cipolla, Carlo M. 1962/1964. *The Economic History of World Population.* Harmondsworth, Middlesex, England: Penguin Books, Ltd.

Clark, Ian. 1996/1999. "Traditions of Thought and Classical Theories of International Relations." In Clark, Ian and Iver B. Neumann, eds. *Classical Theories of International Relations.* New York, NY: St. Martin's Press, Inc.

Cockburn, Alexander and Jeffrey St. Clair. 1998. *Whiteout: The CIA, Drugs and the Press.* London & New York: Verso.

Chomsky, Noam. 1991/1992. *Deterring Democracy.* New York: Hill and Wang.

Cohan, A. S. 1975. *Theories of Revolution: An Introduction.* New York: John Wiley & Sons.

Cohen, Ariel. 2000. "Spreading Freedom: Building Democracy and Public Diplomacy." In Butler, Stuart M. and Kim R. Holmes, eds. *Issues 2000: The Candidate's Briefing Book.* Washington, DC: The Heritage Foundation, pp. 845-860.

Cohn, Elizabeth. July 9, 1999. "U.S. Democratization Assistance." *The Progressive Response,* V. 3, No. 24. Washington, D.C.: Foreign Policy In Focus.

Coker, Christopher. 1989. *Reflections on American Foreign Policy Since 1945.* New York, NY: St. Martin's Press.

Colby, Gerard and Charlotte Dennett. 1995. *Thy Will Be Done, The Conquest of the Amazon: Nelson Rockefeller and Evangelism in the Age of Oil.* New York, NY: HarperCollins Publishers, Inc.

Colletti, Lucio. 1969/1972. *From Rousseau to Lenin: Studies in Ideology and Society*. Trans. by John Merrington and Judith White. New York & London: Monthly Review Press.

Commager, Henry Steele. *Freedom and Order: A Commentary on the American Political Scene*. New York: G. Braziller, 1966.

Connell-Smith, Gordon. 1966. *The Inter-American System*. London & New York & Toronto: Royal Institute of International Affairs, Oxford University Press.

Conry, Barbara. November 8, 1993. "Loose Canon: The National Endowment for Democracy." *Foreign Policy Briefing* No. 27. Washington, DC: The CATO Institute.

Corn, David. April 29, 1991. "Beltway Bandits: A Real Civics Lesson." *The Nation*.

"The Council of the European Union." 1997. Europa home page, URL: <http://europa.eu.int/inst/en/cl.htm#infos>.

Cox, Robert. 1995. "Critical Political Economy." In Bjorn Hettne, ed., *International Political Economy: Understanding Global Disorder*. Halifax, N.S.: Fernwood Pub.; Cape Town: SAPES SA; Dhaka: University Press Ltd.; London & Atlantic Highlands, N.J.: Zed Books, pp. 31-45.

_____, ed. 1997. *The New Realism: Perspectives on Multilateralism and World Order*. New York: St. Martin's Press; Tokyo; New York: United Nations University Press.

_____. 1987. "Production, Power, and World Order: Social Forces in the Making of History." In Jeffrey Harrod, *Power, Production, and the Unprotected Worker*. New York: Columbia University Press.

_____. 1987. *Production, Power, and World Order: Social Forces in the Making*. New York: Columbia University Press.

Cullather, Nicholas. 1994. *Operation PBSUCCESS: The United States and Guatemala 1952-1954*. Washington, D.C.: History Staff, Center for the Study of Intelligence, Central Intelligence Agency.

Dahl, Robert A. 1970. *After the Revolution? Authority in a Good Society.* New Haven & London: Yale University Press.

Danaher, Kevin. 1994. *50 Years Is Enough: The Case Against the World Bank and the International Monetary Fund.* Boston, MA: South End Press.

Day, J.P. 1987. *Liberty and Justice.* London & Sydney & Wolfeboro, NH: Croom Helm.

De Brie, Christian. May 1999. "Watch out for MAI Mark Two." Paris, France: *Le Monde Diplomatique* <http://www.monde-diplomatique.fr/en/1999/05/?c=13mai>.

Democracy Intervention in Haiti: The USAID Democracy Enhancement Project. March, 1994. Washington, D.C.: Washington Office on Haiti.

Der Derian, James, ed. 1995. *International Theory: Critical Investigations.* New York, NY: New York University Press.

_____. 1987. *On Diplomacy: A Genealogy of Western Estrangement.* Oxford & New York: Basil Blackwell.

Derrida, Jacques. 1993/1994. *Specters of Marx: The State of the Debt, the Work of Mourning, and the New International.* Translated by Peggy Kamuf. New York and London: Routledge.

Devetak, Richard. 1996. "Postmodernism." In Burchill, Scott and Andrew Linklater, eds. *Theories of International Relations.* New York, NY: St. Martin's Press, pp. 179-209.

DeYoung, Karen. February 21, 2000. "Rifts in Hard Line on Cuba. But Lawmakers Who Question Sanctions Can Face 'Bad Day'." *Washington Post,* p. A02.

Diamond, Larry and Marc F. Plattner, eds. 1996. *The Global Resurgence of Democracy.* Baltimore, MD: Johns Hopkins University Press.

Dicken, Peter. 1992. *Global Shift: The Internationalization of Economic Activity, Second Edition.* New York & London: The Guilford Press.

Dixon, Keith. 1986. *Freedom and Equality: The Moral Basis of Democratic Socialism.* London, Boston and Henley: Routledge & Kegan Paul.

Dobbs, Michael. December 11, 2000. "U.S. Advice Guided Milosevic Opposition." *Washington Post*. Washington, D.C.: Washington Post Foreign Service.

Dos Santos, Theotonio. May, 1970. "The Structure of Dependence." *The American Economic Review*, Vol. LX, No. 2: pp. 231-6.

Dougherty, James E. and Pfaltzgraff, Jr., Robert L. 1981. *Contending Theories of International Relations: A Comprehensive Survey*. New York: Harper & Row, Publishers, Inc.

Doyle, Michael W. 1986a. *Empires*. Ithaca & London: Cornell University Press.

_____. Summer 1983a. "Kant, Liberal Legacies, and Foreign Affairs, Part I." *Philosophy & Public Affairs*, Vol. 12, No. 3:205-235.

_____. Fall 1983b. "Kant, Liberal Legacies, and Foreign Affairs, Part 2." *Philosophy & Public Affairs*, Vol. 12, No. 4:323-353.

_____. December, 1986b. "Liberalism and World Politics." *American Political Science Review*, Vol. 80, No. 4:1151-1169.

Driscoll, David D. July, 1997. "What is the International Monetary Fund?" Washington, D.C.: IMF External Relations Department, Publications Services. From IMF home page URL: <http://www.imf.org/external/pubs/ft/exrp/what.htm>.

Du Bois, William Edward Burghart. 1945/1975. *Color and Democracy: colonies and peace*. Introduction by Herbert Aptheker. Millwood, NY: Kraus-Thomson Organization.

_____. 1947. *The World and Africa: An Inquiry Into the Part Which Africa Has Played in World History*. New York: The Viking Press.

Duff, Andrew, John Pinder and Roy Pryce, eds. 1994. *Maastricht and Beyond: Building the European Union*. London and New York: Routledge.

Easton, David. 1953. *The Political System*. New York: Knoph.

Eden, Anthony, Earl of Avon. *Freedom and Order: Selected Speeches, 1939-1946.* Boston: Houghton Mifflin Co., 1948.

El-Agraa, Ali, et al. 1997. *Economic Integration Worldwide.* New York: St. Martin's Press.

Engels, Frederick. 1877-8/1894/1978. *Anti-Dühring: Herrr Eugen Dühring's Revolution in Science.* Moscow: Progress Publishers.

_____. 1884/1979. *The Origin of the Family, Private Property, and the State.* New York: Pathfinder Press, Inc.

_____. 1888/1978. *Ludwig Feuerbach and the Outcome of Classical German Philosophy.* New York: International Publishers.

Erlanger, Steven. September 20, 2000. "Milosevic, Trailing in Polls, Rails Against NATO." New York, NY: *The New York Times.*

European Free Trade Association. April 10, 1997. "Establishment and Functions." EFTA web site: <http://www.imf.org/external/np/sec/decdo/efta.htm>.

"*Fact Sheet*: Summit of the Americas." May, 1995. *U.S. Department of State Dispatch Supplement.* Washington, D.C.: Office of Public Communication, Bureau of Public Affairs, V. 6, N. 2, pp. 31-2.

"*Fact Sheet*: Uruguay Round Agreement Reforms and U.S. Trade Policy." July, 1995. *U.S. Department of State Dispatch Supplement.* Washington, D.C.: Office of Public Communication, Bureau of Public Affairs, V. 6, N. 4, pp. 20-22).

Falcoff, Mark. April 1999. "Dollarization for Argentina? For Latin America?" In *Latin American Outlook.* Washington, DC: American Enterprise Institute for Public Policy Research.

Fejes, Fred. 1986. *Imperialism, Media, and The Good Neighor: New Deal Foreign Policy and United States Shortwave Broadcasting to Latin America.* Norwood, NJ: ABLEX Publishing Corporation.

Ferguson, Adam, L.L.D. 1767/1966. *An Essay on the History of Civil Society.* Edinburgh: Edinburgh University Press.

Feuerbach, Ludwig. 1841/1989. *The Essence of Christianity*. Translated by George Eliot. Buffalo, NY: Prometheus Books.

Fineman, Mark. May 1, 1998. "Aristide is still Haiti's No. 1 man." Los Angeles, CA: *The Los Angeles Times*.

Finlay, David J. and Hovet, Jr., Thomas. 1975. *7304: International Relations On The Planet Earth*. New York: Harper & Row.

Finley, M. I. 1968/1972. *Slavery. International Encyclopedia of the Social Sciences*, Vols. 13 & 14, David L. Silla, ed. New York: The Macmillan Company & The Free Press.

Flathman, Richard E. 1972. *Political Obligation*. New York: Atheneum.

_____. 1980. *The Practice of Political Authority: Authority and the Authorative*. Chicago & London: The University of Chicago Press.

_____. 1976. *The Practice of Rights*. Cambridge, London, New York & Melbourne: Cambridge University Press.

Fontaine, Pascal. 1997. "Seven key days in the making of Europe." Part of the "40th anniversary of the Treaties of Rome" commemoration. Europe Home Page: <http://europa.eu.int/search97cgi/>.

"Foreign Affairs Reorganization Fact Sheet." December 30, 1998. Washington, DC: White Office of the Press Secretary <http://www.state.gov/www/global/general_foreign_policy/fs_981230_reorg.htm>.

"Former Communist Rulers Swept Back Into Power." July 4, 2000. Reuters in Ulan Bator. *South China Morning Post* <http://www.extmin.mn/what_new.htm#Former communist rulers swept back into power>.

Forsey, Eugene Alford. 1974. *Freedom and Order*. Toronto: McClelland and Stewart.

"Forum: International Forum for Democratic Studies, National Endowment for Democracy." March, 1999. Washington, DC: International Forum for Democratic Studies <http://www.ned.org/page_1/forumbro.html>.

Fossedal, Gregory A. 1989. *The Democratic Imperative: Exporting the American Revolution*. New York: Basic Books, Inc., Publishers.

Foucault, Michel. 1979/1984. "What Is An Author?" In Rabinow, Paul, ed. *The Foucault Reader*. New York, NY: Pantheon Books, pp. 101-120.

"The four major objectives of the new Treaty for Europe." July 31, 1997. Europe Home Page: <http://europa.eu.int/en/agenda/igc-home/intro/intro/en.htm>.

Frank, Andre Gunder. September, 1966. "The Development of Underdevelopment" in *Monthly Review*, Vol. 18, No. 4: pp. 17-31.

_____. 1969/1970. *Latin America: Underdevelopment or Revolution; Essays on the Development of Underdevelopment and the Immediate Enemy*. New York: Monthly Review Press.

_____. 1998. *ReOrient: Global Economy in the Asian Age*. Berkeley, CA: University of California Press.

Frank, Andre Gunder and Barry K. Gills, eds. 1993. *The World System: Five Hundred Years or Five Thousand?* New York & London: Routledge

Franklin, James L. November 17, 1991. "Churches told patriotism has role in creating global unity." The *Boston Sunday Globe*.

French, Howard W. October 22, 1991. "Ex-Backers of Ousted Haitian Say He Alienated His Allies." *The New York Times*, p. A10.

Fresia, Jerry. 1988. *Toward and American Revolution: Exposing the Constitution & Other Illusions*. Boston, MA: South End Press.

Freud, Sigmund. 1900/1950. *The Interpretation of Dreams*. Trans. by A.A. Brill. New York, NY: Modern Library.

Freud, Sigmund and Josef Breuer. 1895/1957. *Studies On Hysteria*. Trans. from the German and edited by James Strachey, in collaboration with Anna Freud, assisted by Alix Strachey and Alan Tyson. New York, NY: Basic Books.

Friedman, Thomas L. March 28, 1999. "A Manifesto for the Fast World: From supercharged financial markets to Osama bin Laden, the emerging global order demands an enforcer. That's America's new burden." *The New York Times Magazine*, Section 6, pp. 40, 42-44, 61, 70-71, 84, 96-97.

_____. November 13, 1992. "The New Team: Clinton Selects a Diverse Team of Advisers." *The New York Times*, p. A19.

"FTAA Declaration of Ministers Fifth Trade Ministerial Meeting, Toronto, Canada." November 4, 1999. FTAA web site <http://www.ftaa-alca.org/ministerials/minis_e.asp>.

Fukuyama, Francis. Summer, 1989. "The End of History." *The National Interest*, N. 16, pp. 3-18.

_____. 1992. *The End of History and the Last Man*. New York: Free Press.

_____. December 1991. "Liberal Democracy as a Global Phenomenon." *PS: Political Science & Politics*, Vol. XXIV, No. 4:659-664.

Fuller, Graham E. 1991. *The Democracy Trap: The Perils of the Post-Cold War World*. New York, NY: Dutton.

Furtado, Celso. 1963. *The Economic Growth of Brazil: A Survey From Colonial To Modern Times*. Berkeley, CA: University of California Press.

Gaboury, Fred. October 25, 1997. *Rank & file Teamsters: 'Probe Hoffa, Jr. Finances'*. New York, NY: People's Weekly World.

Galbraith, John Kenneth. 1954/1961. *The Great Crash 1929*. Boston, MA: Houghton Mifflin Company.

Gamble, Andrew. 1981/1994. *Britain in Decline: Economic Policy, Political Strategy and the British State. Fourth Edition*. New York, NY: St. Martin's Press.

Gastil, Raymond D. 1987. *Freedom in the World: Political Rights and Civil Liberties 1986-1987*. New York: Greenwood Press.

Gelbspan, Ross. 1991. *Break-ins, Death Threats and the FBI: The Covert War Against the Central America Movement*. Boston: South End Press.

Gellman, Barton. March 11, 1992. "Keeping the U.S. First: Pentagon Would Preclude a Rival Superpower." Washington, D.C.: *Washington Post*, p. A1.

Gervasi, Sean. Winter, 1991-92. "Western Intervention in the USSR." *Covert Action Quarterly*, Issue 39, pp. 4-9.

Gibson, Richard. 1992. "CIA Leaders and the NEA-AFT Merger Plans." From *ACTIV-L* listserv, the *Activists Mailing List*.

Giddens, Anthony. 1995. *A Contemporary Critique of Historical Materialism*, Second Edition. Stanford, CA: Stanford University Press.

_____. 1985. *The Nation-State and Violence: Volume Two of A Contemporary Critique of Historical Materialism*. Berkeley & Los Angeles: University of California Press.

Gill, Stephen, ed. 1997. *Globalization, Democratization, and Multilateralism*. New York: St. Martin's Press.

_____. 1993. *Gramsci, Historical Materialism and International Relations*. Cambridge & New York, NY: Cambridge University Press.

Gill, Stephen and James H. Mittelman, eds. 1997. *Innovation and Transformation in International Studies*. Cambridge & New York: Cambridge University Press, 1997.

Gilpin, Robert. 1981/1983. *War and Change in World Politics*. Cambridge, UK: Cambridge University Press.

_____. 1987. *The Political Economy of International Relations*. Princeton, NJ: Princeton University Press.

Godson, Roy. 1976. *American Labor and European Politics: The AFL as a Transnational Force*. New York: Crane, Russak & Company, Inc.

Goff, Stan. July 29, 1999. "'Narco-guerrillas': alibi for intervention." Raleigh, NC: *The News-Observer*.

Goldstein, Fred. December 9, 1999. "Big Powers, Big Banks: Behind the World Trade Organization." New York, NY: *Workers World Newspaper*.

Gonzalez Casanova, Pablo. 1970. *Democracy in Mexico*. Translated by Danielle Salti. New York: Oxford University Press.

Gorovitz, Samuel, ed. *Freedom and Order in the University. Essays by Paul Goodman and Others*. Cleveland: Western Reserve University, 1967.

Goshko, John M. May 21, 1996. "Iraq accepts strict terms for sale of oil." *The Washington Post*, V. 119, N. 168, pp. A1 & A14.

Gramsci, Antonio. 1955. *Note Sul Machiavelli, Sulla Politica e Sullo Stato Moderno*. Fourth Edition. Torino: Giulio Einaudi Editore S.P.A.

_____. 1929-1935/1971/1987. *Selections from the Prison Notebooks*. Edited and translated by Quinton Hoare and Geoffrey Nowell Smith. New York: International Publishers.

_____. 1926-1937/1957/1983. *The Modern Prince and Other Writings*. New York, NY: International Publishers.

Green, Philip. August 1985. "Equality Since Rawls: Objective Philosophers, Subjective Citizens, and Rational Choice." *The Journal of Politics*, 47:970-997.

_____. 1985. *Retrieving Democracy: In Search of Civic Equality*. Totowa, NJ: Rowman & Allanheld.

Greene, Laurence. 1937. *The Filibuster: The Career of William Walker*. Indianapolis & New York: the Bobbs-Merrill Company.

Greider, William. 1997. *One World, Ready Or Not: The Manic Logic of Global Capitalism*. New York, NY: Simon & Schuster.

Grey, Barry. May 21, 1998. "How Washington builds its second line of defense: US funding for opposition groups in Indonesia." *World Socialist Web Site* <http://www.wsws.org/news/1998/may1998/indo-m21.shtml>.

Grotius, Hugo. 1625/1646/1957. *Prolegomena to the Law of War and Peace*. Translated by Francis W. Kelsey. Indianapolis, New York, & Kansas City: The Bobbs-Merrill Company, Inc.

Gujral, M.L. 1975. *U.S. Global Involvement: A Study of American Expansionism*. New Delhi: Arnold-Heinemann Publishers.

218

Gurr, Ted Robert. December 1991. "America as a Model for the World? A Skeptical View." *PS: Political Science & Politics*, Vol. XXIV, No. 4:664-67.

Haas, Ernst. 1982. "Words can hurt you; or, Who said what to whom about regimes." *International Organization*, 36:207-243.

Haden, Allen. November, 1945. "In Defense of Rockefeller." *The Inter-American*, p. 48.

Hadley, Arthur Twining. 1925/1969. *The Conflict Between Liberty and Equality*. Freeport, NY: Books for Libraries Press.

Hajnal, Peter. June 11, 1998. The Documentation of the G7/G8 System. *G7 Governance*, No. 4. Toronto, Canada: G8 Research Group at the University of Toronto <http://www.library.utoronto.ca/g7/governance/gov4/>.

Haliday, Fred. 1999. *Revolution and World Politics: The Rise and Fall of the Sixth Great Power*. Durham, NC: Duke University Press.

Hall, John A. 1997. "The Tyranny of History: An Analysis of Britain's Decline." In Clesse, Armand and Christopher Coker, eds. *The Vitality of Britain*. Luxembourg: Luxembourg Institute for European and International Studies, pp. 5-20.

Hansen, Mogens Herman. 1989. *Was Athens a Democracy? Popular Rule, Liberty and Equality in Ancient and Modern Political Thought*. Copenhagen: The Royal Danish Academy of Sciences and Letters.

Haraway, Donna Jeanne. 1991. *Simians, Cyborgs, and Women: The Reinvention of Nature*. New York: Routledge.

Harris, R. W. 1966. *Absolutism and Enlightenment, 1660-1789*. New York: Harper & Row, Publishers, Inc.

Hays, Tom. January 28, 2000. "Wife of Army anti-drug officer pleads guilty to drug charges." Seattle, WA: *Seattle Times* <http://seattletimes.nwsource.com/news/natio n-world/html19 8/wife_20000128.html >.

Heimann, Eduard. 1947. *Freedom and Order: Lessons From the War.* New York: C. Scribner's Sons.

Hegel, Georg Wilhelm Friedrich. 1807/1977. *Phenomenology of Spirit.* Trans. By A.V. Miller. Oxford & New York: Oxford University Press.

_____. 1821/1967. *Philosophy of Right.* Trans. by T.M. Knox. London: Oxford University Press.

_____. 1830/1975/1989. *Hegel's Logic: Being Part One of the Encyclopaedia of The Philosophical Sciences (1830).* Trans. by William Wallace.

Held, David. 1987. *Models of Democracy.* Cambridge: Polity in association with Blackwell.

Held, David and Christopher Pollitt, eds. 1986. *New Forms of Democracy.* Beverly Hills and London: Sage Publications, in association with the Open University.

Henkin, Louis, Richard Crawford Pugh, Oscar Schachter and Hans Smit. 1987. *Basic Documents Supplement to International Law, Cases and Materials, Second Edition.* St. Paul, MN: West Publishing Co.

Hempel, Carl G. 1966. *Philosophy of Natural Science.* Englewood Cliffs, NJ: Prentice-Hall, Inc.

Henkin, Louis, Richard Crawford Pugh, Oscar Schachter and Hans Smit. 1987/1993. *Basic Documents Supplement to International Law, Cases and Materials, Third Edition.* St. Paul, MN: West Publishing Co.

Herman, Edward S. and Frank Brodhead. 1984. *Demonstration Elections: U.S.-Staged Elections in the Dominican Republic, Vietnam, and El Salvador.* Boston: South End Press.

Herodotus. c. 490-425 B.C.E. *The Histories.* Trans. By Aubrey de Sélincourt. Harmondsworth, Middlesex, England & New York, NY: Penguin Books.

Herzog, Don. 1989. *Happy Slaves: A Critique of Consent Theory.* Chicago and London: The University of Chicago Press.

Hettne, Bjorn, ed. 1995. "Introduction: The International Political Economy of Transformation." *International Political Economy: Understanding Global Disorder.* Halifax, N.S.: Fernwood Pub.; Cape Town: SAPES SA; Dhaka: University Press Ltd.; London & Atlantic Highlands, N.J.: Zed Books, pp. 1-31.

Hilferding, Rudolf. 1910/1981. *Finance Capital: A Study of the Latest Phase of Capitalist Development.* Translated by Morris Watnich and Sam Gordon. London: Routledge & Kegan Paul.

Hirsch, Fred and Richard Fletcher. 1977. *The CIA and the Labour Movement.* Nottingham: Spokesman Books.

Hoagland, Jim. January 15, 1998. "Clinton forgetfulness shapes policy toward Iraq." Springfield, MA: *Union-News*, p. A14.

Hobbes, Thomas. 1651/1980. *Leviathan.* Edited by C. B. Macpherson. New York: Penguin Books.

Hobson, J.A. 1902. *Imperialism: A Study.* London: James Nisbet & Co., Ltd.

_____. 1902/1967. "The Economic Taproot of Imperialism." In *Imperialism: A Study.* Ann Arbor, MI: University of Michigan Press, pp. 71-93.

Hoffman, Arthur S., ed. 1968. *International Communication and the New Diplomacy.* Bloomington & London: Indiana University Press.

Holsti, K.J. 1967. *International Politics: A Framework for Analysis.* Englewood Cliffs, NJ: Prentice-Hall.

_____. 1993. "International Relations at the End of the Millennium." *Review of International Studies*, V. 19, No. 4, pp. 401-8.

Hopkins, Terence K. 1982. "The Study of the Capitalist World-Economy: Some Introductory Considerations." In Hopkins, Terence K. and Immanuel Wallerstein. *World-Systems Analysis: Theory and Methodology.* Beverly Hills, London, & New Delhi: Sage Publications, pp. 9-38.

Horie, Tadao. 1991. *Marx's Capital and One Free World: A Fundamental Reappraisal of his Political Economy.* New York, NY: St. Martin's Press.

Horwitz, Tony. December 1988. "Bodies; after the last battle of the Iran-Iraq war." *Harper's Magazine*, V. 277, N. 1663, pp. 73-76.

Hoselitz, Berthold F. 1960. *Sociological aspects of economic growth*. Glencoe, IL: Free Press.

Houston, Robert. 1984. *The Nation Thief*. New York: Pantheon Books.

Hunt, Alan, ed. 1980. *Marxism and Democracy*. London: Lawrence and Wishart, Ltd.

Hunt, Michael. 1987. *Ideology and U.S. Foreign Policy*. New Haven: Yale University Press.

Huntington, Samuel P. November/December, 1996. "The West Unique, Not Universal." *Foreign Affairs*, V. 75, N. 6, pp. 28-46.

"IMF Bail Outs: Truth and Fiction." January 12, 1998. IMF Factsheet. From the IMF home page, URL: <http://www.imf.org/external/np/exr/facts/bailout.hTM>.

"IMF Adopts a Decision on New Arrangements to Borrow." January 27, 1997. IMF Press Release No. 97/5. Washington, D.C.: IMF. From the IMF home page, URL: <http://www.imf.org/external/np/sec/pr/1997/pr9705.htm>.

James, Lawrence. 1994. *The Rise and Fall of the British Empire*. London, UK: Little, Brown and Company.

Janis, Irving. 1982/1983. *Groupthink: Psychological Studies of Policy Decisions and Fiascoes*. Boston, MA: Houghton Mifflin.

Janoski, Thomas. 1998. *Citizenship and Civil Society: A Framework of Rights and Obligations in Liberal, Traditional, and Social Democratic Regimes*. Cambridge, UK: Cambridge University Press.

Jessop, Bob. 1978. "Capitalism and Democracy: The Best Possible Political Shell?" In Gary Littlejohn, Barry Smart, John Wakeford and Nira Yuval-Davis, eds., *Power and the State*. London: Croom Helm Ltd. for the British Sociological Association.

_____. 1982. *The Capitalist State: Marxist Theories and Methods*. New York and London: New York University Press.

_____. 1990. *State Theory: Putting the Capitalist State in its Place*. University Park, PA: The Pennsylvania State University Press.

Johnson, Carlos. 1983. "Ideologies in Theories of Imperialism and Dependency." In Chilcote, Ronald H. and Dale L. Johnson. *Theories of Development: Mode of Production or Dependency?* Beverly Hills, London, & New Delhi: Sage Publications, pp. 75-104.

Joint Declaration of the Seventy-Seven Developing Countries Made at the Conclusion of the United Nations Conference on Trade in Development. June 15, 1964. Geneva, Switzerland. G77 home page, URL: <http://www.g77.org/Docs/Joint%20Declaration.html>.

Joint Declaration, Summit of the Americas Second Ministerial Trade Meeting. March 21, 1996. Cartagena, Colombia. AmericasNet Summit of the Americas Implementation Page, URL: <http://americas.fiu.edu/documents/960321a.htm>.

Jones, Charles A. 1983. *The North-South Dialogue: A Brief History*. New York: St. Martin's Press.

Jones, Ian. December 1996/January 1997. "What is the World Trade Organization and why all the ruckus about it?" *World Trade Magazine*, <http://www.worldtrademag.com/199701/>.

Kant, Immanuel. 1784/1983. "Idea for a Universal History with a Cosmopolitan Intent." In *Perpetual Peace and other essays on Politics, History, and Morals*. Translated by Ted Humphrey. Indianapolis, IN: Hackett Publishing Company.

_____. 1795/1983. "To Perpetual Peace: A Philosophical Sketch." In *Perpetual Peace and other essays on Politics, History, and Morals*. Translated by Ted Humphrey. Indianapolis, IN: Hackett Publishing Company.

Karatnycky, Adrian. 1996. "The Comparative Survey of Freedom 1995-1996; Democracy and Despotism: Bipolarism Renewed?" In Adrian Karatnycky, et al., *Freedom in the World: The Annual Survey of Political Rights and Civil Liberties 1995-1996*. New York, NY: Freedom House.

_____. 1998. "The Comparative Survey of Freedom 1997-1998: Freedom in the 'Democratic Age'." In Adrian Karatnycky, et al., *Freedom in the World: The Annual Survey of Political Rights & Civil Liberties 1997-1998*. New Brunswick & London: Transaction Publishers.

_____. 2000. "The 1999-2000 Freedom House Survey of Freedom: A Century of Progress." In Adrian Karatnycky, et al., *Freedom in the World: The Annual Survey of Political Rights and Civil Liberties 1999-2000*. Freedom House web site <http://www.freedomhouse.org/survey/2000/>.

Keane, John. 1988. *Democracy and Civil Society: On the Predicaments of European Socialism, the Prospects for Democracy, and the Problem of Controlling Social and Political Power*. London & New York: Verso.

Kegley, Charles W., Jr. and Eugene R. Wittkopf. 1981/1985. *World Politics: Trend and Transformation, Second Edition*. New York: St. Martin's Press.

_____. 1981/1989. *World Politics: Trend and Transformation, Third Edition*. New York: St. Martin's Press.

_____. 1981/1993. *World Politics: Trend and Transformation, Fourth Edition*. New York: St. Martin's Press.

Kennan, George [Kennan wrote this article under the pseudonym "X"]. July 1947. "The Sources of Soviet Conduct." *Foreign Affairs*, Vol. 25, No. 4: 566-582.

_____. April 18, 1996. "George Kennan." Transcript of interview with David Gergen. *Online NewsHour: Essays & Dialogues*. Public Broadcasting System. <http://www.pbs.org/newshour/gergen/kennan.html>.

224

Kennedy, Edward M. October 17, 1970. "Beginning Anew In Latin America: The Alianza in Trouble." *Saturday Review*, pp. 18-9.

Keohane, Robert O. 1984. *After Hegemony: Cooperation and Discord in the World Political Economy*. Princeton, NJ: Princeton University Press.

_____. 1980. "The Theory of Hegemonic Stability and Changes in International Economic Regimes, 1966-77." In O.R. Holsti, R.M. Siversen, and A.L. George, eds., *Change in the International System*. Boulder, CO: Westview.

Keynes, John Maynard. 1936. *The General Theory of Employment, Interest, and Money*. New York: Harcourt, Brace and Company.

Kindleberger, C. 1973. *The World in Depression*. Berkeley, CA: University of California Press.

Kiss, Arthur. 1982. *Marxism and Democracy: A Contribution to the Problems of the Marxist Interpretation of Democracy*. Trans. by Peter Tamasi and Ivan Sellei. Budapest: Akademiai Kiado.

Kissinger, Henry A. 1964. *A World Restored—Europe After Napoleon: The Politics of Conservatism in a Revolutionary Age*. New York: Grosset and Dunlap.

Kogan, Richard and Robert Greenstein. January 6, 1997. *A Legacy of Debt? The Balanced Budget Amendment and the Next Generation*. Washington, D.C.: Center on Budget and Policy Priorities.

Kolko, Gabriel. 1988. *Confronting the Third World: United States Foreign Policy, 1945-1980*. New York, NY: Pantheon Books.

Kornbluh, Peter & Malcolm Byrne, eds. 1993. *The Iran-Contra Scandal: The Declassified History*. New York, NY: W.W. Norton & Co.

Krader, Lawrence. 1968. *Formation of the State*. Englewood Cliffs, NJ: Prentice-Hall, Inc.

Krasner, Stephen D., ed. Spring, 1982. "International Regimes." *International Organization*, 36:185-510.

_____. 1983. *International Regimes*. Ithaca, NY: Cornell University Press.

Krasner, Stephen D. 1985. *Structural Conflict: The Third World Against Global Liberalism*. Berkeley: University of California Press.

Kubálková, V. and A. A. Cruickshank. 1980. *Marxism-Leninism and Theory of International Relations*. London: Routledge & Kegan Paul.

_____. 1985. *Marxism and International Relations*. Oxford: Clarendon Press.

Kwitney, Jonathan. 1984. *Endless Enemies*. New York: Congdon & Weed : Distributed by St. Martin's Press.

Laclau, Ernesto and Chantal Mouffe. 1985. *Hegemony and Socialist Strategy: Towards a Radical Democratic Politics*. Translated by Winston Moore and Paul Cammack. London: Verso.

LaFeber, Walter. 1993. *Inevitable Revolutions: The United States in Central America*. New York, NY: W.W. Norton.

Lancaster, John. September 19, 2000. "U.S. Funds Help Milosevic's Foes In Election Fight." Washington, DC: *Washington Post*, p. A1.

Lapid, Yosef. 1989. "The Third Debate: On the Prospects of International Theory in a Post-positivist Era." *International Studies Quarterly*, V. 33, No. 3, pp. 235-54.

"The Last African Frontier." August 30, 1998. *Business Times*. South Africa: Sunday Times <http://www.btimes.co.za/98/0830/survey/survey21.htm#top>.

Lee, Martin A. 1993. Interview by Robert Knight on WBAI (99.5) in New York City.

_____. 1997. *The Beast Reawakens*. New York, NY: Little Brown Publishers.

"Left-Right Coalition Comes Together To Defend U.S. Sovereignty in Trade Issues." September 18, 1997. Press Release from the U.S. House of Representatives <http://www.house.gov/bernie/Pressrel/9-18-97.htm>.

Lenin, V.I. 1896. "Biographical Article on Fredrick Engels." In the miscellany *Rabotnik*, No. 1-2. Moscow, Russia.

_____. 1929/1961/1972. "Conspectus of Hegel's Book *The Science of Logic.*" *Lenin: Collected Works*, Volume38, pp. 85-238.

_____. 1905/1972. "Two Tactics of Social-Democracy in the Democratic Revolution." *Collected Works, Vol. 9.* Moscow: Progress Publishers.

_____. 1909/1970. *Materialism and Empirio-Criticism: Critical Comments On A Reactionary Philosophy.* New York, NY: International Publishers.

_____. 1916/1982. *Imperialism: The Highest Stage of Capitalism.* New York, NY: International Publishers.

_____. 1917/1971. *State And Revolution.* New York: International Publishers.

Lernoux, Penny. 1982. *Cry of the People: The Struggle for Human Rights in Latin America.* New York: Doubleday.

Leuchtenburg, William E. 1963. *Franklin D. Roosevelt and the New Deal: 1932-1940.* New York, NY: Harper & Row Publishers.

"The Levellers and Irish Freedom." 1997. Originally published in *Worker's News Paper* of the Workers International League. San Francisco, CA: Republican Socialist Publications <http://www.irsm.pair.com/general/history/levellers.htm>.

Levy, Marion J., Jr. 1952. *The Structure of Society.* Princeton, NJ: Princeton University Press.

Lewis, Diane. Wednesday, August 20, 1997. "UPS accord seen lifting Teamsters, other unions." *The Boston Globe*, p. A1.

Lichtenstein, Peter M. 1983. *An Introduction to Post-Keynesian and Marxian Theories of Value and Price.* Armonk, NY: M. E. Sharpe.

Lipset, Seymour Martin. 1959. "Some Social Requisites of Democracy: Economic Development and Political Legitimacy." *American Political Science Review*, Vol. 53, No. 1:69-105.

Lister, Ruth. 1997. *Citizenship: Feminist Perspectives.* Washington Square, NY: New York University Press.

Locke, John. 1690/1965. *Two Treatises of Government.* New York: The New American Library, Inc.

Lotz, Corinna and Gerry Gold. 1996. "Matter, God, and the New Physics: A Review Essay on the Popular Books of Cosmologist Paul Davies." *Nature, Society, and Thought,* V. 9, No. 2:227-249.

Lowe, Adolph. 1988. *Has Freedom a Future?* New York, NY: Praeger Publishers.

Lukacs, Georg. 1923/1976. *History and Class Consciousness: Studies in Marxist Dialectics,* translated by Rodney Livingstone. Cambridge, MA: The MIT Press.

MacEwan, Arthur. 1990. *Debt and Disorder: International Economic Instability and U.S. Imperial Decline.* New York: Monthly Review Press.

Machiavelli, Niccolo. 1532/1935/1952. *The Prince.* New York, NY & Scarborough, Ontario: New American Library.

Maclean, John. 1981. "Marxist Epistemology, Explanations of 'Change' and the Study of International Relations." In Buzan, Barry and R.J. Barry Jones. *Change and the Study of International Relations: The Evaded Dimension.* New York, NY: St. Martin's Press, pp. 46-67.

Macpherson, C.B. 1977/1987. *The Life and Times of Liberal Democracy.* Oxford: Oxford University Press.

_____. 1962/1988. *The Political Theory of Possessive Individualism: Hobbes to Locke.* Oxford & New York: Oxford University Press.

Madeley, John. 1992. *Trade and the Poor: The impact of international trade on developing countries.* New York: St. Martin's Press.

Magdoff, Harry. 1978. *Imperialism: From the Colonial Age to the Present.* New York & London: Monthly Review Press.

Mandel, Michael. July 20, 1999. "Will NATO be held accountable for war crimes? Alliance leaders can't be permitted to wash their hands of responsibility for NATO's contribution to the Kosovo tragedy." Toronto, Canada: *The Globe and Mail*.

Mann, Michael. 1988. *States, War and Capitalism: Studies in Political Sociology*. Oxford, UK: Basil Blackwell Ltd.

Mansbach, Richard W., Yale H. Ferguson, and Donald E. Lampert. 1976. *The Web of World Politics: Nonstate Actors in the Global System*. Englewood Cliffs, NJ: Prentice-Hall, Inc.

Marcuse, Herbert. 1972. *Counterrevolution And Revolt*. Boston, MA: Beacon Press.

_____. 1941/1960. *Reason and Revolution: Hegel and the Rise of Social Theory*. Boston, MA: Beacon Press.

Marek, Franz. 1969. *Philosophy of World Revolution: A Contribution to an Anthology of Theories of Revolution*. London: Lawrence & Wishart.

Martin, Thomas R. 1996. *Ancient Greece: From Prehistoric to Hellenistic Times*. New Haven, CT & London: Yale University Press.

Marx, Karl. 1843/1975. "Critique of Hegel's Doctrine of the State." *Karl Marx: Early Writings*. Translated by Rodney Livingstone and Gregor Benton. New York, NY: Vintage Books.

_____. 1843a/1975. *Early Writings*. Translated and edited by T.B. Bottomore. New York: McGraw-Hill Book Company.

_____. 1843b/1844. "Letter from Marx to Arnold Ruge." *Marx Engels Internet Archive* <http://marxists.org/archive/marx/letters/ruge/43_03.htm>.

_____. 1843-4/1975. "Critique of Hegel's Philosophy of Right." Introduction. *Karl Marx: Early Writings*. New York: Vintage Books.

_____. 1844/1975. "Economic and Philosophical Manuscripts." *Karl Marx: Early Writings*. Translated by Rodney Livingstone and Gregor Benton. New York, NY: Vintage Books.

_____. 1844/1978. "Economic and Philosophic Manuscripts of 1844." Robert C. Tucker, ed. *The Marx-Engels Reader.* New York: W. W. Norton & Co.

_____. 1844a/1975. "Excerpts from James Mill's *Elements of Political Economy.*" *Karl Marx: Early Writings.* Translated by Rodney Livingstone and Gregor Benton. New York, NY: Vintage Books.

_____. 1845/1978. "Alienation and Social Classes." Robert C. Tucker, ed. *The Marx-Engels Reader.* New York: W. W. Norton & Company.

_____. 1845/1986. "Theses on Feuerbach." C. J. Arthur, ed., *The German Ideology.* New York: International Publishers.

_____. 1849 & 1865/1933 & 1935/1985. *Wage-labour and Capital & Value, Price, and Profit.* New York, NY: International Publishers, Co., Inc.

_____. 1850/1978. "The Class Struggles in France, 1848-1850." Robert C. Tucker, ed. *The Marx-Engels Reader.* New York: W. W. Norton & Company.

_____. 1852/1978. "The Eighteenth Brumaire of Louis Bonaparte." In Tucker, Robert C., ed. *The Marx-Engels Reader*, Second Edition. New York & London: W.W. Norton & Company, pp. 594-617.

_____. 1852a/1978. "Marx to Weydemeyer, 5 March 1852." David McLellan, ed. *Karl Marx: Selected Writings.* Oxford: Oxford University Press.

_____. 1857/ 1953/1973. *Grundrisse: Foundations of the Critique of Political Economy.* New York: Vintage Books.

_____. 1859/1975. "Preface to A Contribution to the Critique of Political Economy." *Karl Marx: Early Writings.* Translated by Rodney Livingstone and Gregor Benton. New York, NY: Vintage Books.

_____. 1859/1981. *A Contribution to the Critique of Political Economy.* New York: International Publishers.

_____. 1867/1977. *Capital: A Critique of Political Economy, Volume I.* New York: Vintage Books.

_____. 1871/1968. *The Civil War in France: The Paris Commune.* New York: International Publishers.

_____. January 5, 1879. "Interview With Karl Marx." Chicago, IL: *Chicago Tribune* < http://history.hanover.edu/modern/marx/marxint.htm>.

_____. 1894/1981. *Capital: A Critique of Political Economy, Vol. Three.* Translated by David Fernbach. New York, NY: Vintage Books.

Marx, Karl & Frederick Engels. 1846-47/1986. *The German Ideology.* New York: International Publishers.

_____. 1848/1948/1998. *The Communist Manifesto.* New York: International Publishers.

Marx, Karl & V. I. Lenin. 1871/1968. *The Civil War in France: The Paris Commune.* New York, NY: International Publishers.

Maynes, Charles William. Spring 1990. "America Without the Cold War." *Foreign Policy*, No. 78: 3-25.

McAfee, Brian. March 23, 1994. "Repeal Torricelli's Cuba-bashing law." In *Movimiento Cubano por la Paz.*

McClelland, David C. 1961. *The Achieving Society.* Princeton, NJ: Van Nostrand.

McColm, R. Bruce. 1991. "The Comparative Survey of Freedom 1990-1991: The Democratic Moment." In R. Bruce McColm, et al., *Freedom in the World: Political Rights & Civil Liberties 1990-1991.* New York, NY: Freedom House.

McColm, R. Bruce. 1993. "The Comparative Survey of Freedom 1992-1993: Our Crowded Hour." In R. Bruce McColm, et al., *Freedom in the World: The Annual Survey of Political Rights & Civil Liberties 1992-1993.* New York, NY: Freedom House.

McCormally, John and Hanna Skandera. April 2000. "Class of 2000: Cuba Policy Capstone Project." Pepperdine School of Public Policy. Malibu, CA: Pepperdine University Press.

McCoy, Alfred W. and Cathleen B. Read and Leonard P. Adams II. 1972. *The Politics of Heroin in Southeast Asia.* New York, NY: Harper & Row

McCoy, Alfred W. 1991. *The Politics of Heroin : CIA Complicity in the Global Drug Trade.* New York, NY: Lawrence Hill Books.

McGehee, Ralph W. 1983. *Deadly Deceits: My 25 Years in the CIA.* New York: Sheridan Square Press.

_____. S eptember 6 , 1 996. "Worldwide Covert O perations." Infowar.com listserv. *Cloaks and Daggers* <http://www.infowar.com/ iwftp/cloaks/090696.html-ssi >.

McGowan, David. 2000. *Derailing Democracy: The America the Media Don't Want You to See.* Monroe, ME: Common Courage Press.

Mcleod, Ross. January 28, 2000. "Goodbye Rupiah? Indonesia should consider the case for dollarization." V. 26, No. 3. *CNN.com Asia Now.* <http:// cnn.com/ASIANOW/asiaweek/magazine/2000/0128/viewpoint.html>.

Mead, Lawrence. 1986. *Beyond Entitlement: The Social Obligations of Citizenship.* New York: The Free Press.

Meditz, Sandra W. and Dennis M. Hanratty, eds. 1989. *Islands of the Commonwealth Caribbean: a regional study.* U.S. Government as represented by the Secretary of the Army. Federal Research Division, Library of Congress. Washington, D.C. U.S. Government Printing Office.

_____, eds. 1989. *Panama: A Country Study.* U.S. Government as represented by the Secretary of the Army. Federal Research Division, Library of Congress. Washington, D.C. U.S. Government Printing Office.

Meyerson, Emile. 1930/1962. *Identity & Reality.* Translated by Kate Loewenberg. New York: Dover Publications, Inc.

Mikkelsen, Adam. Summer 1998/99. "Electronic Money and the Market Process." In *Policy*, Vol. 14, No. 4. St. Leonards, NSW, Australia: The Centre for Independent Studies.

Mills, Patricia Jagentowicz. 1987. *Woman, Nature, and Psyche.* New Haven: Yale University Press.

_____, ed. 1996. *Feminist Interpretations of G.W.F. Hegel.* University Park, PA: Pennsylvania State University Press.

Mommsen, Wolfgang J. 1977/1980. *Theories of Imperialism*. Translated by P.S. Falla. Chicago, IL: The University of Chicago Press.

Moore, Stanley W. 1957/1969. *The Critique of Capitalist Democracy: An Introduction to the Theory of the State in Marx, Engels, and Lenin*. New York: Augustus M. Kelley Publishers.

Mora, Miquel Montana I. 1993. "A GATT With Teeth: Law Wins Over Politics in the Resolution of International Trade Disputes." *Columbia Journal of Transnational Law*: 31:103-180.

Morgenthau, Hans Joachim. 1948/1967. *Politics Among Nations: The Struggle for Power and Peace*. Fourth Edition. New York, NY: Alfred A. Knopf.

Morris, George. 1967. *CIA and American Labor: The Subversion of the AFL-CIO's Foreign Policy*. New York, NY: International Publishers.

Moseley, Fred. 1993. *Marx's Method in* Capital: *A Reexamination*. Atlantic Highlands, NJ: Humanities Press International Inc.

The Most Repressive Regimes of 1998: A Special Report to the 55th Session of the United Nations Commission on Human Rights in Geneva, 1999. New York, NY: Freedom House.

Mouffe, Chantal. 1979. *Gramsci and Marxist Theory*. London & B oston: Routledge & Kegan Paul.

Muller, Herbert J. 1961/1964. *Freedom in the Ancient World*. New York: Bantam Books.

Multilateral Agreement on Investment: Win, Lose or Draw for the U.S.? Hearing before the Subcommittee on International Economic Policy and Trade of the Committee on International Relations, House of Representatives, One Hundred Fifth Congress, second session. March 5, 1998. Washington, DC: U.S. Government Printing Office.

Muravchik, Joshua. 1991. *Exporting Democracy: Fulfilling America's Destiny*. Washington, D.C.: The AEI Press.

National Endowment for Democracy Act. Title V, Public Law 98-164. November 22, 1983. 97 Stat., pp. 1039-1042.

NED 1991 Annual Report: October 1, 1990-September 30, 1991. 1992. Washington, DC: NED Public Information Office.

National Endowment for Democracy Annual Report 1998. 1999. Washington, DC: National Endowment for Democracy.

National Endowment for Democracy Annual Report 1999. 2000. Washington, DC: National Endowment for Democracy.

"NED Statement of Principles and Objectives." March 1992. *Strengthening Democracy Abroad: The Role of the National Endowment for Democracy*. Washington, D.C.: NED Public Information Office.

NED Strategy Document. January 1992. Washington, D.C.: NED Public Information Office.

Nelson, William N. 1980. *On Justifying Democracy*. London, Boston and Henley: Routledge & Kegan Paul.

Neufeld, Mark. 1993. "Reflexivity and International Relations Theory." *Millennium*, V. 22, No. 1, pp. 53-76.

New Advent Catholic Encyclopedia, "Heresy", 1913/1996. <http://www.knight.org/advent/cathen/07256b.htm>.

New Catholic Encyclopedia: An International Work of Reference on the Teachings, History, Organization, and Activities of the Catholic Church, and on All Institutions, Religions, Philosophies, and Scientific and Cultural Developments Affecting the Catholic Church from Its Beginning to the Present. Prepared by an Editorial Staff at The Catholic University of America, Washington, Dictrict of Columbia. 1967. New York, NY: McGraw-Hill Book Company.

Newman, William J. 1968. *The Balance of Power in the Interwar Years, 1919-1939*. New York, NY: Random House.

Nichols, John Spicer. October 24, 1988. "Cuba: The Congress. The Power of the Anti-Fidel Lobby." *The Nation*: 389-92.

_____. February 26, 1990. "Electoral Meddling: Get the N.E.D. Out of Nicaragua." *The Nation*: 266-67.

Nicholson, Ann. September 1, 2000. "Monitoring Mongolian Elections: Eddie F. Brown Heads Up International Delegation." In *Record*, V. 25, No. 1. St. Louis, MO: Washington University in St. Louis.

Nielsen, Kai. 1985. *Equality and Liberty: A Defense of Radical Egalitarianism.* Totowa, NJ: Rowman & Allanheld.

Njoku, Felix 'Machi. January 27, 1998. "Watch Out: Globalisation is Re-drawing Africa's Borders." Dakar, Senegal: Pan African News Association (PANA).

"Normal Trade Relations (Formerly known as Most Favored-Nation status) (MFN)." June 4, 1999. Statement of the U.S. Treasury's International Trade Data System (ITDS) <http://itds.treas.gov/ITDS/ITTA/mfn.html>.

Norton, Michael. October 1, 1991. "Haiti's leader seized in revolt by army troops: Negotiators seek to save his life; at least 26 killed." The *Boston Globe*, pp. 1, 8.

Novak, Michael, et al. 1987. *A Community of Self-Reliance: The New Consensus on Family and Welfare.* Milwaukee, WI: American Enterprise Institute for Public Policy Research.

"NSC-68: A Report to the National Security Council." 1950/1975. *Naval War College Review*, Vol. XXVII, No. 6/Sequence No. 255, May/June 1975: 51-108.

NSDD 77. Management of Public Diplomacy Relative to National Security. A declassified summary presented to the Subcommittee on International Operations of the House Committee on Foreign Affairs. Hearings and Markup Before the Committee on Foreign Affairs and its Subcommittee on International Operations, House of Representatives, Ninety-Eighth Congress, First Session on H.R. 2915. Washington, D.C.: U.S. Government Printing Office, 1984. [Original document, NSDD 77, was signed on January 14, 1983.]

Nye, Joseph S., Jr. 1992. "What New World Order?" *Foreign Affairs*, Vol. 71, No. 2: 83-96.

O'Brien, Conor Cruise. 1979. "Modernisation, Order and the Erosion of a Democratic Ideal." In David Lehmann, ed., *Development Theory: Four Critical Studies.* London: Cass, pp. 49-76.

O'Brien, Mary. 1989. "Hegemony Theory and the Reproduction of Patriarchy," in *Reproducing the World: Essays in Feminist Theory.* Boulder, CO: Westview Press.

O'Connor, James. August, 1996. "No Way Out? The U.S. Economy in the Nineties." *Democracy, Economics & Politics: Essays on the Political Economy of Globalisation*, First Edition, pp. 48-75.

Oddo, Gilbert Lawrence. 1979. *Freedom and Equality: Civil Liberties and the Supreme Court.* Santa Monica, CA: Goodyear Publishing Co.

O'Donnell, Guillermo, Phillippe C. Schmitter and Laurence Whitehead, eds. 1986. *Transitions from Authoritarian Rule: Prospects for Democracy.* Baltimore & London: The John Hopkins University Press.

Ogden, Christopher. April 1, 1991. "In From The Cold." *Time*, V. 137, N. 13, p. 36.

"On New Development of US Hegemonism." May 27, 1999. *People's Daily Online.* <http://www.peopledaily.com.cn/english/199905/27/enc_990527001007_TopNews.html>.

"OPEC FACT SHEET." January 1998. United States Department of Energy: Energy Information Administration <http://www.eia.doe.gov/emeu/cabs/contents.html>.

Operation Zapata: the "ultrasensitive" report and testimony of the Board of Inquiry on the Bay of Pigs. 1981. Frederick, MD: Aletheia Books. University Publications of America, Inc.

Orszag, Peter and Robert Greenstein. February 22, 1999. *Federal Debt: What Matters and Why.* Washington, D.C.: Center on Budget and Policy Priorities.

Ostwald, Martin. 1986. *From Popular Sovereignty to the Sovereignty of Law: Law, Society, and Politics in Fifth-Century Athens.* Berkeley, Los Angeles & London: University of California Press.

"Overt Meddling." October 16, 1989. *The Nation*, Vol. 249, No. 12: 407-8.

236

"Overview of APEC." May 12, 1997. APEC Human Resource Development in Industrial Technology <http://www.apec-hurdit.org/overview-of-apec.html>.

Parenti, Michael. 1995. *Against Empire: The Brutal Realities of U.S. Global Domination.* San Francisco: City Lights Books.

_____. 1971. *Trends and Tragedies in American Foreign Policy.* Boston: Little, Brown and Company.

Park, James William. 1995. *Latin American Underdevelopment: A History of Perspectives in the United States, 1870-1965.* Baton Rouge & London: Louisiana State University Press.

Parsons, Talcott and Edward A. Shils, eds. 1951. *Toward a General Theory of Action.* New York: Harper & Row, Publishers.

Pateman, Carole. 1970/1981. *Participation and Democratic Theory.* Cambridge: Cambridge University Press.

_____. 1979/1985. *The Problem of Political Organization: A Critique of Liberal Theory.* Berkeley & Los Angeles: University of California Press.

Paul, Ellen Frankel, Fred D. Miller, and Jeffrey Paul. 1985. *Liberty and Equality.* Oxford & New York: Basil Blackwell for the Social Philosophy and Policy Center, Bowling Green State University.

Perkins, Dexter. 1941/1946. *Hands Off: A History of the Monroe Doctrine.* Boston, MA: Little, Brown And Company.

Perroux, Francois. 1968. "Multinational Investment and the Analysis of Development and Integration Poles." In Perroux, *Multinational Investment in the Economic Development and Integration of Latin America.* Bogata, Columbia: Inter-American Development Bank, pp. 95-125.

Petras, James. Fall 1986. "The Redemocratization Process." *Contemporary Marxism*, No. 14.

Petras, James and Morris Morley. 1990. *US Hegemony Under Siege: Class, Politics and Development in Latin America.* London & New York: Verso.

Phillips, D. L. 1993. *Looking Backward: A Critical Appraisal of Communitarian Thought*. Princeton, NJ: Princeton University Press.

Pike, Fredrick B. 1995. *FDR's Good Neighbor Policy: Sixty Years of Generally Gentle Chaos*. Austin, TX: University of Texas Press.

The Pike Report on the CIA. Introduction by Philip Agee. Nottingham, Great Britain: Bertrand Russell Peace Foundation Ltd., Spokesman Books.

Pincus, Walter. March 17, 1998. "Inspector: CIA Kept Ties With Alleged Traffickers." *The Washington Post*, p. A12.

Plato. 427-347 B.C.E./1941/1970. *The Republic*. Translated by Francis MacDonald Cornford. London: Oxford University Press.

____. 427-347 B.C.E./1970/1988. *The Laws*. Translated by Trevor J. Saunders. London: Penguin Books.

"Polls Show Ex-Communist Wins Romanian Vote." December 10, 2000. *CNN.com* <http://europe.cnn.com/2000/WORLD/europe/12/10/romania.elections.02/index.html>.

Polybius. c. 200-118 B.C.E./1979/1986. *The Rise of the Roman Empire*. Translated by Ian Scott-Kilvert. Selected with an Introduction by F.W. Walbank. Harmondsworth, Middlesex, England: Penguin Books.

Pomeroy, William. January 28, 1995. "New U.S. attempts to control world economy." New York, NY: *Peoples Weekly World*, p. 7.

"Poor Countries Debt Rises" (Subidas deuda de países pobre). January 27, 1998. La Paz, Bolivia: (AFP) *Los Tiempos*, p. B5.

Prakash, Gyan. 1990. *Bonded Histories: Genealogies of Labor Servitude in Colonial India*. Cambridge & New York: Cambridge University Press.

Prebisch, Raúl. 1971. *Change and Development—Latin America's Great Task: Report Submitted to the Inter-American Development Bank*. New York, Washington, & London: Praeger Publishers.

238

Pregelj, Vladimir N. June 10, 1998. "Most-Favored-Nation Status of the People's
Republic of China." *Congressional Research Service (CRS) Issue Brief*
<http://www.fas.org/man/crs/980717CRSMFN
.htm>.

"Presidency Conclusions." March 24-5, 1999. European Council. Berlin, Germany <http://europa.eu.int/council/off/conclu/mar99_en.
pdf>.

Quester, George H. December 1991. "America as a Model for the World?" *PS:
Political Science & Politics*, Vol. XXIV, No. 4:658-59.

Ratnesar, Romesh. October 6, 2000. "Vojislav Kostunica: Tough Intellectual."
CNN.com <http://europe.cnn.com/2000/WORLD/europe/10/05/
etime.kostunica/>.

Raum, Tom. January 19, 1996. "Buchanan Hits WTO Ruling, Forbes Flat Tax."
Associated Press.

Reagan, Ronald W. "Address to Members of Parliament, June 8, 1982" In *Weekly
Compilation of Presidential Documents*, V. 18, No. 23 (June 14, 1982):
pp. 764-70.

Reich, Robert B. 1991. *The Work of Nations: Preparing Ourselves for 21st-
Century Capitalism*. New York: A.A. Knopf.

Remnick, David. 1993. *Lenin's Tomb: The Last Days of the Soviet Empire*. New
York: Random House.

Rennie, David. July 4, 2000. "Landslide Victory for Far Left in Mongolia."
London, UK: *The Daily Telegraph* <http://www.telegraph.co.uk:80/
et?ac=003988802900272&rtmo=
qxqussq9&atmo=rrrrrrrq&pg=/et/00/7/4/wmong04.html>.

Resnick, Stephen A. and Richard D. Wolff. 1987. *Knowledge and Class: A
Marxian Critique of Political Economy*. Chicago & London: The University of Chicago Press.

_____. Summer 1993. "State Capitalism in
the USSR? A High-Stakes Debate." *Rethinking MARXISM*, V. 6, No. 2,
pp. 46-68.

Rezendes, Michael. October 9, 1994. "A hemisphere transformed: Democracy now predominates over dictatorship in the Americas." *The Boston Sunday Globe*, p. 75.

Riessman, Frank and Erik Banks. Spring 1996. "The Mismeasure of Civil Society." In *Social Policy*, V. 26, No. 3, pp. 2-5.

Robaina, Roberto. March 6, 1996. "Address by the Minister of Foreign Affairs of Cuba, Mr. Roberto Robaina, at the Resumption of the 50th Session of the U.N. General Assembly, March 6, 1996." New York: New York Transer News Collective.

Robb, Senator Charles S. June 17, 1997. "Payment of Dues to United Nations." U.S. Senate website < http://www.senate.gov/member/va/robb/statements/floor/undues.html>.

Robbins, Lionel, Baron and Lord. 1977. *Liberty and Equality*. London: Institute of Economic Affairs.

Robinson, William I. 1996. *Promoting Polyarchy: Globalization, US Intervention, and Hegemony*. Cambridge & New York: Cambridge University Press.

Rodney, Walter. 1982. *How Europe Underdeveloped AFRICA*. Washington, D.C.: Howard University Press.

Ronell, Avital. 1989. *The Telephone Book: Technology—Schizophrenia—Electric Speech*. Lincoln, NB & London: University of Nebraska Press.

Rosenberg, Arthur. 1938/1965. *Democracy And Socialism: A Contribution to the Political History of the Past 150 Years*. Boston, MA: Beacon Press.

Rosenberg, Justin. 1994. *The Empire of Civil Society: A Critique of the Realist Theory of International Relations*. London & New York: Verso.

Ross, Sonya. May 18, 2000. "Clinton Pushes for Improved Africa Trade." CNN.com. <http://www.cnn.com/2000/ALLPOLITICS/stories/05/18/africa.ap/index.html>.

Rostow, Walt W. 1960. *The Stages of Economic Growth: A Non-Communist Manifesto*. Cambridge: Cambridge University Press.

240

Rousseau, Jean Jacques. 1755/1987. *A Discourse on Inequality*. Translated by Maurice Cranston. Harmondsworth, Middlesex, England: Penguin Books.

_____. 1762/1954. *The Social Contract*. Translated by Willmore Kendall. Chicago, IL: Henry Regnery Company.

Ruggie, John Gerard. 1984. "Another Round, Another Requiem? Prospects for the Global Negotiations." Jagdish N. Bhagwati and John Gerard Ruggie, eds., *Power, Passions, and Purpose: Prospects for North-South Negotiations*. Cambridge, MA: The MIT Press.

Rühle, Otto. 1924/1970/1974. *From the Bourgeois to the Proletarian Revolution*. London: Socialist Reproduction in co-operation with Revolutionary Perspectives. Based on a German edition of the text published by Institut fur Praxis und Theorie des Ratekomminismus (IPTR) in Berlin, 1970. [Online text at <http://www.geocities.com/~johngray/borpro.htm>]

Sagan, Eli. 1991. *The Honey and the Hemlock: Democracy and Paranoia in Ancient Athens and Modern America*. New York, NY: Basic Books.

Sandström, Sven. October 1, 1997. Remarks at the Preparatory Meeting for the Summit of the Americas. Santiago, Chile. AmericasNet Summit of the Americas Implementation Page <http://americas.fiu.edu/documents/971006d.htm>.

Scheer, Robert. 1982. *With Enough Shovels: Reagan, Bush and Nuclear War*. New York, NY: Random House.

Schiller, Friedrich. 1901. *The History of the Thirty Years' War in Germany*. Translated by Rev. A. J. W. Morrison, M. A. New York: A.L. Burt, Publisher.

Schlesinger, Steven and Stephen Kinzer. 1982. *Bitter Fruit: The Untold Story of the American Coup in Guatemala*. Garden City, NY: Doubleday.

Scholl, Russell B. July 1999. "The International Investment Position of the United States at Yearend 1998." In *Survey of Current Business*. Washington, D.C.: U.S. Department of Commerce, Bureau of Economic Analysis, pp. 36-47.

Schott, Jeffrey J. September 1996. *WTO 2000: Setting the Course for World Trade*. Washington, D.C.: Institute for International Economics.

Schoultz, Lars. January-March, 1980. "Freedom in the World: Political and Civil Liberties," (Review). In *Universal Human Rights*, V. 1, N. 2, pp. 94-6.

Schumpeter, Joseph. 1950. *Capitalism, Socialism, and Democracy*. New York: Harper Torchbooks.

_____. 1951. *Imperialism and Social Classes*. Translated by Heinz Norden. Edited by Paul M. Sweezy. New York, NY: Augustus M. Kelley, Inc.

Schweller, Randall L. January 1992. "Domestic Structure and Preventive War: Are Democracies More Pacific?" *World Politics*, Vol. 44, No. 2:235-269.

Scipes, Kim. July 8, 1999. "Current AFL-CIO Foreign Operations." Labor Research and Action Project. *Labor-Rap* discussion list < http://csf.colorado.edu/forums/labor-rap/current-discussion/msg00178.html >.

Scoble, Harry and Laurie Wiseberg. 1981. "Problems of Comparative Research on Human Rights." In V.P. Nanda, J.R. Scarritt, and G.W. Shepherd, *Global Human Rights: Public Policies, Comparative Measures, and NGO Strategies*. Boulder, CO: Westview Press.

Scott, Jack. 1978. *Yankee Unions, Go Home!: How the AFL Helped the U.S. Build an Empire in Latin America*. Vancouver, Canada: New Star Books.

Scott, Peter Dale. 1999. *The Official Story: What the Government Has Admitted About CIA Ties to Drug Traffickers*. With Introduction by Martha Honey. Washington, D.C.: Institute for Policy Studies & the Drug Policy Project.

Sealey, Raphael. 1987. *The Athenian Republic: Democracy or the Rule of Law?* University Park & London: The Pennsylvania State University Press.

Shah, S.A. August, 1996. "The Impasse of Mass Democracy." *Democracy, Economics & Politics: Essays on the Political Economy of Globalisation*, First Edition, pp. 1-24.

Shannon, Don. December 20, 1991. "Freedom Eludes Many in World." *Los Angeles Times*.

Shannon, Thomas Richard. 1989. *An Introduction to the World-System Perspective*. Boulder, San Francisco, & London: Westview Press.

Sheehan, Neil, et al. 1971. *The Pentagon Papers as Published by The New York Times. The Pentagon history was obtained by Neil Sheehan*. New York: Quadrangle Books.

Sherr, Alan B. 1986. *A Legal Analysis of the "New Interpretation" of the Anti-Ballistic Missile Treaty*. Boston, MA: Lawyers Alliance for Nuclear Arms Control.

Shlapentokh, Vladimir. In collaboration with Neil F. O'Donnell. 1993. *The Last Years of the Soviet Empire: Snapshots from 1985-1991*. Westport, CT & London: Praeger Publishers.

Shultz, George P. February 23, 1983. *Statement before the Subcommittee on International Operations of the House Committee on Foreign Affairs. Hearings and Markup Before the Committee on Foreign Affairs and its Subcommittee on International Operations, House of Representatives, Ninety-Eighth Congress, First Session on H.R. 2915*. Washington, D.C.: U.S. Government Printing Office, 1984.

Sims, Beth. 1992. *Workers of the World Undermined: American Labor's Role in U.S. Foreign Policy*. Boston, MA: South End Press.

Singer, J. David. 1961. "The Level-Of-Analysis Problem in International Relations." In Knorr, Klaus Eugen and Sidney Verba, eds. *The International System: Theoretical Essays*. Princeton, N J: Princeton University Press, pp. 77-92.

Sjöstrand, Wilhelm. 1973. *Freedom and Equality as Fundamental Educational Principles in Western Democracy; from John Locke to Edmund Burke*. Stockholm: Föreningen för svensk undervisningshistoria.

Sklar, Holly, ed. 1980. *Trilateralism: The Trilateral Commission and Elite Planning for World Management*. Boston: South End Press.

Sklar, Holly and Chip Berlet. Winter 1991-92. "NED, CIA, and the Orwellian Democracy Project." *Covert Action Quarterly*, No. 39.

Slater, David. 1997. "Geopolitical Imaginations Across the North-South Divide: Issues of Difference, Development and Power. In *Political Geography*, V. 16, N. 8, pp. 631-653.

Slomanson, William R. 1990/95. *Fundamental Pespectives on International Law, Second Edition*. St. Paul, MN: West Publishing Co.

Smith, James Morton and Paul L. Murphy. 1965. *Liberty and Justice*. New York: Knopf.

Snyder, Richard C., H.W. Bruck, and Burton Sapin, eds. 1962. *Foreign Policy Decision-Making: An Approach to the Study of International Politics*. New York, NY: Free Press of Glencoe.

Soros, George. February, 1997. "The Capitalist Threat." *The Atlantic Monthly*, V. 279, N. 2, pp. 45-58.

_____. Winter 1998-99. "Capitalism's Last Chance?" *Foreign Policy*, No. 113, pp. 55-66. Washington, DC: Carnegie Endowment for International Peace.

Spelman, Elizabeth V. 1988. *Inessential Woman: Problems of Exclusion in Feminist Thought*. Boston: Beacon Press.

Spero, Joan Edelman. 1981. *The Politics of International Economic Relations, Second Edition*. New York: St. Martin's Press.

_____. March 7, 1994. "The International Economic Agenda And the State Department's Role." *U.S. Department of State Dispatch*. Washington, D.C.: Office of Public Communication, Bureau of Public Affairs, V. 5, N. 10, pp. 123-25).

Sprout, Harold and Margaret Sprout. 1971. *Toward a Politics of the Planet Earth*. New York: Van Nostrand Reinhold.

Stearns, Cliff (R-FL). May 14, 1996. "We Told You So." (Remarks Made Before the U.S. House of Representatives by Rep. Cliff Stearns on the threat to U.S. national sovereignty incurred by the U.S. membership in the World Trade Organization.) *Congressional Record*, p. H4904.

de Ste. Croix, G.E.M. 1981. *The Class Struggle in the Ancient Greek World: From the Archaic Age to the Arab Conquests*. London: Gerald Duckworth & Company, Limited.

Stockwell, John. 1978. *In Search of Enemies: a CIA Story.* New York, NY: Norton.

"The Strategic Compact: A Summary Note." 1997. The World Bank Group <http://www.worldbank.org/html/extdr/backgrd/ibrd/comsum.htm>.

Stråth, Bo and Rolf Torstendahl. 1992. "State Theory and State Development: States as Network Structures in Change in Modern European History." In Rolf Torstendahl, ed. *State Theory and State History.* London: Sage Publications.

Sunkel, Osvaldo. April, 1972. "Big Business and 'dependencia.'" *Foreign Affairs* 50, pp. 517-531.

Tarullo, D.K. 1985. "Logic, Myth, and the International Economic Order." *Harvard International Law Journal*, 26:533-53.

Therborn, Goran. 1978. *What Does the Ruling Class Do When It Rules? State Apparatuses and State Power under Feudalism, Capitalism and Socialism.* London: NLB.

Thucydides. c. 460-404 B.C.E./1954/1985. *History of the Peloponnesian War.* Translated with an Introduction by Rex Warner. Harmondsworth, Middlesex, England & New York, NY: Penguin Books.

Tilly, Charles. 1990. *Coercion, Capital, and European States, AD 990-1990.* Cambridge, MA & Oxford, UK: Basil Blackwell.

de Tocqueville, Alexis. 1835/1956/1984. *Democracy in America.* Edited and abridged by Richard D. Heffner. New York: Mentor Books.

Trend, J. B. 1951. *Bolívar and the Independence of Spanish America.* Clinton, MA: Colonial Press Inc.

Trotsky, Leon. 1932. *History of the Russian Revolution.* Translated from the Russian by Max Eastman. London: V. Gollancz.

_____. 1931/1969. *The Permanent Revolution & Results and Prospects.* New York, NY: Pathfinder Press, Inc.

Tunkin, G. I. 1970/1974. *Theory of International Law.* Translated by William E. Butler. Cambridge, MA: Harvard University Press.

Tyler, Patrick E. March 8, 1992. "U.S. Strategy Plan Calls for Insuring No Rivals Develop: A One-Superpower World. Pentagon's Document Outlines Ways to Thwart Challenges to Primacy of America." *New York Times,* pp. 1, 14.

"U.S. Direct Investment Position Abroad on a Historical-Cost Basis: Country Detail." March 12, 1999. Bureau of Economic Analysis International Investment Data. BEA website < http://www.bea.doc.gov/bea/di/diapos66.htm>.

U.S. General Accounting Office. April 30, 1996. *AIFLD Funding and Programs.* GAO/NSIAD-96-142R. Washington, D.C.: U. S. General Accounting Office.

_____. September 1990. *Central America: Assistance to Promote Democracy and National Reconciliation in Nicaragua.* GAO/NSIAD-90-245. Washington, D.C.: U.S. General Accounting Office.

_____. January 1994. *Promoting Democracy: Foreign Affairs and Defense Agencies Funds and Activities—1991 to 1993.* GAO/NSIAD-94-83. Washington, D.C.: U.S. General Accounting Office.

_____. January 1992. *Promoting Democracy: National Endowment for Democracy Efforts to Improve Grant Management.* GAO/NSIAD-92-89. Washington, D.C.: U.S. General Accounting Office.

_____. March 1991. *Promoting Democracy: National Endowment for Democracy's Management of Grants Needs Improvement.* GAO/NSIAD-91-162. Washington, D.C.: U.S. General Accounting Office.

_____. February 1996. *P romoting Democracy: Progress Report on U.S. Democratic Development Assistance to Russia.* GAO/NSIAD-96-40. Washington, D.C.: U.S. General Accounting Office.

_____. September 1986. *Promoting Democracy: The National Endowment for Democracy's Management of Grants Overseas.* GAO/NSIAD-86-185. Washington, D.C.: U.S. General Accounting Office.

_____. September 1996. *U.S. Information Agency: Options for Addressing Possible Budget Reductions.* GAO/NSIAD-96-179. Washington, D.C.: U.S. General Accounting Office.

_____. July 6, 1984. *Report To Senator Malcolm Wallop: Events Leading To The Establishment Of The National Endowment For Democracy*. GAO/NSIAD-84-121. Washington, D.C.: U.S. General Accounting Office.

Viner, J. 1952. "America's Aims and the Progress of Underdeveloped Countries." In Berthold F. Hoselitz, ed., *The Progress of Underdeveloped Areas*. Chicago, IL: University of Chicago Press, pp. 175-202.

Viotti, Paul R. and Mark V. Kauppi. 1987. *International Relations Theory: Realism, Pluralism, Globalism*. New York, NY: Macmillan Publishing Company.

Volume II: The Contra Story. Allegations of Connections Between CIA and the Contras in Cocaine Trafficking to the United States. (96-0143-IG) October 8, 1998. Washington D.C.: Central Intelligence Agency Inspector General. This is an unclassified version of a classified Report of Investigation of the same title, issued by the Inspector General (who at the time was Frederick Hitz) on April 27, 1998.

Wade, Robert. Winter 1998-99. "The Coming Fight Over Capital Flows." *Foreign Policy*, No. 113, pp. 41-54. Washington, DC: Carnegie Endowment for International Peace.

Wade, Robert and Frank Veneroso. September/October 1998. "The Gathering World Slump and the Battle Over Capital Controls." *New Left Review*, No. 231, pp. 13-42. United Kingdom: New Left Review, Ltd.

Wæver, Ole. 1997. "Figures of International Thought: Introducing Persons Instead of Paradigms." In Neumann, Iver B. and Ole Wæver, eds. *The Future of International Relations: Masters in the Making?* London and New York: Routledge.

Walker, Gen'l William. 1860/1985. *The War in Nicaragua*. With a Foreword by Robert Houston. Tucscon, AZ: The University of Arizona Press.

Walker, Thomas, ed. 1991. *Revolution and Counterrevolution in Nicaragua*. Boulder, CO: Westview Press.

Wallerstein, Immanuel. 1974. *The Modern World System: Capitalist Agriculture and the Origins of the European World-Economy in the Sixteenth Century*. New York & London: Academic Press.

_____. 1980. *The Modern World System II: Mercantilism and the Consolidation of the European World-Economy, 1600-1750.* New York, NY: Academic Press, Inc.

Waltz, Kenneth N. 1959. *Man, the State, and War: A Theoretical Analysis.* New York, NY: Columbia University Press.

_____. 1979. *Theory of International Politics.* Reading, MA: Addison-Wesley Publishing Company.

_____. 1986. "Reductionist and Systemic Theories." In Keohane, Robert O. *Neorealism and Its Critics.* New York, NY: Columbia University Press, pp. 47-69.

_____. December 1991. "America as a Model for the World? A Foreign Policy Perspective." *PS: Political Science & Politics*, Vol. XXIV, No. 4:667-670.

Waters, Malcolm. 1995. *Globalization.* London and New York: Routledge.

Wastson, Adam. 1992. *The Evolution of International Society: A Comparative Historical Analysis.* London and New York: Routledge.

Weaver, Eric and William Barnes. 1991. "Opposition Parties and Coalitions." In Thomas W. Walker, ed., *Revolution & Counterrevolution in Nicaragua.* Boulder, CO: Westview Press.

Webster's Ninth New Collegiate Dictionary. 1898/1984. Springfield, MA: Merriam-Webster, Inc., Publishers.

Wedgwood, Cicely Veronica. 1938/1969. *The Thirty Years War.* Gloucester, MA: Peter Smith Publisher, Inc.

Weiner, Tim. August 29, 1993. "C.I.A. Opening Files on Cold War Role: Secret Operations in Cuba, Iran and Guatemala to Be Among Those Revealed." *The New York Times*, p. L7.

Weissman, Robert. January/February, 1996. "The WTO Strikes (What the WTO actually does)." *Multinational Monitor*, editorial, p. 5.

Wells, Tom. With a foreward by Todd Gitlin. 1994. *The War Within: America's Battle over Vietnam.* Berkeley, CA: University of California Press.

Wendt, Alexander. Spring 1992. "Anarchy Is What States Make of It: The Social Construction of Power Politics." *International Organization*, Vol. 46, No. 2.

Wesolowsky, Tony. October 11, 2000. "Belarus: Will Elections Reflect Yugoslav Example?" Washington, D.C.: Radio Free Europe/Radio Liberty Inc. <http://www.rferl.org/nca/features/2000/10/111011143420.asp>

Wessel, David. December 26, 1997. "Korean bailout raises tough questions, critics worry U.S. and IMF are protecting investors, lenders in private sector." *The Wall Street Journal*, p. A2.

Wiarda, Howard J. 1990a. *The Democratic Revolution in Latin America: History, Politics, and U.S. Policy.* New York & London: Homes & Meier Publishers, Inc.

_____. 1990b. *Foreign Policy Without Illusion: How Foreign Policy-Making Works and Fails to Work in the United States.* Glenview, IL: Scott, Foresman/Little, Brown Higher Education.

_____. 1986. "Can Democracy Be Exported? The Quest for Democracy in U.S.-Latin American Policy." In Middlebrook, Kevin J. and Carlos Rico, eds. *The United States and Latin America in the 1980s: Contending Perspectives on a Decade of Crisis.* Pittsburgh, PA: The University of Pittsburgh Press.

Wick, Charles Z. March 3, 1983. *Statement Before the Subcommittee on International Operations of the House Committee on Foreign Affairs. Hearings and Markup Before the Committee on Foreign Affairs and its Subcommittee on International Operations, House of Representatives, Ninety-Eighth Congress, First Session on H.R. 2915.* Washington, D.C.: U.S. Government Printing Office, 1984.

Widmer, Edward L. 1999. *Young America: The Flowering of Democracy in New York City.* New York, NY: Oxford University Press.

Wight, Martin. 1966a. "Why Is There No International Theory?" In Butterfield, Herbert and Martin Wight, eds. *Diplomatic Investigations: Essays in the Theory of International Politics.* London: George Allen & Unwin, Ltd., pp. 17-34.

_____. 1966b. "Western Values in International Relations" In Butterfield, Herbert and Martin Wight, eds. *Diplomatic Investigations: Essays in the Theory of International Politics*. London: George Allen & Unwin, Ltd., pp. 17-34.

_____. 1977. *Systems of States*. Edited by Hedley Bull. Leicester: Leicester University Press.

Wightman, David. 1984. "Why Economic History?" In Strange, Susan, ed. *Paths to International Political Economy*. London, Boston, & Sydney: George Allen & Unwin, pp. 23-32.

Williams, William Appleman. 1959/1972. *The Tragedy of American Diplomacy*. New York, NY: Dell Publishing Co., Inc.

Willoughby, John. Spring 1992. "Debt and Disorder: International Economic Instability and U.S. Imperial Decline (book review)." *Science & Society*, Vol. 56, No. 1:111-113.

Wills, Garry. January 31, 1999. "O Democracy! Did Hawthorne, Whitman and Melville belong to a youth cult?" Review article appearing in *The New York Times Book Review*, p. 15.

Wolfe, Alan. 1973. *The Seamy Side of Democracy: Repression in America*. New York, NY: David McKay Company, Inc.

Wood, Ellen Meiksins. 1999. *The Origin of Capitalism*. New York, NY: Monthly Review Press.

Wood, Ellen Meiksins and Neal Wood. 1978. *Class Ideology and Ancient Political Theory: Socrates, Plato, and Aristotle in Social Context*. New York: Oxford University Press.

Woodcock, George. 1974. *Who Killed the British Empire? An Inquest*. London, UK: Jonathan Cape Ltd.

World Investment Report 1999: Foreign Direct Investment and the Challenge of Development. 1999. New York, NY: United Nations Conference on Trade and Development.

250

"World trade growth accelerated in 1997, despite turmoil in some asian financial markets." March 19, 1998. Geneva, Switzerland: World Trade Organization Press Release <http://www.wto.org/english/news_e/pres98_e/pr98_e.htm>.

Young, Iris. 1990. *Justice and The Politics of Difference*. Princeton, NJ: Princeton University Press.

Young, Oran R. 1972. "The Actors in World Politics." In Rosenau, James N., Vincent Davis, and Maurice A. East, eds. *The Analysis of International Politics: Essays in Honor of Harold and Margaret Sprout*. New York & London: The Free Press.

Zaks, Dmitry. March 9-16, 1997. "'Dismantler of the System' Shatalin Dead at Age 62." *The St. Petersburg Times*.

Index

About the Author

Colin S. Cavell, Ph.D. is currently an Assistant Professor of Political Science at the University of Bahrain in the Kingdom of Bahrain, teaching in the Department of Foreign Languages and Literature. Born and raised in Baton Rouge, Louisiana, Dr. Cavell earned his Bachelor of Arts degree in Political Science from Louisiana State University in 1982, his Masters of Arts degree in Political Science from the University of New Orleans in 1987, and his Doctorate of Philosophy degree in Political Science from the University of Massachusetts in Amherst, Massachusetts in February 2001. Dr. Cavell has taught at the University of New Orleans, the University of Massachusetts, Merrimack College in North Andover, Massachusetts, and Holyoke Community College in Holyoke, Massachusetts. In addition, Dr. Cavell has taught political science with the Junior Statesmen Foundation Summer Program at Yale University in New Haven, Connecticut. A frequent guests on radio programs, Dr. Cavell as well reviews articles for the journal *RETHINKING Marxism* and is a member of the Editorial Advisory Board for *The New World of Politics: An Introduction to Political Science*.